THE COMPLETE ILLUSTRATED GUIDE TO GROWING

CACTI

& SUCCULENTS

THE COMPLETE ILLUSTRATED GUIDE TO GROWING

CACTI

& SUCCULENTS

THE DEFINITIVE PRACTICAL REFERENCE ON IDENTIFICATION, CARE AND CULTIVATION, WITH A DIRECTORY OF 400 VARIETIES AND 700 PHOTOGRAPHS

MILES ANDERSON

CONSULTANT: TERRY HEWITT

LORENZ BOOKS

This edition is published by Lorenz Books, an imprint of Anness Publishing Ltd,
Hermes House, 88–89 Blackfriars Road, London SE1 8HA;
tel. 020 7401 2077; fax 020 7633 9499
www.lorenzbooks.com; www.annesspublishing.com

If you like the images in this book and would like to investigate using them for publishing, promotions
or advertising, please visit our website www.practicalpictures.com for more information.

UK agent: The Manning Partnership Ltd; tel. 01225 478444;
fax 01225 478440; sales@manning-partnership.co.uk
UK distributor: Grantham Book Services Ltd; tel. 01476 541080;
fax 01476 541061; orders@gbs.tbs-ltd.co.uk
North American agent/distributor: National Book Network;
tel. 301 459 3366; fax 301 429 5746; www.nbnbooks.com
Australian agent/distributor: Pan Macmillan Australia;
tel. 1300 135 113; fax 1300 135 103; customer.service@macmillan.com.au
New Zealand agent/distributor: David Bateman Ltd; tel. (09) 415 7664; fax (09) 415 8892

Publisher Joanna Lorenz
Senior Editor Cathy Marriott
Designers Lisa Tai and Simon Wilder
Photgrapher Peter Anderson

ETHICAL TRADING POLICY

Because of our ongoing ecological investment programme, you, as our customer, can have the pleasure and reassurance
of knowing that a tree is being cultivated on your behalf to naturally replace the materials used to make the book
you are holding. For further information about this scheme, go to www.annesspublishing.com/trees

A CIP catalogue record for this book is available from the British Library.

Previously published as *The Complete Guide to Growing Cacti and Succulents*

contents

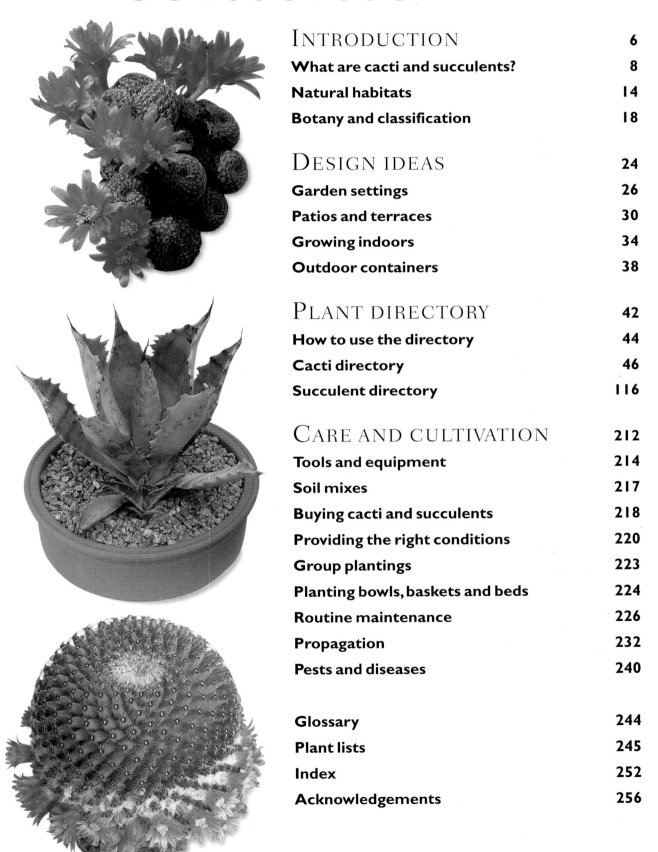

introduction

There is a vast range of cacti and succulent plants in an infinite variety of shapes, sizes and colours. Some groups are cultivated for their flowers, while many are grown for their shape or form. Some are very small and slow-growing, needing just a 5cm/2in pot, while others are large and bizarre. No matter how long you have been collecting, there are always new and fascinating cacti and succulents to catch your eye. The purpose of this book is to help you enjoy and care for your plants, so that they will reward you by growing into magnificent specimens, producing lots of beautiful flowers.

◁ *These cacti are all part of the* Mammillaria *group, a genera that includes many easy-to-cultivate species.*

WHAT ARE CACTI AND SUCCULENTS?

In some publications, the term "cacti and succulents" is used as if the two were separate, distinct groups. This has led to much confusion. A simple rule can be used to clarify this, however: all cacti are succulents, but not all succulents are cacti.

Plants adapted to dry or desert conditions are collectively known as xerophytes. Xerophytic plant species number in the tens of thousands and are members of many different plant families. Succulents are xerophytes that have developed storage structures, in which they hoard water, enabling them to survive periods of drought. The degree of succulence varies considerably, as do the organs used to store the tissue, namely, the leaves, stems and roots.

The cactus family, or Cactaceae, is one of the largest families of succulents in the world, containing around 2,500 species or about one quarter of the succulent plant species.

Of roughly 10,000 species of succulents worldwide, most are members of six families; the Asclepiadaceae, Asphodeliceae, Cactaceae, Crassulaceae, Euphorbiaceae and Mesembryan-themaceae. These and several other families of note are discussed, explained and illustrated in this book.

STEM SUCCULENTS

Because of their popularity and availability, cacti tend to be the first stem succulents with which people come in contact. This association is so strong (and the general knowledge about succulents is so lacking) that, when presented with any succulent, stem succulents in particular, such as a stapeliad or *Euphorbia*, they assume it is a cactus. However, two other families of plants have evolved succulent stems reminiscent of those of cacti. The Asclepiadaceae and Euphorbiaceae both contain some species which superficially resemble cacti; they have thickened stems with reduced or absent leaves and, in the Euphorbiaceae, many have developed spines.

The reduction of leaves is not a prerequisite for stem succulents as many stem succulents maintain large leaves during the growing season, losing them during dry periods. Of the six major families, those that are predominantly stem succulents are the Asclepiadaceae, Cactaceae and Euphorbiaceae.

CAUDICIFORMS

Within the group of stem succulents are species popularly referred to as caudiciforms. These plants form fleshy, thick stems and/or roots. The caudex, or storage organ, does not develop many, if any, woody fibres and can be easily cut. These storage structures thicken each season and, in some species, may ultimately reach several metres/yards in diameter. The annual growth for caudiciforms is generally leafy herbaceous stems or vines. This foliage is often non-succulent and produced

8

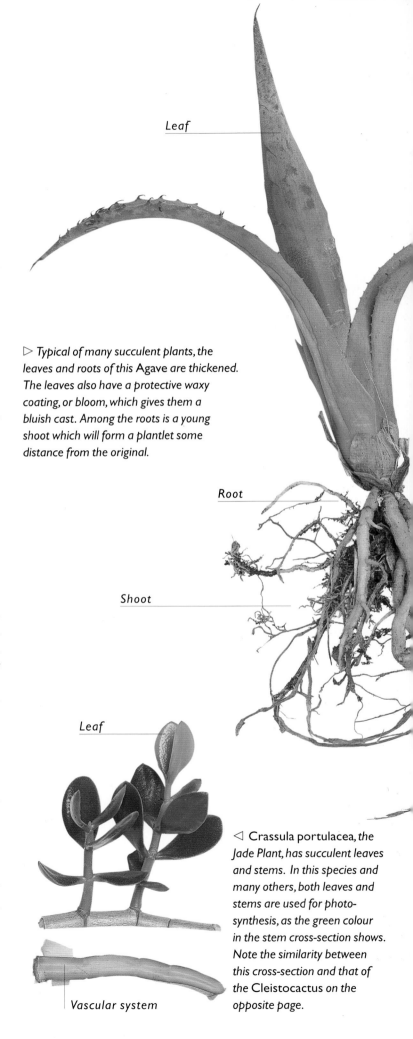

▷ *Typical of many succulent plants, the leaves and roots of this* Agave *are thickened. The leaves also have a protective waxy coating, or bloom, which gives them a bluish cast. Among the roots is a young shoot which will form a plantlet some distance from the original.*

Leaf

Root

Shoot

Leaf

◁ Crassula portulacea, *the Jade Plant, has succulent leaves and stems. In this species and many others, both leaves and stems are used for photo-synthesis, as the green colour in the stem cross-section shows. Note the similarity between this cross-section and that of the* Cleistocactus *on the opposite page.*

Vascular system

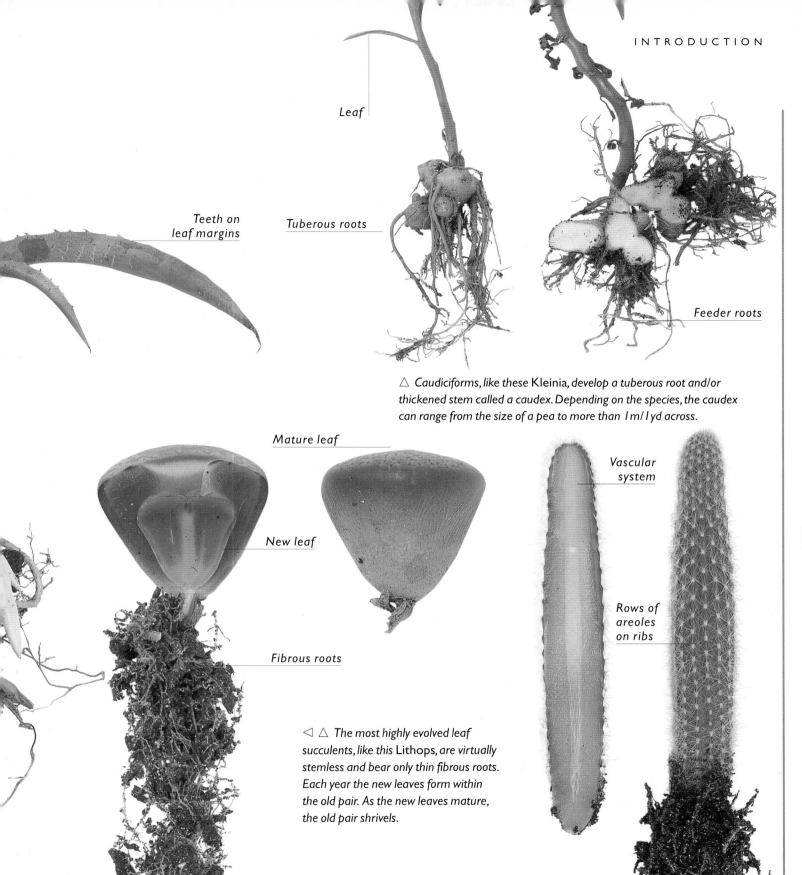

Leaf

Teeth on
leaf margins

Tuberous roots

Feeder roots

△ *Caudiciforms, like these Kleinia, develop a tuberous root and/or thickened stem called a caudex. Depending on the species, the caudex can range from the size of a pea to more than 1m/1yd across.*

Mature leaf

New leaf

Fibrous roots

Vascular
system

Rows of
areoles
on ribs

9

◁ △ *The most highly evolved leaf succulents, like this Lithops, are virtually stemless and bear only thin fibrous roots. Each year the new leaves form within the old pair. As the new leaves mature, the old pair shrivels.*

Roots

▷ *Typical of most cacti, this Cleistocactus consists of a thickened stem bearing many spines. Since most cacti are leafless, the stem must manufacture the plant's food. The vascular tissue, which transports food and water, is clearly visible in the cross-section.*

in great quantities. Most or all of this is shed at the end of the growing period. The caudex can be entirely subterranean, varying from a single bulb, corm or tuber to a cluster of thickened, dahlia-like roots. Some subterranean caudices (or caudexes) can grow to 2m/6½ft long or almost 1m/1yd across, weighing many kilograms. Often these species die back to the ground when dormant, leaving little above ground to indicate their presence. Other caudiciforms have trunks that are partially buried while still others form shrubs and trees with greatly thickened trunks. The major families of succulents with numerous caudiciform species are the Asclepiadaceae and Euphorbiaceae. Caudices can be raised by the grower for an interesting effect.

LEAF SUCCULENTS

As species evolved succulence, some depended on the stems or roots as the major storage organ, while others developed fleshy leaves. The extreme examples of the latter group are species which consist of stemless pairs of leaves. Most of the leaf succulents, however, consist of fleshy leaves borne on thin, somewhat fleshy stems. The most common growth habit in this group of succulents is a rosette of fleshy leaves. However, many extremely succulent species are composed of pairs of leaves which form small clusters, as is found in the Mesembryanthemaceae. Of the six major families of succulents, those that are predominantly leaf succulents are the Asphodeliceae, Crassulaceae and Mesembryanthemaceae.

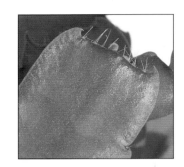

◁ The areole is the feature most commonly associated with cacti. It is essentially a flattened stem, with each spine produced in front of a microscopic leaf. Like most stems, areoles generally have dormant buds which can produce other stems or flowers.

△ The ribbed stems of cacti allow them to swell and shrink without bursting or wilting. The stomates, microscopic pores which allow plants to breathe, are located along the stems of cacti and open only at night to avoid dehydration.

▷ Spines not only protect cacti from being eaten by animals, but also provide shade from intense sun, impede air movement over the epidermis to decrease water loss, and insulate against cold weather. In areas with regular fog, the spines collect moisture from the air and channel it to the roots.

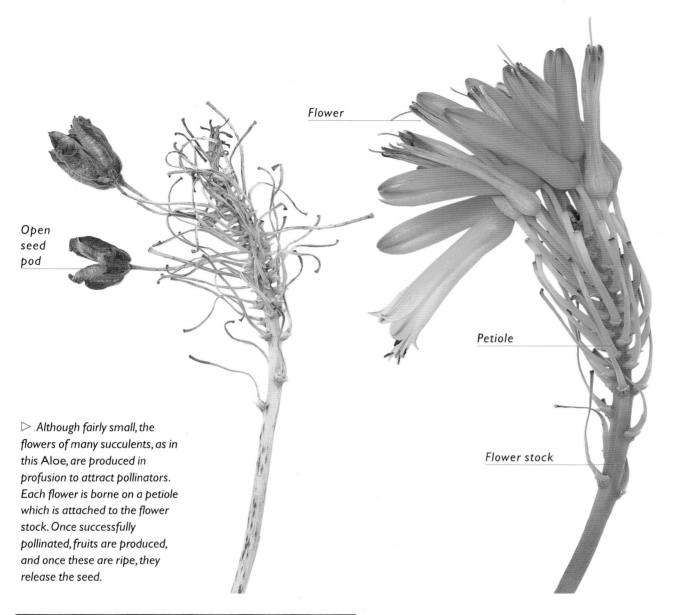

Flower

Open
seed
pod

Petiole

Flower stock

▷ .Although fairly small, the
flowers of many succulents, as in
this Aloe, are produced in
profusion to attract pollinators.
Each flower is borne on a petiole
which is attached to the flower
stock. Once successfully
pollinated, fruits are produced,
and once these are ripe, they
release the seed.

△ In the Euphorbia family the flowers are greatly reduced, without
petals or sepals, and are borne in a cup-shaped flowering head called a
cyathium. To attract pollinators, some species, like this Euphorbia milii,
produce large, brightly coloured bracts from the base of the cyathia.

SUCCULENT METABOLISM

Together with their swollen storage organs, succulent plants
have evolved other features that enable them to conserve water.
Their surface area has been reduced, in several plant families to
the extreme: a simple spherical body which has the lowest
possible surface-area-to-volume ratio. Stomates, the small pores
that allow the plant to breathe, are kept to a minimum. Many of
the most advanced succulents have developed a specific
metabolism which allows them to thrive in arid environments. In
typical non-succulent plants, the stomates must be open during
the day for photosynthesis to take place. Succulents using
Crassulacean Acid Metabolism or CAM, keep their stomates
closed during the day and still manufacture food. By "holding
their breath" during the hottest part of the day, they reduce their
water loss. The stomates then open at night and acquire the next
day's supply of carbon dioxide.

EPIDERMIS

Besides limiting the number of stomates, succulents have other
epidermal modifications. Often the epidermis is covered with a
thick, waxy cuticle. In some succulents, this powdery bloom rubs

△ *Many other succulents besides the cacti also have fierce spines for protection. In some species the spines are the remnants of the petiole or leaf base, in others they form from the pointed end of a branch. In Pachy-podium species, like this* P. namaquanum, *stipular spines grow from near the leaf base.*

▷ *Many succulents rely on wind or water for seed dispersal. Some seeds are thin with papery edges or have downy hairs to carry them away from the parent plant. Others are dust fine and are thrown from the dried capsules as the wind whips the flower stock. Other species rely on water to splash the seeds from the capsules.*

off when the plant is handled or watered overhead. The trichomes, small hairs on the leaves and stems, have also been modified. Depending on its density, colour and length, this covering of hairs is referred to by several terms including "pubescent", "hirsute" and "tomentose". This covering can serve several functions. Primarily, it slows air movement over the leaf surface, further slowing evaporation. It can also serve as protection from the sun's rays, both in tropical species and alpine species. In some cases, it offers some protection from frost.

SPINES, THORNS AND OTHER PROTECTIVE DEVICES

While many species of succulents have poisonous or irritating sap for protection, others bear armaments. There is some confusion regarding the various sharp projections on succulents.

Spines are modified leaves and are the most recognizable feature on cacti. The armaments borne by most *Euphorbia* and *Pachypodium* are stipular spines, formed from the projections at the base of the leaves. Species in the *Didiereaceae* and *Fouquieriaceae* bear spines formed from leaf bases. Uniquely in the genus *Avonia*, the stipules form a papery sheath that covers most or all of the leaf.

Thorns are formed from modified branches; these are less common among succulents. Many species of *Commiphora* bear thorns, however.

In several species of *Euphorbia*, persistent peduncles (flower stalks) can be confused with spines.

FLOWERS

Since succulents occur in many families, the flowers vary widely but often echo those of non-succulent plants. In the succulent genera *Adenium* and *Pachypodium*, the flowers are as large and brightly coloured as any member of their family, which includes

△ *To disperse their seed, some succulent fruits are designed to be eaten by animals, others use wind . Many plants in the Mesembryanthemaceae family have dry capsules which open once wetted. The seeds are then splashed out by subsequent raindrops.*

the common oleander and periwinkle. In some instances, the flowers are greatly reduced in size, to conserve water and energy. The caudiciform genus *Adenia* (not related to *Adenium*) is closely related to the common passionflower vine; however, its flowers are dull and quite small in comparison. In the Cactaceae and Mesembryanthemaceae, the flowers are often relatively large and brightly coloured. Producing large flowers requires a great deal of energy and the loss of precious water. To make the most of this expenditure, species have evolved the ability to flower simultaneously. Whole populations of the same species will flower together, often for a very short time. This ensures their mutual pollination and, for the onlooker, can create a magnificent spectacle. Succulent flowers are generally pollinated by insects, although some are visited by birds, and a few are wind pollinated.

FRUITS AND SEEDS

The fruits and seeds of succulents vary even more widely than their flowers. The members of the Apocynaceae, Asclepiadaceae and Asteraceae have inedible fruit, containing seeds which bear many long, often downy, hairs and are borne away on the wind. Fruits in the Cactaceae are often edible and brightly coloured when ripe. They are eaten by birds and mammals and the many small seeds they contain are dispersed. The fruits of the Mesembryanthemaceae are generally dry, many-celled capsules. They have hinged lids which, when moistened by a drop of water, open to the sky for the minute seeds to be splashed out by the next drop. Most species in the Euphorbiaceae produce three-celled fruits which explode when ripe, throwing the seeds up to 1m/1yd or more. The ripe fruits of the Crassulaceae and Portulacaceae are dry, open-ended capsules, held upright. As the wind whips the flower stalks about, the small seeds are thrown from the capsule.

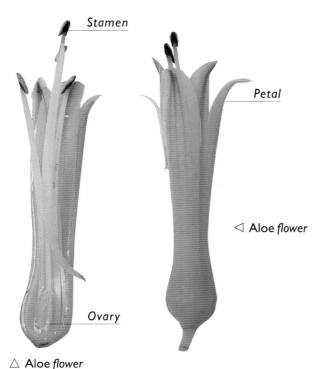

△ **Aloe** *flower*

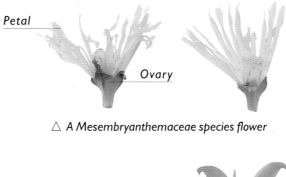

◁ *Succulent fruits and seeds vary even more than their flowers. This fruit of the* Momordica rostrata *resembles small, dark orange peppers.*

13

▽ *The flowers of these different succulents (clockwise from left: Aloe, species in Mesembryanthemaceae, and Echeveria) are quite similar, containing essentially the same parts: the sepals, the colourful petals, several stamens (made of a filament topped with an anther), and pistil(s), composed of an ovary, style and stigma.*

△ *A Mesembryanthemaceae species flower*

◁ **Aloe** *flower*

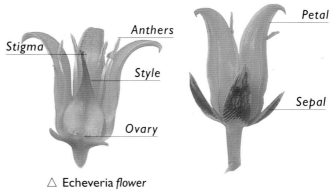

△ **Echeveria** *flower*

Natural habitats

Succulents occur throughout much of the world. They often exist in environmental niches that would otherwise be unoccupied. They have a varied and rich range of habitats.

Adapting to the Environment

While a few succulent species make up the dominant flora in some arid areas, growing along with or in the place of shrubs and trees, more often they are found growing in the protection of larger plants or in the shelter of rocks. Whatever precipitation occurs must then be shared by all. Since succulents can survive on a minimum of water, this situation is generally advantageous to the succulent without being deleterious to the shade plant. This is not always true as can be shown in the relationship between *Carnegiea gigantea*, the giant saguaro cactus and *Cercidium microphyllum*, the Foothills Palo Verde, a small tree from the Sonoran Desert in Arizona, USA and Mexico. Saguaro seedlings begin life under the protection of several species of "nurse" plants. When a saguaro seedling germinates under a Foothills Palo Verde, it may grow in harmony with it for more than 50 years. However, this association can end during years of lower than average rainfall. The feeder roots of the saguaro occur in the first 30cm/12in of the surface, and can take up most of the moisture from light rains. The nurse tree is literally starved, or at least made more vulnerable to insect or fungal attack.

Desert Plains

Since the bulk of succulents is found in arid regions, they are most often associated with deserts but, in fact, only a small percentage of succulent species actually occur in extremely arid areas. Most species grow in areas receiving from 5–50cm/2–20in of precipitation annually. Many grow in areas that receive a generous annual rainfall in one season but which then undergo six or more months of drought. Here, succulent species, the caudiciforms in particular, produce large quantities of growth during the rainy season, becoming dormant during the dry season.

Mountainous Regions and Rain Forests

Succulents occur widely through hilly and mountainous regions, growing in cracks in the rock, sometimes on sheer cliffs or on rock shelves with little soil. This survival strategy works as well in areas of high rainfall as it does in arid ones. By surviving in these

△ *Although many rare succulents are threatened by unscrupulous collectors, overgrazing by livestock, urbanization and agricultural development pose a far greater danger. Several weeks before this photograph was taken, this had been the habitat for* Carnegiea, *and several species of* Echinocereus, Mammillaria *and* Opuntia.

◁ *Many succulents occur on rocky hillsides and cliffs. This affords them better drainage during wet years and allows them to survive periods of drought better than competing species. This colony of* Agave *has established itself on a rocky slope. The oldest plant is nearly ready to produce its only flower stalk. If successful, it will produce thousands of seeds and then die.*

△ This dense population of Carnegiea gigantea, *the giant saguaro cactus, should continue to dominate this landscape because of the presence of nurse plants.*

△ Here, several succulents share the same niche: three Fouquieria splendens (centre), Carnegiea, Ferocactus, Echinocereus, Mammillaria *and several* Opuntia *species.*

◁ As drainage and soil type change, so do the species of succulents. Here, some species of Opuntia *occupy the lower areas, while others dominate the rocky outcrops.*

△ *This* Stenocereus thurberi, *or Organ Pipe Cactus, is growing on the Gulf of California. Many succulents occur along dry coastlines like this one. Although these habitats can have low annual rainfall, high humidity and occasional fog make it possible for a great number of species to survive.*

▷ *In Organ Pipe Cactus National Monument* Carnegiea gigantea *and* Stenocereus thurberi *grow together, along with* Fouquieria splendens. *In the Americas, Africa and Madagascar there are areas where several species of large succulents dominate the landscape.*

△ *The desert briefly comes into bloom in the spring in Joshua Tree National Monument. Even in a very arid climate succulents can form dense colonies if they are sufficiently drought-hardy, like these* Opuntia bigelowii *or Teddy Bear Cholla.*

▷ *Living up to its common name, the Mexican Fence Post,* Stenocereus marginatus, *is planted in rows to make a living fence. In other areas* Fouquieria splendens, *species of* Opuntia, *and certain* Euphorbia *are grown as hedges and fences.*

◁ *These ancient* Carnegiea
gigantea *are perhaps 150–200
years old and may only live
another 50 years. The smaller
plants growing nearby are from
later generations that will replace
the older plants in the years to
come.*

△ *In the Mohave Desert, only a
few centimetres of rain fall
during each winter. This limits
the numbers of species which
can survive as well as their
density.* Yucca brevifolia, *the
Joshua tree, dominates the
sparse landscape.*

well drained, low-soil locations, they avoid excess moisture and
thrive in niches where other species cannot. Succulents from
mountainous regions must be adapted to survive cold as well as
drought. There are specialized tropical succulents that occur in
humid rain forests, as well. Many of these are epiphytes, plants
that grow without soil, using other species, particularly trees, for
support. These feed on the nutrients the rain washes down the
bark of their host plants.

NATURAL DISTRIBUTION

Some succulent species do survive in hyper-arid areas, along the
coast of Chile and the south-west coast of Africa, where rainfall
is quite rare and the plants have evolved to survive on the daily
fog off the ocean that moistens the top centimetre or two of soil.
Africa, including the Arabian peninsula, contains the greatest
concentration of succulents in the world. Southern Africa, in
particular, has very ancient deserts which have allowed species
from many families to develop succulence in a wide variety of
forms. Madagascar, because of its isolation, has developed a
great diversity of succulents rivalling those in Africa, but not in
the number of species. In the Americas, the greatest
concentration of succulents is found in Mexico, although
succulent species occur from the USA to southern Argentina.
A number of succulent species occur in southern Europe but,
generally, most are only suitable for rock gardens.

BOTANY AND CLASSIFICATION

When a budding cactus and succulent collector first opens a book on the subject, he or she is confronted by copious lists of Latin names. To newcomers, these names can seem unintelligible and unpronounceable. The result of the labours of taxonomists for the last 300 years, Latin names are man's attempt to simplify and make sense of the relationships of living things.

Most lay people expect taxonomy to remain static – as though a name is "set in granite" once given to a particular plant or animal. This cannot be, alas, since ever more accurate methods are constantly being developed for analysing the relationships of plants.

Environmental forces have caused plants to evolve into many bizarre and interesting forms. When studying related species, genera or families of flowering plants, taxonomists look at the plants' bodies (leaves, stems, roots, etc.) but this yields only gross data. More importantly, they closely examine the flowers and fruit, and, more recently, genetic markers, all of which more concretely show the relative proximity of species to each other. Even within a single genus, it is possible to have many closely related species that bear little outward resemblance; one only has to look at the genus *Euphorbia* to see this. Upon closer examination, however, the flowers and fruit clearly show their family association.

CACTUS SHAPES

▷ *This is a columnar cactus. This group contains mostly large-growing plants, ultimately becoming the familiar desert "trees". Many will not flower until they are at least 1.2m/4ft tall.*

◁ *This is a rainforest cactus,* Selenicereus chrysocardium. *These plants usually have flattened, leaf-like or cylindrical stems and are often pendant in habit. They are mostly large growing, make ideal subjects for hanging baskets and are cultivated for their flowers.*

◁ *This is the Prickly Pear (*Opuntia). Opuntias *often have flattened, disc-like pads arranged on top of each other like bunnies' ears. These plants are usually collected for their appearance and spination.*

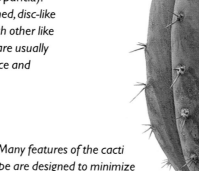

▷ *Many features of the cacti shape are designed to minimize water loss, such as their waxy skin and concertina-like ribbing. The ribbing enables the plant to expand and contract as moisture becomes available, without splitting its skin.*

SUCCULENT SEEDLINGS

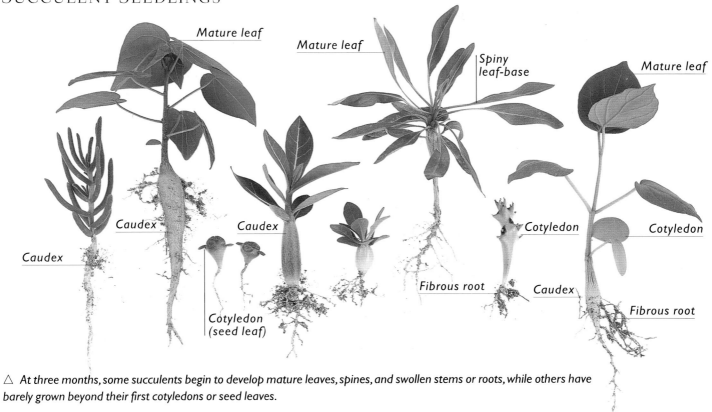

Mature leaf

Mature leaf

Spiny leaf-base

Mature leaf

Caudex

Caudex

Caudex

Cotyledon

Cotyledon

Fibrous root

Caudex

Cotyledon (seed leaf)

Fibrous root

△ *At three months, some succulents begin to develop mature leaves, spines, and swollen stems or roots, while others have barely grown beyond their first cotyledons or seed leaves.*

LEAF SHAPES

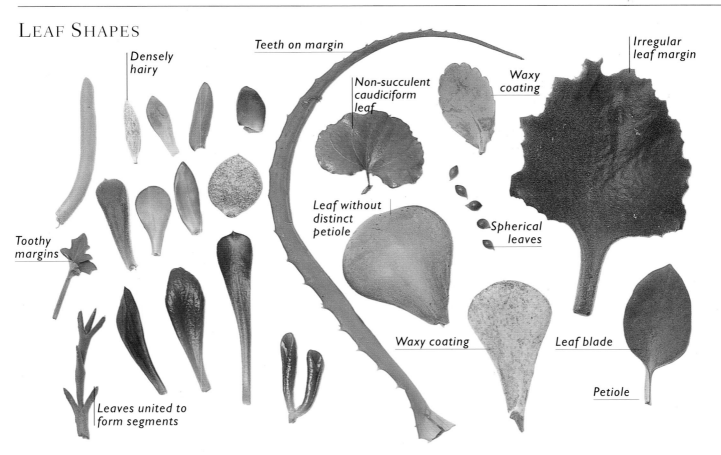

Densely hairy

Teeth on margin

Irregular leaf margin

Non-succulent caudiciform leaf

Waxy coating

Toothy margins

Leaf without distinct petiole

Spherical leaves

Waxy coating

Leaf blade

Leaves united to form segments

Petiole

△ *Succulents have many of the same leaf shapes as non-succulent plants, although they are generally smaller to lessen evaporation, and in some instances have become almost spherical, which gives the lowest surface area to volume ratio.*

Stem Shapes

Areole

Areole

Joints arising
from an areole

Areole

Flower

Flower

Aerial roots

Areole

Areoles with
thin spines

Areole

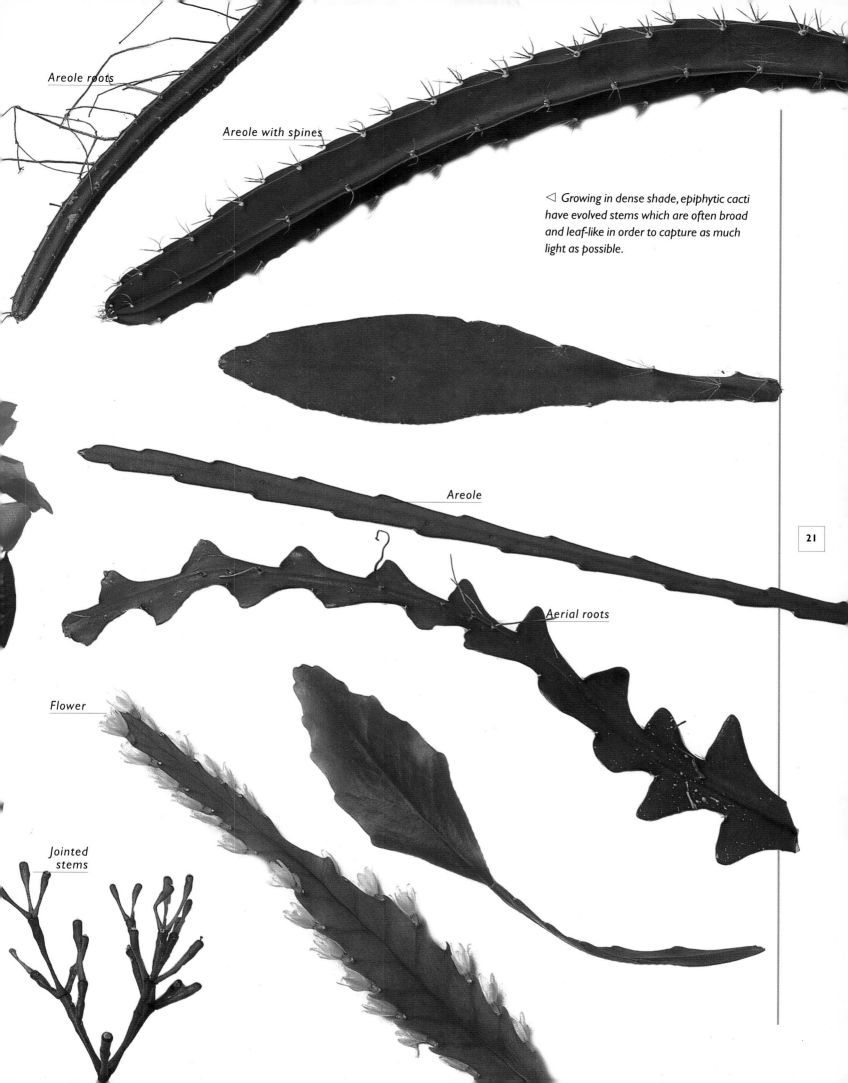

Areole roots

Areole with spines

◁ *Growing in dense shade, epiphytic cacti have evolved stems which are often broad and leaf-like in order to capture as much light as possible.*

Areole

21

Aerial roots

Flower

Jointed stems

FLOWERS

Although a few succulents are wind pollinated, the majority are pollinated by insects and other animals. Many are brightly coloured or sweetly scented and are visited by bees, butterflies, moths, birds or bats. A great number are foul smelling and attractive to flies and ants.

▷ Although without fragrance, the flowers of the Echeveria are coloured to attract bees and other insect pollinators.

△ The brightly coloured flowers of Rebutia heliosa *like many diminutive cacti are important to attract pollinating insects.*

▽ When borne in mass, the flowers of this Crassula are attractive to insects. In addition to the visual display, some Crassula have highly scented flowers in order to draw insects and ensure pollination.

△ In addition to producing showy flowers, cacti within a population flower simultaneously, making the best use of their precious resources.

◁ *Like many cacti, this Schlumbergera produces highly coloured flowers. It is particularly important that the flowers stand out from the leaf boughs of its host tree.*

▽ *Epiphyllum x 'Reward' is the culmination of hybridizing smaller flowered species with coloured flowers to larger, white-flowered species.*

▽ *The daisy-like "flowers" of this Kleinia, like other plants in the Asteraceae, are composed of many small flowers. Although they look inconspicuous individually, when borne together they create a display to draw pollinating insects.*

▷ *Like many other plants, cacti and succulents have been hybridized to improve their flowers. The flower of this Epiphyllum-Disocactus hybrid, Epiphyllum x 'Wendy May', combines the rich colour and shape of the Disocactus parent with the larger size of the Epiphyllum heritage.*

design
ideas

Whether you are growing cacti and succulents in garden settings, on a patio or terrace, in a greenhouse or indoors, this section will provide you with design ideas and inspiration. Discover how to plan and plant an impressive display of cacti and succulents in your garden. If space is at a premium, or climatic conditions not in your favour, you can still enjoy growing the plants in pots, boxes and planters. Whatever you decide, there is certain to be a plant that will thrive in your environment.

◁ *Growing cacti and succulents in containers allows you to control the plants' growing conditions.*

GARDEN SETTINGS

Without a doubt, the most spectacular displays of succulents are well planned outdoor plantings. When planted in the ground and exposed to the elements, cacti and succulents can take on an appearance that is not otherwise possible. The benefits of growing plants in the ground are balanced by the liabilities, however. The degree of control the grower has over the plants is considerably less than in container cultivation and, obviously, the plants cannot be as easily rearranged as in a potted display. In addition, the plants may be subject to abnormal weather conditions and are not as easily protected.

The grower does have a certain amount of control over the environment he or she provides for plants grown outside, but much of this must be thought out before the first succulent is ever put in the ground. To prevent waterlogging, particularly in regions with a high rainfall, succulents can be maintained in raised beds or planted on berms (mounds) formed of a well drained compost (potting soil). In many gardens, a steep slope with shallow soil is all that many succulent species require.

In addition to preparing the site correctly, the particular species for outside growing need to be carefully selected. This does not mean only choosing those with the right tolerances for sun or shade and for the temperatures they are expected to endure; you need to select species that will grow well together for a period of time. By picking the right species, the grower will determine the amount of annual care that must go into a planting. The species chosen will determine if the planting is to be a long-term, low-maintenance display or a hands-on garden, requiring thinning as specimens begin to over-run each other.

△ *Plants that need little more than annual rainfall to survive can be chosen. Here, species of* Agave, Dasylirion *and* Opuntia *provide a relatively care-free landscape. These species have also been selected for their cold and sun hardiness to suit the climate and will require no additional protection once established.*

▽ *The yellow-flowered rosettes of* Aeonium *and pink-flowered* Lampranthus *have been combined for effect in this mass planting. In plantings with relatively fast-growing, spreading succulents, occasional pruning and replanting are necessary. After several years the bed will become untidy and overgrown. When it is time to replant a mass planting, the plants already growing there will provide plenty of cuttings.*

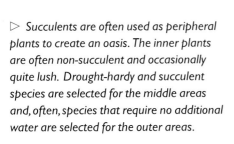
△ The choice of plants for a garden is determined by the local climate and the amount of care the gardener wishes to provide. In the background an Aloe (left) and an Agave (right) provide a backdrop for smaller, bushy species of Mesembryanthemaceae and a large cluster of Aeonium.

▷ Succulents are often used as peripheral plants to create an oasis. The inner plants are often non-succulent and occasionally quite lush. Drought-hardy and succulent species are selected for the middle areas and, often, species that require no additional water are selected for the outer areas.

△ *A display of succulent plants does not require either rare species or expensive pots to look good. Here, common species of* Echinopsis *and* Sempervivum *are attractively displayed in plain clay pots. The location of the shelving provides them with adequate but not excessive light.*

▷ *This attractive planter combines succulents that have different shapes and forms. The pair of round-bodied* Notocactus, *tall* Trichocereus *and thin-leaved* Agave *at the back provide greenery without the care and water that non-succulent species would require.*

◁ *In this planting, non-succulent* Lantana *provides lush greenery and colourful flowers. Species of* Agave, Opuntia *and* Yucca *provide the succulent transition to the native desert flora in the background.*

▷ *Epiphytic cacti can provide a stunning display.* Aporocactus, Epiphyllum *and their hybrids, as well as other epiphytic cacti, require the warmth, shade and humidity of their original tropical habitat. They have been bred for decades and their hundreds of hybrids bear flowers in every shade possible for cacti, with some over 20cm/8in wide. Their pendulous, lightly spined stems provide a tropical look when they are not in flower.*

PATIOS AND TERRACES

When used for outdoor pot culture, cacti and succulents contribute their greatest visual impact for the amount of space and care required. Because of their compact root systems and hardiness to heat, drought, and underpotting (being kept rootbound in a small pot), succulents provide relatively care-free, attractive additions to most outdoor settings. The wide range of species available on the market today ensures that some species will be adaptable for almost every climate.

CHOOSING THE BEST PLANTS

Choosing particular plants for outdoor pot culture depends on the degree of care the grower is willing to provide, the particular exposure for which the plant is intended, the local climate, and the species that are readily available. In extremely wet and/or cold climates, the number of succulents that will be hardy year-round is relatively limited. Of course, if the grower is willing to take extra steps to protect less hardy species, the number of usable species is greatly increased.

CARING FOR OUTDOOR PLANTS

In moderately cold areas, especially those with very wet winters, semi-hardy species can be moved against buildings under overhangs, to keep them dryer and somewhat warmer.

▷ *Succulents can be used in place of non-succulent patio plants. Shade provided by walls, an overhanging roof or an adjacent tree will moderate the environment, giving the grower a greater choice of species that can be used.*

▽ *Given a degree of shade, small clay pots are perfect for succulents. They can be moved easily for display, and the hardy nature of succulents allows them to thrive without frequent watering.*

▽ Raised ground beds, like this greenhouse cactus planting with various species of Parodia in the foreground, make a more natural display than individually potted plants.

△ Narrow, tall-growing succulents like these Opuntia and Sansevieria are good accent plants for narrow locations. However, care should be taken not to position spiny plants in high traffic areas.

△ The relatively small amount of care required by succulents makes them excellent for display on patio tables. Care must always be taken to ensure they will tolerate the new exposure and are sufficiently acclimatized.

◁ Spreading species will require the same occasional maintenance in a raised greenhouse bed as they do outside. The faster growing species will eventually overtake and smother slower-growing ones. If this spreading Opuntioid has outgrown its allotted space, it can be judiciously pruned, or dug up, separated, and a portion of it replanted.

Additionally, a covering of hessian (burlap) or an old sheet will add several degrees of frost protection. Where winters are too severe, growers are forced to move frost-tender or even semi-hardy plants indoors during the winter months. Provided the grower accepts this inconvenience, the number of species that can be grown in any given region is greatly increased. Generally, these outdoor plants require minimal care through the winter; infrequent watering and no fertilization.

However, care must be taken when placing plants back outside. During the period indoors or under cover, the plants will lose their acclimatization to the outdoor sun and can easily suffer from sunburn. This can be remedied by moving them into the sun gradually, or by placing them out with a covering of 30–50 per cent shade cloth (3–4 layers of muslin/cheesecloth) for several weeks until they have acclimatized. Taking care and time at this stage will be worth it in the future.

GREENHOUSE CULTIVATION

Once a grower has invested in a greenhouse, the range of species that can be maintained successfully considerably increases. With the correct artificial environment, virtually any species can be cultivated anywhere, from cacti in the far north to orchids in the desert. The time when most structures of this type were literally glass houses is largely over. New materials and better knowledge of growing requirements have allowed growers worldwide to tailor their buildings to provide the proper conditions for optimum growth. This does not apply only to commercial growers, since some of the most impressive collections under glass belong to hobbyists.

Types of Greenhouse

These structures can vary from the most rudimentary to extremely elaborate, depending on the degree of effort needed to control their artificial climate. The most basic greenhouse is the cold frame, which offers protection from excess moisture and, to some degree, from excessive cold. The difference between a cold frame and state-of-the-art greenhouse is that further steps are taken to modify the interior climate (for example, heating, cooling, air circulation and so on). While necessity often requires that the appearance of greenhouses is utilitarian, they can be designed to be attractive as well, but this is generally not as important to the grower as the contents.

Displaying in Greenhouses

In addition to allowing the grower to cultivate exotic species in otherwise adverse climates, greenhouses permit more varied and attractive displays. Aside from masses of potted specimens, exotic species can be cultivated in ground beds, creating impressive effects. Occasionally, a greenhouse is specifcally designed and landscaped with succulents for a stunning display but, for the most part, one of the main functions of the greenhouse is as a retreat from the busy world, where the grower can be surrounded by plants.

▽ *Leafy succulents such as* **Adenium**, **Pachypodium** *and many other species like this* **Euphorbia** *can provide the illusion of lush tropical greenery without the frequent watering required by non-succulent species.*

△ *Clusters of pots – whether plain, painted or patterned – always make an attractive display in a greenhouse or patio. To protect the display area from water damage, saucers are placed under the pots.*

33

GROWING INDOORS

Cacti and succulents are found most often as houseplants and in other interior settings, such as shopping centres and offices. Because of their tenacity, they endure, sometimes thriving, where other plants languish and fail. Their strange appearance and often geometrical forms add an unusual beauty that other houseplants cannot offer. There are succulent species that will survive all but the most dimly lit interior and, if the grower is willing to rotate plants from lighter to darker locations and vice versa, even settings with inadequate light can be occupied by living succulents.

Typically, the windowsill is the indoor home of the cactus or succulent, but they also work well in doorways. Tall-growing species of *Cereus* or *Euphorbia* provide height with little spread, for example. Interior planter boxes are fairly popular but they require more care than individually potted plants since the large volume of soil takes longer to dry out, making root rot a possibility. Alternatively, fill a large planter with bark, gravel or another inert material and plant the succulents (in their pots) in this medium. If the plant needs to be relocated, simply move it in its pot.

Many hanging species that are too tender to survive a patio exposure survive well indoors, and will thrive under the illumination of a skylight. Growing under artificial light has become common for residences without adequate indoor sunlight. Although the newer halide lights are considerably more expensive than the fluorescent lights originally designed for indoor growing, the difference in growth that halide lights make is remarkable, and plants can be grown from seed to flower in the total absence of real sunlight.

▽ *If adequate levels of light cannot be provided in a reasonably well-lit location, plants can be rotated from a better growing area to a display location and back again. While this requires additional attention, it does ensure flowering, healthy plants for a less than ideal situation.*

△ *Selecting pots to match plants is always important. This Cereus species nicely accents the tall pot in which it is planted. When planting in extremely deep containers, watering should be closely monitored since they will dry out more slowly than shallow pots.*

34

◁ Decorative pots are more useful indoors, where they can be selected both to match the plant and complement the interior. The blue colouring of this Pilosocereus goes well with the pot and the surroundings. It is also staged in a bright location. An effort should always be made to select plants that will grow well in the amount of light available.

▷ Even this small windowsill provides adequate lighting to keep a tiny collection of succulents healthy. Some growers are tempted to turn their plants periodically as they lean towards the light, but care should be taken that the previously shaded side of the plant does not get sunburned by its new exposure.

△ A potted Opuntia, or Prickly Pear, provides the spread and greenery of a conventional houseplant, while requiring less frequent watering. The choice of lightly spined species of succulents is especially important for busy indoor areas.

37

◁ Light is the most important factor to consider when growing plants indoors. Where adequate illumination is provided, the plants will be much healthier and require less care.

◁ Ornate planters can create a stunning visual effect, but they also have some drawbacks. Often, matching saucers are not available so the plants have to be watered elsewhere. Sometimes the pots lack a drainage hole. The compost (potting soil) should always be allowed to dry out between waterings. The compost (potting soil) may need to be changed periodically to prevent salts from building up.

▷ Extreme temperatures can be a problem when growing succulents near a window. Plants kept too close to a window can be exposed to temperatures over 38°C/100°F or they can freeze in winter without adequate air movement and insulation.

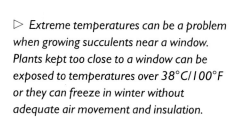

OUTDOOR CONTAINERS

The durability of succulents allows them to be grown in virtually any container. They will survive, and thrive, even when under-potted and root-bound; hence there is little need to transplant them annually or even every couple of years. Underpotted specimens make excellent displays with their pots nested in larger pots with no drainage, and in ornate containers not normally suitable for potting.

WHICH CONTAINER?

Many growers choose to grow their plants exclusively in porous clay pots. The availability of high-quality potting composts (potting soils) allows succulents to be grown successfully in glazed and plastic pots just as easily. The only drawback of many attractive containers is their excessive depth, which can be remedied by filling them partially with gravel or other coarse inert material before planting. Most succulents are perfectly adapted for shallow pots or bonsai-style planters since they can tolerate both periodic drought and restricted root growth and can survive many years in the same pot. Displaying caudiciform succulents in bonsai pots is becoming increasingly popular.

WINDOW BOXES

These planters have long been popular in urban areas, particularly for those enthusiasts with little growing space. Although originally developed for flowering annuals, the good drainage and shallow soil they provide make window boxes ideal for cacti and succulents. In hot, arid regions, people new to the area often begin by planting the tender, leafy plants with which they are familiar, only to see them perish from the harsh conditions. With luck, they later find that succulents flourish in this situation. Of course, the succulent species need to be selected for their specific light and temperature requirements. Generally, those species that will tolerate intense light and heat can be put in settings with lower light and planted together with those which require more shade.

HANGING BASKETS

Many succulents make fine specimens in hanging baskets, once again because of the shallow soil and good drainage baskets provide. The succulents that make particularly nice displays are, obviously, those with pendulous or vining stems. Of these, there are far more that require shade than there are sun-loving species. This is largely because many of them, the cacti in particular, tend to grow naturally in the shade of trees, often using these for support. Hence, most hanging baskets do better and last longer on a sheltered patio. Although a single specimen will eventually fill a hanging basket, most of the time several cuttings are planted together. These will more quickly fill the pot and tend to create a denser, more attractive effect.

△ *This display of cacti and succulents demonstrates the visual effect of matching tall plants and pots with shorter species in lower containers. Whichever container is selected, its size should be only as large as necessary. Succulents rarely die from being underpotted.*

△ *Expensive ceramic planters are not essential for creating an attractive display. When nicely arranged, plain clay pots are quite adequate. Garishly coloured planters generally detract from the plant.*

▷ *An Agave americana 'Medio-picta alba' has been staged effectively in this planter. Not only do the colours of the plant and pot complement each other, but the shape of the pot mirrors that of the plant. Equally importantly, the pot is not too large; a large pot can lead to problems with root rot.*

△ *Traditional wooden window box planters have largely been replaced by long clay planters, which are relatively portable and long lasting. This also allows them to be displayed in garden settings among plants that have totally different watering requirements.*

▷ *For display in a corner or against a wall, this bowl garden was planted with the taller plants towards the back. A bowl intended for a central location can be planted with the tallest plants in the middle. These plants have been adequately spaced to allow for growth, with stones placed between them to fill gaps.*

△ *Here several different species are planted in a window box. In time, if planters become grossly overgrown as the different plants grow at different rates, they can be removed and replanted.*

◁ *When several different species are combined in the same planter, care must be taken to select those with similar watering requirements. These succulents will flourish together needing the same amount of care.*

▽ *Unless terracotta pots are treated with a sealant, salts will eventually accumulate on the lower sides. Much of this can be removed with a stiff brush. Many growers prefer not to use a sealant on their porous clay pots, since this prevents the clay from "breathing" and slows down drying out.*

PLANT DIRECTORY

cacti

To many people, a cactus is the tall, spiny plant that they have seen in films of the wild west. There are, in fact, nearly 2,500 different species and an even greater number of distinctive forms. They range from small, button-like plants, less than 2.5cm/1in across, to barrel-shaped plants and tall, columnar cacti, which are grown for their magnificent flowers. This cacti directory provides a full photographic catalogue of the most common species.

◁ *A group of* **Echinocereus** *or "hedgehog cacti", so-called because of the hemispherical mounds typical of some of the species (seen far left).*

How to Use the Directory

The plant directory is divided into two sections: cacti and succulents. Within each section the genera, or plant groups, are arranged by the Latin or plant names in alphabetical order.

Plant Names

With each of the entries in this section are several, often long, Latin names. These provide information about their taxonomic status, or, who is related to whom and how closely. A family of plants (the name ending in -aceae) is made up of many different genera (the plural of genus). Within each genus, there are often a number of closely related species. If there is only one species in a genus, it is said to be monotypic.

Additionally, a species can also be divided into subspecies, varieties, cultivars and forms. Subspecies (written as ssp.) and varieties (written as var. or v., as in *Agave parryi* var. *truncata*) are quite similar. These distinguish variations in different populations of a species. These populations can be nearby, or separated by hundreds of kilometres. A form refers to minor differences within a species, often one characteristic, like flower colour. Cultivar, short for cultivated variety, is used for one individual with unusual features, either of cultivated or wild origin. Occasionally a species name will be preceded by aff., an abbreviation for affinity, meaning than an unnamed species is closely related to an already named species, e.g. *Kalanchoe* aff. *marmorata*.

The name of hybrid succulents is listed two ways, depending on their origin. When an "x" precedes the genus, it denotes an intergeneric hybrid, e.g. x *Graptoveria*, which is a *Graptopetalum* crossed with an *Echeveria*. If the "x" precedes the hybrid name it denotes the cross of two species in the same genus, e.g. *Crassula* x 'Morgan's Pink', a hybrid of two Crassula species.

Finally, there are some mutations which are commonly cultivated and this additional name appears after the

species: cristate (or crest), monstrosa (or monstrose), and variegate, e.g. *Cereus hildmannianus monstrosus*

Although the Latin names of cacti and succulents may appear confusing to the beginner, they provide valuable information about plants' features, their habitat, and are often a tribute to those who discovered them or were prominent at the time they were named. Names can also change over time which can make things even more complicated for the collector.

For example, *Carnegiea gigantea* was originally named *Cereus giganteus*: '*Cereus*' for its columnar growth habit and white tubular flowers and '*giganteus*' for its gigantic stature. However, eminent taxonomists N.L. Britton and J.N. Rose determined that it was distinct enough to warrant its own genus. In 1908 in *The New York Botanical Garden*, they published it under the new genus Carnegiea in honour of the distinguished philanthropist of the time, Andrew

Genus name
Botanical or Latin name of the plant group.

Genus introduction
Main features and common characteristics of the group.

Latin plant name
If applicable, the common plant name is included below.

Natural habitat
Information is included, where relevant, on the natural habitiat

---

Mammillaria

One of the largest genera, with about 250 species, this is, understandably, one of the most common in cultivation. The species vary from dwarf species no more than 2cm/¾in in size to massive clusters more than a metre/yard across. While many of the species are somewhat tender, others will tolerate heavy frost and a few thrive in full sun. The flowers, although small, are often borne in rings around the crowns of the stems for several weeks. There are many species that are easy to cultivate as well as those of interest to the advanced collector and they range from the south-western USA into Mexico.

△ **Mammillaria bocasana**

Often sold as the "powder puff" cactus, this species gets its common name from the white, hair-like spines that often hide the stiff radial spines and hooked central spine. The 6cm/2½in wide stems can form a 25cm/10in wide, flattened cluster. Its pinkish-yellow flowers are produced during the summer. A woollier form, *M. bocasana* fma. *multilanata*, is also commonly available. *M. bocasana* is somewhat prone to rot, particularly in larger plants. It tolerates temperatures of −7°C/20°F for short periods and it is propagated from seed.

Natural habitat: Mexico

△ **Mammillaria bombycina**

Its attractive spination and many pink spring flowers have made this species very popular. The 6cm/2½in wide stems can make clusters to 30cm/12in or more. It has no special requirements but will not withstand long periods below −4°C/25°F. It is grown from seed.

Natural habitat: Mexico

△ **Mammillaria duwei**

Often considered a form of *M. nana*, this species has dense, pubescent radial spines and occasionally produces pubescent hooked central spines. The 4cm/1½in wide stems can form a small cluster with age. The small yellow flowers are produced for many weeks in the spring. It can tolerate temperatures down to −7°C/20°F, but will not put up with excess moisture during the winter. It is propagated from seed.

Natural habitat: Mexico

84

44

PLANT DIRECTORY *cacti*

△ *Mammillaria candida*

Generally solitary, the 10cm/4in wide stems of this species will occasionally cluster with age. When grown in adequate light, the dense, white spines completely hide the stem. Light pink flowers are borne in rings in late spring. It will tolerate temperatures of –7°C/20°F, for short periods. It is grown from seed.

Natural habitat: Mexico

△ *Mammillaria carmenae*

Rediscovered in the 1970s, this choice species has become quite common. Although dwarf and mostly solitary in its habitat, the stems will grow to 5cm/2in and make 15cm/6in wide clusters in cultivation. It will tolerate some frost, but is particularly rot-prone if kept too wet in cool weather. It is, primarily, grown from seed.

Natural habitat: Mexico

85

◁ *Mammillaria geminispina*

Clumping to form plants up to 40cm/16in across, this species is commonly available in two fairly distinct forms. Known as *M. geminispina nobilis*, this is the more recent introduction and has thinner stems than the older form, 7cm/2⅝in wide as opposed to 10cm/4in wide; it can have central spines up to 5cm/2in long. Both forms produce rings of 7mm/¼in wide, dark pink flowers in the spring and make good landscape plants in areas where the temperature doesn't drop below –7°C/20°F, or stay below freezing for more than 24 hours. Outstanding clones of this species are propagated from offsets, but it is generally grown from seed.

Natural habitat: Mexico

Caption

Includes details on the form, growth, flower type, unusual features and cultivation advice.

Photograph

Each species is illustrated with a photograph.

Symbols

There are five different symbols which indicate the best growing situation for the plant.

Carnegie. When it was changed, '*giganteus*' was changed to '*gigantea*' in order to agree with the suffix of the new Latin genus name.

Growing Symbols

After each species description are symbols to help the grower choose the plant location. There are five different symbols which indicate the following locations: house, windowsill, outdoor pot culture, greenhouse, landscaping.

Temperature

The temperatures provided represent the minimum temperature these species will tolerate for brief periods of time. The same species, however, may be damaged from these or even less severe temperatures when exposed for prolonged periods or if they have tender new growth. Similarly, some species will tolerate even lower temperatures than those given, when properly acclimatized and protected from excess moisture.

Key to Growing Symbols

There are five different symbols which help the grower to choose the best growing situation for the plant.

House

Species with the house symbol should survive, if not thrive, given the limited light and temperature levels in a bright indoor location.

Windowsill

These species often require more light than typical houseplants, but should otherwise grow well indoors when placed in a sunny window.

45

Outdoor pot culture

Plants labelled for use in pots outdoors will generally tolerate a wider range of temperatures and brighter light than houseplants. Many of these species do, however, have special requirements which are included in their descriptions. Not all species listed as patio plants will be appropriate for all areas, and most will have to be protected.

Greenhouse

Virtually any plant can be cultivated in a greenhouse, although some rapidly become too large. If this is the sole icon for a plant, it has light and temperature requirements which will be difficult to provide elsewhere.

Landscaping

Species with the landscape symbol are particularly well suited for outdoor plantings, provided the local climate is appropriate. Many of these species will tolerate hot, direct half-day sun, once they are acclimatized.

ACANTHOCALYCIUM

This small genus is closely related to *Echinopsis*. Consisting of around ten species, these are generally unbranched and, initially, spherical, but with age become columnar. While the most common species are easily grown, several species are more dwarf, slow-growing and fairly rot-prone. All species tolerate some frost and fairly hot, intense sunlight. The flowers are diurnal and can be white, yellow, pink, orange or red.

▷ **Acanthocalycium violaceum**

The most common species in this genus, this is also the largest. Initially spherical, it can eventually form a solitary column 15cm/6in in diameter and 60cm/2ft tall. It is a good beginner's plant, flowering at 6cm/2½in in size. It also tolerates very strong light and cold for short periods (down to –10°C/15°F). It is propagated only by seed.

Natural habitat: Argentina

APOROCACTUS

One of the easiest of the epiphytic genera to grow, this genus has thin stems that bear highly coloured flowers and are perfectly adapted for hanging baskets. They have been hybridized with several other genera of epiphytes; the most common result is the hybrid genus x *Aporophyllum*, from crosses with *Epiphyllum*. They will grow in a standard cactus potting compost (potting soil).

▷ **Aporocactus flagelliformis**

Cultivated for decades, this species is often called the "rat-tail cactus". Its 1cm/½in thick stems hang down to 60cm/2ft, making this cactus one of the outstanding plants for hanging baskets. Bright pink flowers, 4cm/1½in across and 6cm/2½in long, are produced randomly along the stems. While this species will not tolerate any frost, it does well outdoors in the summer, provided it is protected from the full afternoon sun. It is grown from cuttings or seed.

Natural habitat: Mexico

46

ANCISTROCACTUS

A genus aptly named "ancistro", which means "hooked": many hooked central spines protect the club-shaped stems of these plants. As cultivated seedlings they generally grow quickly and easily but, as they mature, they become increasingly rot-prone. Some species defy cultivation as mature plants on their own roots, and so are grafted.

▷ **Ancistrocactus uncinatus var. *wrightii***

The solitary, bluish body becomes shortly columnar with age, 7cm/2¾in wide by 20cm/8in tall. The maroon flowers are borne in the spring. This species is slow-growing and must be grown in a very porous compost (potting soil). If it is kept dry, it will take temperatures down to −12°C/10°F, for short periods.

Natural habitat: Texas (USA), Mexico

ARIOCARPUS

A small but popular genus of very slow-growing species. The stems range from solitary dwarf species 2cm/¾in wide to flattened clusters up to 30cm/12in across; they are composed of a rosette of triangular, spineless tubercles, arising from a tuberous taproot. The woolly crowns give rise to flowers, which are white, yellow, pink or purple. All species are protected in habitat and, while some have large ranges, a few are restricted to small, isolated populations. All require a very coarse, well-drained compost (potting soil), and are exceedingly slow-growing, unless provided with bright light and fairly high temperatures. *Ariocarpus* seedlings are often grafted, which can reduce the period of growth to maturity by years. Although one species is found in Texas (USA), the rest of the genus occurs only in Mexico and some are very localized and have been seriously endangered by collectors. *A. retusus* and *A. fissuratus* occur much more widely but many of the populations and areas of original habitat have been destroyed by agriculture and ranching.

△ **Ariocarpus fissuratus var. *fissuratus***

Growing flat to the ground, the tubercles of this species are heavily fissured. It is very slow-growing but may reach 15cm/6in in diameter eventually. This species will take temperatures down to −10°C/15°F, for short periods, if kept dry. It requires heat and a very porous potting soil. Although grown from seed, it is often grafted to accelerate its growth.

Natural habitat: Texas (USA), Mexico

ARIOCARPUS

△ ***Ariocarpus fissuratus** var. lloydii*

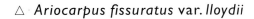

This variety differs from the previous species in having much smoother tubercles, often totally lacking a fissure, and by growing wider, taller and faster. The 9cm/3½in wide plant pictured is only nine years old. It will take −4°C/25°F briefly, if kept dry. It is grown from seed.

Natural habitat: Mexico

◁ ***Ariocarpus retusus** var. retusus*

The largest member of the genus, this species is also the most variable. The northernmost form, *A. retusus* var. *furfuraceus*, bears rough, fat, grey tubercles, about as wide as they are long. As the species ranges farther south, the tubercles become increasingly long, as pictured here. It varies from grey-green to a chalky, whitish grey. Individual stems can grow to 25cm/10in in diameter, but generally remain fairly flat, clustering with age. White flowers up to 5cm/2in across are produced in a ring near the apex of the plant. A specimen of the fastest-growing species in the genus, the 15cm/6in wide plant pictured is eight years old, grown from seed. This species can take some frost, if kept dry. It is propagated from seed and rarely grafted.

Natural habitat: Mexico

◁ *Ariocarpus trigonus*

This species has a body consisting of dark green, claw-like tubercles, set on top of a thick, short root. The yellow, scented flowers are borne in a ring around the centre of the plant in the autumn (fall). Still uncommon in cultivation, it is fairly fast-growing. The 14cm/5½in wide plant pictured is 11 years old. It does not tolerate frost, and is grown from seed.

Natural habitat: Mexico

△ *Ariocarpus kotschoubeyanus* var. *elephantidens*

The crown of this species can be 10cm/4in wide, growing flush to the soil. The bulk of the body is underground as a fat conical root. Other forms of this species have smaller bodies, some only 2cm/¾in wide, and have smooth tubercles; the tubercles of this large form are rough and often longer than wide. To keep the taproot from rotting, underpotting (keeping it rootbound in a small pot) in a very coarse compost (potting soil), is recommended. The 4cm/1½in wide, dark pink flower emerges from the crown in the autumn (fall). It will take some frost and is propagated by seed.

Natural habitat: Mexico

△ *Ariocarpus scapharostrus*

One of the rarest of the genus, this species is limited to a few hillsides. The tubercles are rough and dark green, standing erect from a thick, underground root. A few flowers are produced in the autumn (fall) and are among the nicest in the genus, a dark purple. Pictured here is a nine-year-old 3.5cm/1⅜in wide, mature specimen, grown from seed. Because it is rot-prone and slow-growing, it is the most frequently grafted species of *Ariocarpus*. It will tolerate some frost, but prefers warmth. It is grown or grafted.

Natural habitat: Mexico

ARROJADOA

Consisting of fewer than ten species, this unique genus forms long, rambling stems, which produce a blunt, bristly flowering end. After flowering for, perhaps, a season, new stems grow from this area and repeat the process. On mature plants, the flowers occur in flushes throughout the summer. The flowers are generally pink.

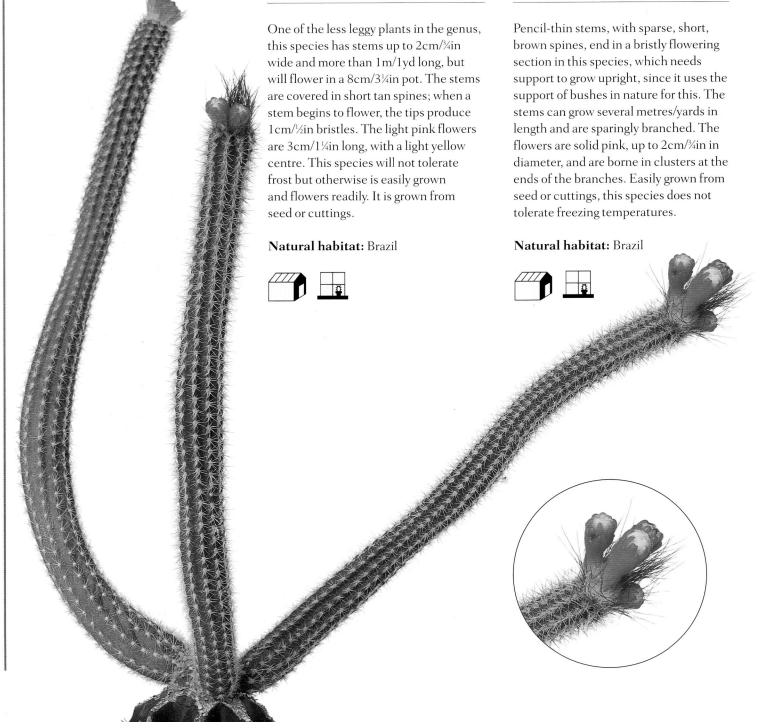

◁ *Arrojadoa dinae*

One of the less leggy plants in the genus, this species has stems up to 2cm/¾in wide and more than 1m/1yd long, but will flower in a 8cm/3¼in pot. The stems are covered in short tan spines; when a stem begins to flower, the tips produce 1cm/½in bristles. The light pink flowers are 3cm/1¼in long, with a light yellow centre. This species will not tolerate frost but otherwise is easily grown and flowers readily. It is grown from seed or cuttings.

Natural habitat: Brazil

△ *Arrojadoa penicillata*

Pencil-thin stems, with sparse, short, brown spines, end in a bristly flowering section in this species, which needs support to grow upright, since it uses the support of bushes in nature for this. The stems can grow several metres/yards in length and are sparingly branched. The flowers are solid pink, up to 2cm/¾in in diameter, and are borne in clusters at the ends of the branches. Easily grown from seed or cuttings, this species does not tolerate freezing temperatures.

Natural habitat: Brazil

ASTROPHYTUM

This is an incredibly popular genus, despite having fewer than six species and perhaps a dozen varieties. Its popularity lies in the geometrical form of the plants: several are spineless and all produce nice flowers throughout the summer. Unique to this genus is the presence of small white flecks on the stems. This "flocking" is variable and many cultivars now being propagated have well-developed flocking, often in attractive patterns.

△ *Astrophytum asterias* **cultivar Super Kabuto**

Bred from a wild sport, with unusually large flecks, this beautiful cultivar is quite variable. Seedlings of Super Kabuto can have anything from almost no flocking to flocking that covers virtually the whole body. Some individuals have intricate markings and chevrons made from lines of flecks. This cultivar seems to be slower in growing than the normal species and is often grafted to speed growth, later being degrafted and rerooted.

△ *Astrophytum coahuilense*

This spineless, five-ribbed species is covered with dense flocking and can reach 15cm/6in wide and 30cm/12in tall, but is quite slow-growing. In summer, flowers appear intermittently, 4cm/1½in wide, yellow with an orange throat. It will tolerate −7°C/20°F briefly, if kept fairly dry. It is grown from seed.

Natural habitat: Mexico

△ *Astrophytum asterias*

This is a very popular species because of its perfect symmetry. The low, spineless body has eight flat ribs, with small white flecks hardly noticeable in some plants, whereas others are fairly densely covered in flecks. Although slow-growing it can reach over 18cm/7in. It will produce 5cm/2in wide, yellow flowers, with a red centre, throughout the summer. While this species will take some frost, it must be dry, as it is the most prone to root rot; additionally, it will not tolerate so much sun as the other members of the genus. It is grown from seed and often grafted.

Natural habitat: Texas (USA), Mexico

ASTROPHYTUM

△ **Astrophytum ornatum**

The largest member of the genus, and the easiest to grow. The columnar body has eight ribs, with yellow to brown, 3cm/1¼in long spines. It can grow to 15cm/6in wide and 1m/1yd or more tall, producing 3cm/1¼in yellow flowers during the summer. There are several forms of this species, all of which will tolerate –7°C/20°F, briefly. It is grown from seed.

Natural habitat: Mexico

◁ **Astrophytum myriostigma monstrose cultivar Lotusland**

This unusual cultivar has always been offered grafted but offsets heavily and grows so quickly that it will often kill the grafting stock in a year or two, particularly *Myrtillocactus*. If it is grafted on a thick stock of *Stenocereus griseus* (*S. victoriensis*), it will last for several years, as least. Since the offsets will often produce roots, there may be a chance that they can be rooted as well.

△ ▽ **Astrophytum myriostigma**

The most common of the genus, the "bishop's cap", generally has five spineless, sharp ribs, but will produce seven, six, four and, occasionally, three ribs. There are several natural forms of this species, which vary in size (up to 15cm/6in across by 40cm/16in tall) and in the amount of flocking, including *A. myriostigma* var. *nudum*, which is devoid of flecks. The 4cm/1½in, pure yellow flowers are produced all summer. Several cultivars from Japan are now becoming available, including Onzuka, with Super Kabuto-like flocking. *A. myriostigma* and its varieties will tolerate –4°C/25°F, briefly. While mostly propagated from seed, some of the cultivars are grafted to speed their growth.

Natural habitat: Mexico

PLANT DIRECTORY cacti

AUSTROCEPHALOCEREUS

Meaning literally "the southern head-bearing cereus", this small genus is made of more or less branching plants that cluster from the base. True flowering cephalia (densely spined crowns) are borne on the sunny side of the plant. The flowers are nocturnal and close with the rising of the sun. This genus requires warmth in winter and is somewhat rot-prone. Once the stems start flowering, the orientation of the plant should be maintained as, if the plant is turned, a new cephalium will form on the new sunny side.

△ *Austrocephalocereus lehmannianus*

△ *Austrocephalocereus dybowskii*

The columnar stems of this clustering species are up to 10cm/4in in diameter and can be more than 2m/6½ft tall. Covered with soft white hair and short, brittle tan spines, it will produce a woolly lateral cephalium 20–40cm/8–16in long, from which emerge 3cm/1¼in wide, whitish flowers. Mature plants are rare in cultivation. The plant pictured here is one of the more common clustering cultivars and makes a nice potted specimen. It will not tolerate long periods of cold or frost, and is cultivated from seed or cuttings.

Natural habitat: Brazil

The 2–3cm/¾–1¼in thick stems of this attractive species only grow to a metre/yard or more in height, and will produce the woolly, brownish, lateral cephalium when it is only 30–50cm/12–20in tall. The 3cm/1¼in, broad, off-white flowers emerge from the cephalium at night and close early in the morning. The non-flowering stems are light blue and are lightly covered with thin, brittle, tan spines. It is grown from seed or cuttings and will not tolerate frost or extended periods of cold weather.

Natural habitat: Brazil

53

AZTEKIUM

This was a monotypic genus until a second species, *A. hintonii*, was described in the 1980s. Both species are slow-growing and grow only on pure gypsum in the wild.

▷ *Aztekium ritteri*

This unusual, clustering species is composed of flattened stems up to 3–4 cm/1¼–1½in in diameter, arising from a short, thick taproot. The stems have grooves along the ribs. The 7mm/⅓in wide, white to light pink flowers form sporadically throughout the summer. *A. ritteri* is most often available as a grafted plant.

Natural habitat: Mexico

BORZICACTUS

Fairly thin-stemmed, this small genus is made up of mostly upright species but some become pendant. Bright red flowers are often borne in several flushes during the summer. Given warmth and bright, but not intense, light, these plants are among the best columnar, flowering cacti. They are easily grown from cuttings. They are found in Peru and Bolivia.

▷ *Borzicactus samaipatanus*

Popular due to its freely flowering nature, this species has 2–3cm/¾–1¼in thick stems densely covered in stiff golden spines and will grow to more than 1m/1yd long, hanging from the pot. The 3cm/1¼in wide, blood-red flowers are produced, in several flushes, along the stems, in early summer. It will not tolerate prolonged cold or frost, but is easily grown from seed or cuttings.

Natural habitat: Bolivia

CARNEGIEA

This monotypic genus (having only one species) ranges from far south in Sonora, Mexico, north into Arizona, USA. Unarguably, it is one of the giants of the cactus family, but it is neither the tallest nor the heaviest. It is, however, the most promoted, more often used as scenery in movies at the cinema and on television than any other cactus species. In its natural habitat, it is home to many birds, and provides food for great numbers of species, with its pollen, nectar and seeds.

◁ △ △ *Carnegiea gigantea*

This species can grow to over 15m/50ft tall, with a main trunk up to 60cm/2ft thick, and weighing many thousands of kilograms. Commonly thought to grow very slowly, its growth rate is, in fact, an average 20cm/8in per year. Grown only from seed, the seedlings appear quite different from the adult plants, being unbranched and much more heavily spined. As a mature plant, it will tolerate −7°C/20°F briefly, but seedlings should be protected from excessive cold.

Natural habitat: Arizona (USA), Mexico

CEPHALOCEREUS

At one time this was a much larger genus, but most of its species have been moved to *Piloso-cereus*. The remaining species, numbering one to two, are tall, columnar and (rarely) branched, forming a woolly cephalium on the side of the stem at the tip.

▷ *Cephalocereus senilis*

Among the most well known cacti, the "old man of Mexico" is generally found in cultivation as a seedling with long white hair. Growing to 40cm/16in thick and 15m/50ft tall in its habitat, it is very slow to grow and quite rot-prone. It is propagated by seed, and will tolerate –4°C/25°F briefly, if kept dry.

Natural habitat: Mexico

CEREUS

Among the first cacti in cultivation, *Cereus* are still some of the most commonly grown cacti. The plants are large, often forming trees in their natural habitat. Although bearing tan to black spines up to 4cm/1½in long in the wild, there are many nearly spineless cultivars available for landscape plants in areas where the weather is mild enough. None of this genus will tolerate temperatures below freezing for prolonged periods but most will tolerate intense heat and sun, if given enough water. In the wild, they range from the West Indies to northern South America and south into Brazil and Argentina.

▷ *Cereus hildmannianus* var. *monstrose*

Also commonly sold as *Cereus peruvianus monstrose*, it is a very fast-growing species. Under optimum conditions, it can grow up to 30cm/12in per year, eventually forming a mass of club-shaped stems 3m/10ft tall. The *monstrose* forms of this species rarely flower, but the normal form produces 15cm/6in wide, white nocturnal flowers which are produced sporadically during the summer. While the normal *Cereus* *hildmannianus* is often grown from seed, *monstrose* and spined cultivars are grown from cuttings. It will tolerate brief periods of frost, but will be damaged by temperatures below –4°C/25°F.

Natural habitat: Brazil

CLEISTOCACTUS

O ne of the most popular genera of columnar cacti, these species are easy to grow and flower in relatively small pots. Named for the "closed" appearance of the blooms, the flowers open barely wider than the floral tube, but they are generally brightly coloured and borne in profusion for several weeks or in flushes several times during the summer. Many of the species have an odd, S-shaped flower, and most are thought to be pollinated by hummingbirds. Most grow quickly from seed or cuttings. Their natural habitat ranges from Peru to Bolivia, south into Argentina, Paraguay and Uruguay.

△ *Cleistocactus baumannii*

An easy species to grow, its 3cm/1¼in thick stems can quickly grow to 2m/6½ft in height, sometimes 30cm/12in in a season. During the summer, the slightly bent flowers are produced randomly from the tip to 40cm/16in down the stem. Grown from seed or cuttings, it will not tolerate more than a brief period of frost.

Natural habitat: Uruguay, Paraguay, northern Argentina, eastern Bolivia

△ ▷ *Cleistocactus straussii*

Among the most popular and attractive of *Cleistocactus*, the stems of this species will reach 6cm/2½in in diameter and 3m/10ft tall. It can grow up to 20cm/8in in a season, but is generally slower and more rot-prone than other species. The purplish-red flowers are borne near the tips of the stems in the spring. It is grown from seed, since cuttings generally will not root. Mature plants will take some frost, but the tips of the stems may be damaged.

Natural habitat: Bolivia

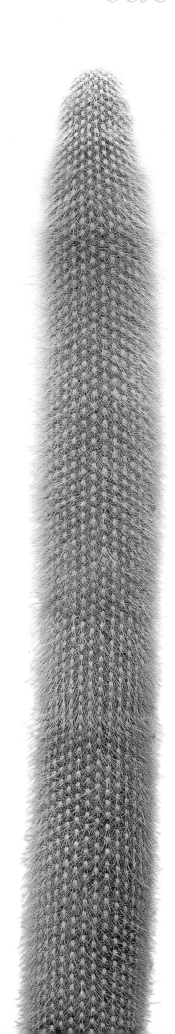

COPIAPOA

From the Atacama desert, these plants rarely receive rain in their habitat; they survive on the moisture from the fog that often blankets the coast. Solitary or clustering, all of the species are slow-growing, many remarkably so. Several species produce a chalky white bloom, a waxy coating which gives them a beautiful, unreal appearance. In cultivation, this coloration is washed away by overhead watering. The flowers are predominantly yellow and produce few seeds. They are grown from seed and/or grafted.

▷ *Copiapoa cinerea*

Among the finest and most sought after in the genus, this is also among the slowest growing. The stems can reach 14cm/5½in in diameter and 30cm/12in tall, but the plant pictured here at 12cm/4½in x 12cm/4½in is already 15 years old. In their habitat, this species and several others have a chalky white epidermis, but overhead watering washes this off. While it can offset with extreme age in cultivation, it is most commonly grown from seed. It requires warmth in the winter and should be kept fairly dry during this season.

Natural habitat: Chile

▽ *Copiapoa tenuissima*

In bright light, this attractive species turns almost black. The 4cm/1½in wide stems can make a 25cm/10in clump eventually. Yellow flowers emerge from the crown of thin black spines and white wool during the summer and spring. It forms a large taproot and must have good drainage. It will not tolerate frost, or prolonged periods of cold. It is grown from seed or offsets.

Natural habitat: Chile

△ *Copiapoa barquitensis*

Considered to be a form of *C. humilis*, this low-growing species will produce a cluster of heads up to 20cm/8in across. The flowers are produced in the spring and summer. Offsets often root while still attached. It must be kept free from frost.

Natural habitat: Chile

△ *Copiapoa lembkei*

Although the plants in habitat produce an attractive greyish bloom on the skin, in cultivation the plants are more of an olive colour. The light yellow flowers are produced in the spring and summer. Rarely offsetting and slow to grow, it is propagated by seed. Somewhat rot-prone, it needs warmth and should be kept fairly dry during the winter.

Natural habitat: Chile

58

CORYPHANTHA

Closely related to *Mammillaria*, this genus differs in its apical flowers (borne at the apex of the stems), fruit which is borne externally throughout its maturation and the presence of a groove that runs along the top of the mature tubercles. Although some species produce red or pink flowers, most tend to be yellow. They are generally fast-growing from seed or offsets and many will tolerate low temperatures for brief periods. Their range extends from the south-west USA into Mexico.

△ *Coryphantha durangensis*

Growing from a thickened taproot, the bluish, club-shaped stems 4cm/1½in across and 10cm/4in tall are solitary at first, and will sparingly offset in age. Yellow flowers emerge from the densely woolly crown in early summer. Although not difficult to grow, it should be planted in a coarse potting soil, to prevent rot. It is propagated from seed. It will tolerate −10°C/15°F, briefly.

Natural habitat: Mexico

◁ *Coryphantha clava*

The club-shaped stems, which are 10cm/4in in diameter, can grow to over 30cm/12in long, often becoming prostrate and clustering with age. The yellow flowers are produced in the summer and give rise to the spineless, green fruit typical of the genus. It is propagated from seed and will tolerate −4°C/25°F, briefly.

Natural habitat: Mexico

CORYPHANTHA

▷ *Coryphantha elephantidens*

The spherical stems of this species can reach 15cm/6in in diameter and will form clumps up to 40cm/16in wide. Sweetly scented pink flowers up to 7cm/2¾in across are borne in late summer. This species will tolerate some light frost, but is prone to an orange surface rot if it is exposed to winter humidity. It is grown from seed or offsets.

Natural habitat: Mexico

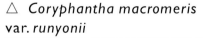

△ *Coryphantha macromeris var. runyonii*

Smaller than var. *macromeris*, this variety also has shorter spines. Both offset heavily, making large, flat clusters up to 25cm/10in across. The pink flowers, up to 6cm/2½in in diameter are produced sparingly throughout the summer. If kept dry, it will tolerate −7°C/20°F, easily. It is propagated by seed or cuttings.

Natural habitat: Texas (USA), Mexico

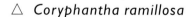

△ *Coryphantha ramillosa*

Mostly solitary, the somewhat flattened stems of this species grow to 9cm/3½in across and 8cm/3¼in tall. The 6cm/2½in wide pink flower is produced in late summer. This species is rare and protected in the wild, but is not difficult in cultivation. It will tolerate −7°C/20°F, briefly. It is grown from seed.

Natural habitat: Texas (USA)

△ *Coryphantha sulcata*

The individual heads of this clustering species can reach 12cm/4½in in diameter. The slightly flattened clusters will produce yellow flowers over 5cm/2in in diameter. This species poses no cultural difficulties, other than preferring low humidity during the winter. It will tolerate −7°C/20°F, briefly. It is only propagated by seed.

Natural habitat: Texas (USA), Mexico

DISCOCACTUS

These small, barrel-like cacti occur in the tropics, where they grow on rock outcrops in the forest. When mature, the stems of these unique cacti cease vegetative growth, and produce a true cephalium at the crown. This flowering head is composed of dense cottony fibres and a few bristles. During the summer, flushes of buds emerge in the late afternoon, opening in the evening as large, often heavily scented, white flowers. The flowers fade with the morning sun. Rot-prone and requiring warmth in the winter, this genus is often grafted on short stocks and planted low, to hide the fact. Many of the *Discocactus* are highly endangered in their natural habitat, coming from small, isolated populations that are easily obliterated by agriculture and development. The genus occurs in Brazil, Paraguay, and Bolivia.

△ *Discocactus albispinus*

△ *Discocactus horstii*

△ *Discocactus pugionacanthus*

This species is closely related to *D. araneispinus*, *D. boomianus*, and *D. zehntneri*, with which it is often combined. Initially solitary, it often clusters with age. The stems can grow to 10cm/4in in diameter, with stiff yellow spines to over 4cm/1½in long. The nocturnal flowers open 3–4cm/1¼–1½in wide and are lightly scented. This species is easier than most to keep on its own roots, but must be kept warm in the winter. It is reasonably easily grown from seed or offsets.

Natural habitat: Brazil

This species is truly one of the gems of the cactus family. The solitary stems are flattened, growing only to 6cm/2½in in diameter. The flowers are not heavily scented but, when borne in profusion in the summer, are quite stunning. It is particularly rot-prone and slow-growing, so grafting is recommended. On a graft, it will tolerate lower temperatures than normal, but no frost. It is generally started from seed, and then grafted.

Natural habitat: Brazil

The solitary heads of this species will grow to 10cm/4in, and develop a pronounced cephalium with time. During the summer, nicely shaped flowers (5cm/2in wide) are produced every few weeks but their scent is not notable. It will not tolerate any frost, and must be kept warm in the winter, if grown on its own roots. It is grown from seed.

Natural habitat: Brazil

ECHINOCACTUS

This genus, together with the closely related *Fero-cactus*, make up the "barrel cacti". There are fewer than ten species and they vary from dwarf plants only 12cm/4½in broad to giants up to 1m/1yd wide and 2m/6½ft tall, weighing more than 1000kg/2200lb. The flowers vary from yellow to pink. Their culture varies considerably; some are easily grown and others are among the slowest and most rot-prone of the *Cactaceae*. This genus is found through New Mexico and Texas (USA) and south into Mexico.

◁ △ *Echinocactus grusonii*

A beautiful and fast-growing species, this can grow to more than a metre/yard wide and tall in a few decades. In full sun, the spines become dense, developing a deep golden colour. Despite being almost extinct in the wild, due mostly to loss of habitat, it is one of the most common cacti commercially. The golden yellow 4cm/1½in flowers are borne from the crown of the plant in the summer, but only on plants of at least 35cm/14in in diameter, and only when grown in intense sunlight. Mature plants will tolerate –4°C/25°F, briefly. It is grown from seed.

Natural habitat: Mexico

ECHINOCEREUS

Many species in this genus will form large, spiny, hemispherical mounds, giving them the common name "hedgehog cacti". This large genus has other body-forms as well, from thin, pendulous, rambling stems to solitary miniature species. They bear flowers in the whole range of cactus colours: white, yellow, pink, orange, red, purple and even green. Several species are good for cac-tus gardens at more northern latitudes, tolerating pro-longed periods below -18°C/0°F. The cold-hardy species will dehydrate in the autumn (fall), even when there is plenty of water; this allows them to take lower tempera-tures. They are mostly grown from seed, although se-lected forms can be grown from cuttings. They range through the south-western USA and Mexico.

△ *Echinocereus coccineus* var. *neomexicanus*

The individual stems of this species grow to 7cm/2¾in in diameter and will offset to make hemispherical clusters up to 35cm/14in across. In late spring, light scarlet flowers 5cm/2in long appear, scattered about the plant. This species will tolerate temperatures down to −10°C/15°F, but must be kept dry if low temperatures persist for extended periods. It is generally grown from seed.

Natural habitat: New Mexico (USA)

△ *Echinocereus papillosus*

This species forms clumps of sprawling 2–3cm/¾–1¼in thick stems. It can be used in a hanging basket, growing 30cm/12in long stems and producing 12cm/4½in, bright yellow flowers, with a red centre, in early summer. It can withstand temperatures down to −7°C/20°F, briefly. Like many closely related species, during the winter it dehydrates, looking limp and unattractive, but this prevents it from freezing. It is grown from cuttings or seed.

Natural habitat: Texas (USA)

△ *Echinocereus pentalophus*

One of the best *Echinocereus* for use in a hanging basket, the 2–3cm/¾–1¼in thick stems can grow to 40cm/16in or more. For a short time in late spring, a profusion of large (10cm/4in) pink flowers with white throats can almost cover the plant. If kept dry, it will tolerate −7°C/20°F, briefly. The stems become limp and purple during the winter, but recover in the spring. It is grown from cuttings or seed.

Natural habitat: Texas (USA)

ECHINOCEREUS

▷ *Echinocereus rigidissimus* var. *rubispinus*

The generally solitary stems grow to 5cm/2in in diameter and up to 20cm/8in tall. The spine colour is variable, but mature plants grown in adequate light will produce dark pink spines. A few flowers are produced in early summer and are 7cm/2¾in across, pink with a white centre. It is rot-prone and will survive light frost. It is grown from seed.

Natural habitat: Mexico

△ *Echinocereus poselgeri*

Moved from the genus *Wilcoxia*, the thin stems (up to 30cm/12in long but less than 1cm/½in thick) emerge from a cluster of tuberous roots. In its habitat, this plant grows amongst shrubs for support, and is only detectable when the flowers open, borne in clusters at the tips of the stems. The 5cm/2in broad flowers are bright pink, with a darker centre. This species will not tolerate much frost and should be potted in a particularly well-drained compost (potting soil), to avoid rot. It is grown from seed, rarely from cuttings.

Natural habitat: Texas (USA), Mexico

△ *Echinocereus pulchellus*

The 5cm/2in wide stems of this dwarf species can eventually form clusters up to 12cm/4½in across. In the wild, the plant is pulled below ground level during times of drought. In early summer, the bright pink flowers can cover the top of the plant for a short time. If kept dry, it will tolerate −10°C/15°F, briefly. It is grown from seed.

Natural habitat: Mexico

△ *Echinocereus reichenbachii*

Generally solitary, the stems of this common species can grow to 6cm/2½in in diameter and 15cm/6in tall. The 7cm/2¾in wide flowers are produced in several flushes in late spring. It will tolerate brief periods at −7°C/20°F. It is grown from seed.

Natural habitat: Texas (USA), Mexico

△ *Echinocereus subinermis*

Generally solitary, this species will offset with age. The stems grow to 7cm/2¾in in diameter and up to 20cm/8in tall. While most species in this genus have one flush of flowers, the lemon yellow 6cm/2½in flowers of *E. subinermis* are produced several times during the summer. Unlike its more northerly relatives, this species does not tolerate much frost, nor full harsh sun. It is grown from seed.

Natural habitat: Mexico

△ *Echinocereus* x (with *Wilcoxia*)

Hybrids of *Echinocereus* are starting to appear on the market. In areas where they can be grown in landscapes, the potential for breeding new and attractive hybrids is great. Because of their attractive spination, hardy nature, and large, colourful flowers, they could make one of the better groups of cacti for hybridization for landscapes.

△ *Echinocereus viridiflorus*

The 4cm/1½in wide, flattened stems of this dwarf species can form small clusters up to 12cm/4½in across. In spring, the lemon-scented, greenish flowers are produced in quantity and over a fairly long period. It shrivels and becomes flat with the onset of autumn (fall). If kept dry, or under a layer of snow, it can withstand –23°C/–10°F, for prolonged periods. It is grown from seed.

Natural habitat: New Mexico, Colorado (USA)

65

◁ *Echinocereus schmollii*

Closely related to *E. poselgeri*, this species was also in the genus *Wilcoxia*. The rather limp stems emerge from a tuberous root, producing 4cm/1½in wide, pale pink flowers, in early summer. The spines are quite variable, from soft white and woolly to stiff black bristles. This has lead to several names and much confusion among collectors over the identity of their plant. It does not tolerate much frost, and should be planted in a very well-drained compost (potting soil). It is grown from seed or cuttings.

Natural habitat: Mexico

ECHINOPSIS

This genus was originally largely composed of species with white nocturnal flowers, but has recently been considerably amplified. In this publication, it includes species *Helianthocereus*, *Lobivia*, *Pseudolobivia*, *Soehrensia*, and *Trichocereus*. The plants vary from low dwarf species a few centimetres across to giants 10m/30ft tall. The flowers range through every colour found in the *Cactaceae*. Many species have been used as parents for the numerous hybrids available today. These rival the large number of *Epiphyllum* hybrids, since *Echinopsis* need no special care. The hybrids vary from brightly flowered windowsill plants to landscape-size cultivars with 20cm/8in wide, coloured flowers. Most *Echinopsis* are easily grown, propagated from seed or cuttings. The genus ranges through much of the southern part of South America.

△ *Echinopsis famatimensis (Lobivia famatimensis, Rebutia famatimensis)*

This slow-growing, dwarf species produces soft, 5cm/2in wide stems, which will form a 9cm/3½in wide cluster. In the spring, woolly brown buds form on the sides of the plant, opening into 5cm/2in wide, yellow flowers. It has a thickened taproot and is particularly rot-prone. If kept dry, it will tolerate −10°C/15°F, briefly. It is grown from seed or cuttings and is occasionally grafted.

Natural habitat: Argentina

△ *Echinopsis aurea*

This variable species has solitary or clustering stems up to 10cm/4in across and 14cm/5½in or more tall. The 3–6cm/1¼–2½in wide flowers can be white, pink, yellow or red, and are produced in several flushes during the summer. It is somewhat rot-prone but, when planted in a shallow pot, this is not a problem. It can tolerate temperatures down to −4°C/25°F for short periods. It is propagated from seed or offsets.

Natural habitat: Argentina

△ *Echinopsis chamaecereus*

Called the "peanut cactus", this species has previously been in collections as *Chamaecereus silvestrii*. The 1cm/½in thick stems hang over the pot, and in late spring, it produces a couple of flushes of 4cm/1½in wide, orange flowers. It will take bright light but suffers in hot sun. If kept dry, it is hardy down to −7°C/20°F for short periods. It is propagated from cuttings and, occasionally, from seed.

Natural habitat: Argentina

◁ *Chamaecereus* x 'Fire Chief'

Many hybrids have been made from *Echinopsis chamaecereus* in the last few decades. Generally they have more numerous, larger flowers and produce more robust growth. They are propagated by cuttings. 'Fire Chief' is the most widespread.

ECHINOPSIS

△ *Echinopsis huascha*

The 5cm/2in thick stems of this species can form upright or prostrate clusters and can be up to 60cm/2ft long. There are several colour forms of this species. This is a yellow form, sometimes found under the name *E. huascha* var. *macrantha*. The yellow, orange or red flowers are produced near the tips of the stems in summer and can be up to 10cm/4in across. If the weather is not too hot and dry, the flowers will last for a couple of days. It will tolerate temperatures down to –4°C/25°F for short periods. Generally, it is propagated from cuttings, to maintain a known flower colour.

Natural habitat: Argentina

△ *Echinopsis smurzianus*

The stems are quite variable in size, 8cm/3¼in–20cm/8in thick and up to 40cm/16in long. White flowers, 12cm/4½in wide, are produced in summer. It will tolerate –4°C/25°F briefly, and is propagated generally from cuttings.

Natural habitat: Argentina

△ *Echinopsis* x 'Green Gold'

Probably a hybrid from *E. aurea* and *E. oxygona*, the 8cm/3¼in wide stems will form 25cm/10in wide clusters. The yellow flowers are 7cm/2¾in wide and 12cm/4½in long and are produced in several flushes during the summer. It will tolerate temperatures down to –4°C/25°F for brief periods. It is propagated from offsets.

▷ *Echinopsis peruvianus*

This lightly spined species can produce stems 12cm/4½in thick and over 2.5m/8ft tall. The stems cluster sparingly and are shy to flower. The flowers are nocturnal, white and open to 15cm/6in, fading in the morning light. It can tolerate bright light, but suffers in full hot sun. It will tolerate brief periods down to –4°C/25°F. It is propagated from seed or cuttings.

Natural habitat: Peru

△ *Echinopsis* x 'Los Angeles'

Probably one of the Paramount hybrids, produced by Harry Johnson at his nursery in Paramount, California, this is certainly one of the largest-bodied hybrids commonly available. If the offsets are removed to allow the main stem to grow, it can reach over 20cm/8in wide and 60cm/2ft tall. In summer, the 8cm/3¼in wide, 16cm/6¼in long, light pink flowers are borne in several flushes, often covering the top of the plant. It will tolerate temperatures to –7°C/20°F for short periods.

△ *Echinopsis* x 'Glorious'

A popular hybrid, probably originating in California, the 5cm/2in thick prostrate stems form a clump up to 40cm/16in wide. In summer, it produces several flushes of 10cm/4in wide, red flowers, with darker highlights at the tips of the petals. It will tolerate brief periods at –7°C/20°F and can also take full sun for half of the day in the hottest climates. It grows quickly from cuttings, making a large cluster in a couple of seasons.

EPIPHYLLUM

Aptly named, this genus, composed of epiphytes, has been popular for many decades. The plants require humidity and warmth, but not excessive heat, and will not tolerate any frost. Often, they are used as hanging patio plants, being brought indoors for the winter. In many cases, they are grafted on species of *Opuntia* or *Selenicereus*, where they flower well without the need for a particular compost (potting soil). Most of the true species have large white flowers but have been bred for decades with smaller-flowered, but highly coloured species, resulting in hundreds of beautifully flowered hybrids. This genus is found from Mexico, through Central America and into northern South America, in Ecuador, Peru, Bolivia, Paraguay and Brazil.

70

△ *Epiphyllum anguliger*

The dark green, flattened stems are heavily notched and can hang down 1m/1yd or more. White flowers, 8cm/3¼in long, are produced in the summer. It prefers bright indirect light with some humidity, and will not tolerate frost. It is grown from seed or cuttings.

Natural habitat: Mexico

△ *Epiphyllum* x 'King Midas'

Still considered to be one of the best yellow/golden-flowered *Epiphyllum* hybrids, this was made available in 1939. The flowers are more than 16cm/6¼in across and are produced in the spring. It is grown from cuttings.

△ *Epiphyllum* x 'Reward'

Produced in the USA and first distributed in 1952, its light yellow flowers will open to 16cm/6¼in or more. It is grown from cuttings.

△ *Epiphyllum* x 'Jennifer Ann'

This very nice yellow hybrid was released in the 1980s. The flowers open to 16cm/6¼in in the spring. It is grown from cuttings.

△ *Epiphyllum* x 'Just Pru'

This was released many years ago by Hollygate Cactus Nursery. The flower is up to 12cm/4½in in diameter. It is grown from cuttings.

71

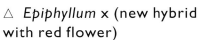

△ *Epiphyllum* x (new hybrid with red flower)

This hybrid by Frank Nunn is as yet unnamed. When breeding plants, it is sometimes easier to produce quality hybrids than to find new names!

△ *Epiphyllum johnsoni*

This old hybrid bears deep red flowers in the spring. It is grown from cuttings.

▷ *Epiphyllum* x 'Wendy May'

A hybrid of *Discocactus* (*Chiapasia*) *nelsonii*, it was produced by Frank Nunn and named for Terry Hewitt's daughter. The long flower opens to about 7.5cm/3in.

EPITHELANTHA

Consisting of anything from one to several species, depending on the taxonomist, all are slow-growing dwarf plants. Often found growing in shallow soil on rocky hillsides, they need excellent drainage in cultivation. Their range extends from the south-western United States into Mexico.

△ *Epithelantha micromeris*

Appropriately called the "button cactus", this miniature species will flower at under 2cm/¾in, but can make clusters up to 14cm/5½in. The 3mm/⅛in wide, white to light pink flowers emerge from the densely spined crown, from early spring to mid-summer. Generally self-fertile, the flowers are followed by 1.5cm/⅝in long, shocking-pink fruit, which last for days. Very rot-prone, it should be planted in a very coarse compost (potting soil) in a shallow pot. If kept dry, it can tolerate brief periods of –7°C/20°F. It is occasionally grafted, but is generally propagated by seed or offsets.

Natural habitat: Arizona, New Mexico, Texas (USA), Mexico

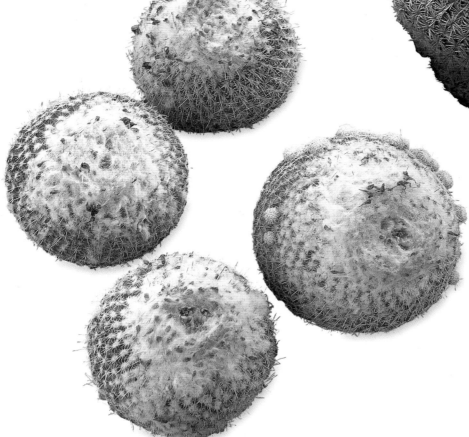

△ *Epithelantha micromeris* **var.** *unguispina*

This variety is distinguished from the one typically found by having a short (4mm/just under ¼in), stiff, black-tipped central spine and by having larger, darker pink flowers. In other respects, the care requirements are much the same, although it may not endure as much cold as its northern relatives. It is propagated by offsets and seed.

Natural habitat: Mexico

72

ERIOSYCE

The genus has recently been increased from its two original species to include all of the species from *Islaya*, *Horridocactus*, *Neochilenia*, *Neoporteria* and *Pyrrhocactus*. Stem shape within this genus varies from low and tuberous to shortly columnar and, eventually, long decumbent. Most species have showy flowers varying from white to red. Many in this genus are somewhat rot-prone, with the dwarf species particularly so. The natural habitat of the genus is Chile.

△ *Eriosyce imitans*

The dark, flattened stems of this uncommon species sit on top of a thick taproot. Growing to 8cm/3¼in wide, the body is only a few centimetres tall. In early summer, glossy, cream-coloured flowers open to 4.5cm/1¾in. It is very slow-growing and rot-prone. If kept dry, it will tolerate −7°C/20°F, briefly. It is grown from seed.

Natural habitat: Chile

▷ *Eriosyce napina*

The grey stems of this dwarf grow to 4cm/1½in thick and 6cm/2½in tall, but sit on top of a root often several times that mass. In summer, the 5cm/2in wide, glossy whitish flowers are borne one or two at a time and cover the top of the plant. To prevent the large taproot from rotting, it needs to be underpotted (kept rootbound in a small pot) and planted in a very coarse compost (potting soil). If kept dry, it will tolerate −7°C/20°F for short periods. It is grown from seed.

Natural habitat: Chile

△ *Eriosyce senilis*

The solitary stem, round at first, becomes elongated, 8cm/3¼in wide and up to 18cm/7in tall; it is covered with wiry, curly spines. The spines range from blond to white, with black tips. The tubular bright red flowers, 3cm/1¼in wide and 5cm/2in long, push through the spines at the tip of the stems in the spring. It will tolerate bright, hot, indirect light and brief periods to −4°C/25°F. It is grown from seed.

Natural habitat: Chile

ERIOSYCE

◁ *Eriosyce subgibbosa* var. *nigrihorrida*

Generally growing less than 25cm/10in tall, the solitary stem bears black to dark tan spines up to 5cm/2in long. The bright pink flowers are borne from the tips, 3cm/1¼in or more wide. It will tolerate hot, bright, indirect light and brief periods to –4°C/25°F. It is grown from seed.

Natural habitat: Chile

◁ *Eriosyce villosa* fma. *laniceps*

The dense, thin, grey spines surround the brownish-green body of this solitary species. The stem can grow to 8cm/3¼in wide and 12cm/4½in tall. In spring, it produces a flush of bright pink, 2cm/¾in wide flowers. It will tolerate –4°C/25°F for short periods. It is grown from seed.

Natural habitat: Chile

△ *Eriosyce occulta*

This dwarf, tuberous species often has black spines up to 17mm/just under ¾in long. The spineless plant pictured here is the more popular form with collectors. The stems tend to cluster with age. It will tolerate –7°C/20°F, briefly. It is grown from seed.

Natural habitat: Chile

ESCOBARIA

Closely related to *Coryphantha*, the plants in this genus are generally smaller. The flowers are often quite small, no more than 1cm/½in across, but can be up to 6cm/2⅓in wide. The flower colour ranges from pink to yellow to tan and even golden brown. Their range extends across the south-western USA into Mexico.

△ **Escobaria leei**

◁ **Escobaria hesteri**

The 4cm/1½in wide stems of this small species will eventually form a cluster 10cm/4in across. Unlike many *Escobaria, E. hesteri* will produce its 3cm/1¼in, dark pink flowers intermittently throughout the summer, often from each stem. Although somewhat rot-prone, if it is kept dry it will tolerate temperatures down to −10°C/15°F. It is propagated from seed or cuttings.

Natural habitat: Texas (USA)

Although the clusters of this species can grow to 15cm/6in or more across, the individual heads are only 1cm/½in thick. It produces brownish-pink flowers, in early summer. This species is highly restricted in the wild, and also highly protected. Fortunately, given a coarse, well-drained compost (potting soil), it is not particularly difficult to propagate. If kept dry, it will tolerate temperatures down to −7°C/20°F. It is grown from seed or offsets and, occasionally, grafted.

Natural habitat: Texas (USA)

◁ **Escobaria minima**

Closely related to *E. leei* and a neighbour in habitat, this species is also restricted in its distribution and highly protected. The stems grow to 2cm/¾in wide and can make clusters up to 20cm/8in in diameter. During early summer, it produces several flushes of showy, 2cm/¾in wide, pink flowers. It requires excellent drainage but, if kept dry, can tolerate temperatures down to −7°C/20°F. It is propagated by seed, cuttings and, occasionally, grafting.

Natural habitat: Texas (USA)

75

ESCOBARIA

△ *Escobaria roseana*

The densely spined stems of this species grow to 3.5cm/1⅜in wide and form small clusters up to 12cm/4½in wide. It is rot-prone, but if kept dry, it will tolerate –7°C/20°F, briefly. It is grown from seed.

Natural habitat: Mexico

◁ *Escobaria vivipara*

This species occurs over a wide area and has several distinct varieties. The 6cm/2½in wide stems offset more or less heavily, to make clusters up to 20cm/8in in diameter. Pink flowers up to 4cm/1½in wide are produced in the spring. Some of the northern varieties will withstand prolonged temperatures down to –23°C/–10°F, especially under a covering of snow. It is grown from seed.

Natural habitat: south-west USA

ESPOSTOA

This columnar genus is quite common and popular, because of the dense, woolly hair that is wrapped around the stems. In their natural habitat, these bushy or tree-like plants can grow more than 6m/20ft tall. At maturity, the plant produces a woolly, grooved cephalium, or flowering zone, at the tips of the stems. In cultivation, they require average care, but are somewhat rot-prone and will not tolerate heavy frost or an intensely hot exposure. They are found from Ecuador to Peru.

▷ *Espostoa lanata*

Although the plants seen in cultivation are generally unbranched seedlings 1m/1yd or less tall, in their habitat the 10cm/4in thick stems branch to make a tree-like plant up to 4m/13ft tall. Good for a sheltered patio in the summer, this species will not tolerate day-long full sun and high temperatures, nor will it tolerate frost. It is also rot-prone, particularly during the winter. It is only propagated by seed.

Natural habitat: Peru

FEROCACTUS

Most commonly known as the "barrel cacti", this genus contains more than 30 species, which range across the south-west USA and northern Mexico. They are generally spherical in youth, later becoming columnar, up to 4m/13ft tall in the largest species. The flowers are borne from the crown, ranging from yellow to red, pink to purple. Many of the species will tolerate frost and intense hot sunlight. Most are grown only from seed.

△ *Ferocactus cylindraceus*

Often found under the old name *F. acanthodes*, this slow-growing species will eventually reach 35cm/14in across and ancient plants can be 2m/6½ft tall. There are several varieties, largely distinguished by spine shape and colour; the spine colour can vary considerably from plant to plant within the same population, going from tan to red. The 4cm/1½in wide flowers appear in a ring at the top of the plant in the summer. It is rot-prone but, if kept dry, will tolerate −7°C/20°F, briefly.

Natural habitat: Arizona, California (USA), Mexico

◁ *Ferocactus glaucescens*

Eventually reaching 35cm/14in across and tall, the bluish stems bear a loose, comb-like arrangement of spines along the ribs. The 3cm/1¼in yellow flowers appear near the crown in late spring, followed by 2cm/¾in white fruit. In age, the lower portions of the stem develop shallow cracks. It will tolerate some frost, but prolonged freezing will burn the edges of the ribs. It is grown from seed.

Natural habitat: Mexico

▷ *Ferocactus herrerae*

The 30cm/12in wide stems of this species can reach 2m/6½ft tall in time. As a seedling, it is, initially, club-shaped, perched on a short stock that disappears as the plant matures. In summer, it produces yellow and red flowers. It is among the easiest and fastest of the *Ferocactus* to grow. Mature plants will tolerate −4°C/25°F, briefly. It is grown from seed.

Natural habitat: Mexico

FEROCACTUS

◁ *Ferocactus macrodiscus*

In its natural habitat, the flat stems can grow to 30cm/12in. Appearing when only 8cm/3¼in across, the candy-striped pink and white flowers open to 3cm/1¼in. It prefers warmth and bright light but will suffer in full hot sun and heavy frost. It is grown from seed.

Natural habitat: Mexico

△ *Ferocactus pilosus*

Both *F. pringlei* and *F. stainesii* are now considered synonyms of this species. It can be solitary or clustering, with stems up to 40cm/16in wide and 1m/1yd tall. The forms of this species differ in size and the presence or lack of fine white radial spines under the heavier red spines. The 2.5cm/1in broad flowers are orange with red-tipped petals, opening only slightly. This species will tolerate −4°C/25°F for short periods and it is propagated from seed.

Natural habitat: Mexico

△ *Ferocactus rectispinus*

The body of this striking species can grow to 35cm/14in wide and more than 1m/1yd tall. Although varying in length from plant to plant, it has some of the longest spines in the family, upwards of 25cm/10in. Tan, often with a pinkish tip, they are also slightly hooked. The light yellow flowers are 5cm/2in wide and are borne in summer. Mature plants will tolerate −4°C/25°F, briefly. It is propagated from seed.

Natural habitat: Baja California (Mexico)

△ *Ferocactus robustus*

While the stems never grow wider than 10cm/4in, they cluster heavily, making hemispherical mounds up to 1m/1yd tall and 3m/10ft wide. The stems are lightly spined and shy to bloom, producing only a few 4cm/1½in wide flowers each year. It prefers shade from the hottest sun and will be damaged by a heavy frost. It is grown from seed or cuttings.

Natural habitat: Mexico

△ *Ferocactus viridescens*

Generally solitary, the stems of this slow-growing species reach 30cm/12in wide and 40cm/16in tall after many years. The 3cm/1¼in wide, greenish yellow flowers are borne in early summer. It is quite rot-prone, particularly during the winter. It will tolerate some frost. It is grown from seed.

Natural habitat: southern coast of California (USA) and into Baja California (Mexico)

△ *Ferocactus wislizeni*

Growing to 50cm/20in thick and over 2m/6½ft tall, the crown tilts to the south, earning it the name "compass barrel cactus". The flowers are variable, even within a single population, going from pure yellow to solid orange-red, by way of intermediates with orange petals edged in yellow. It is somewhat rot-prone. It will tolerate −7°C/20°F, and is grown from seed.

Natural habitat: Arizona (USA) into Mexico

79

FRAILEA

This genus of dwarf species is still relatively un-common. *Frailea* are generally cleistogamous, meaning that the flowers (always yellow) set seed with-out ever opening.

▷ *Frailea castanea*

This solitary miniature grows only to 3cm/1¼in across. The flattened, olive-green to brown stems produce sulphur-yellow flowers that only open for a few hours on a hot afternoon. It is grown from seed and is often grafted.

Natural habitat: Brazil

GYMNOCALYCIUM

Named for the naked flower buds bearing neither hair nor spines (from *gymnos*, meaning "naked", and calyx, the collective term for the sepals), this is one of the largest South American genera. The species range from dwarf solitary stems 4cm/1½in across, to stems 20cm/8in wide and tall. The flowers are generally not intensely coloured, ranging from white to pale yellow and pink. Many species flower quite freely and at an early age. Unlike many genera of cacti, each flower can last for several days. They are common in cultivation, easy to care for, and are often among the first species acquired by budding collectors. The natural habitat of the genus is from Argentina, north to Bolivia, Paraguay, Uruguay and Brazil.

△ **Gymnocalycium andrea var. grandiflorum**

The soft, lightly spined bodies will form a small cluster to 10cm/4in across with age. One of the few yellow-flowered members of the genus, the 3.5cm/1⅜in wide flowers are borne in late spring, for a couple of weeks. It will tolerate briefly temperatures down to −7°C/20°F. It is grown from seed.

Natural habitat: Argentina

△ **Gymnocalycium baldianum**

Generally solitary, this species can reach a flowering size of 3cm/1¼in in 12 months from seed, eventually growing to 9cm/3½in. The flattened stem produces 4cm/1½in wide flowers, which can be white, pink, orange, red or shades in between. Being spring-flowering, it can bloom for several months. It is easily grown and will take temperatures down to −12°C/10°F, briefly. It is grown from seed.

Natural habitat: Argentina

△ **Gymnocalycium bruchii**

Bearing soft pink, 3.5cm/1⅜in flowers, the dainty 4cm/1½in thick stems form many-headed clusters, up to 15cm/6in across. If kept dry, it will tolerate temperatures down to −12°C/10°F. It is grown from seed or offsets.

Natural habitat: Argentina

◁ Gymnocalycium cardenasianum

The solitary grey body will grow slowly to 13cm/5in. Thick and occasionally twisted, the spines can grow to 6cm/2½in long. Plain pink, 4cm/1½in wide flowers are produced sparingly in mid-summer. It will tolerate −7°C/20°F, briefly.

Natural habitat: Bolivia

△ Gymnocalycium erinaceum

The soft stems of this generally solitary species grow to 5cm/2in and are covered with black-tipped white spines. It will tolerate temperatures down to −7°C/ 20°F for short periods.

Natural habitat: Argentina

△ Gymnocalycium eurypleurum

Solitary, the stems of this species grow up to 10cm/4in across. The light pink, 4cm/1½in wide flowers are produced for several weeks in summer. It will tolerate some frost. It is grown from seed.

Natural habitat: Paraguay

△ Gymnocalycium pflanzii var. albopulpa

This large-stemmed, solitary species can grow up to 16cm/6¼in wide and tall. In summer, cup-shaped pink flowers are borne. It will not tolerate long periods of frost, and is grown from seed.

Natural habitat: southern Bolivia, northern Argentina

81

◁ Gymnocalycium manzanense

The flattened stems of this attractive species can grow to 13cm/5in. During several weeks in the summer, light pink flowers are produced some distance from the centre of the plant. It will tolerate −4°C/25°F, briefly. It is grown from seed.

Natural habitat: Argentina

GYMNOCALYCIUM

△ *Gymnocalycium quehlianum*

The solitary, flat stems of this species only grow to 7cm/2¾in broad and are grey-green or reddish in colour. The flower is borne on a slender tube to 6cm/2½in long and is white with a reddish throat. It is slow-growing and somewhat rot-prone. It is propagated by seed.

Natural habitat: Argentina

△ *Gymnocalycium saglione*

The giant of the genus, the solitary stem grows to 30cm/12in wide and tall. The cup-shaped pale pink flowers, borne in a ring around the crown, are produced for a couple of weeks in early summer. This species takes more sun than many of the smaller species and will tolerate −7°C/20°F, briefly. It is grown from seed.

Natural habitat: Argentina

△ *Gymnocalycium tillianum*

Solitary, the stem of this species grows to 13cm/5⅛in wide and high. Unusually for this genus, it bears bright orange flowers, which darken to red on their second or third day. It will tolerate −7°C/20°F, briefly, and it is grown from seed.

Natural habitat: Argentina.

HATIORA

Only one species is commonly available of this small genus of Brazilian epiphytes. The small flowers are borne at the ends of the branches and range from yellow to red.

▷ *Hatiora salicornioides*

The bottle-shaped joints of this epiphyte form hanging stems more than 16cm/6¼in long. In summer, the small orange flowers, 1cm/½in long, are borne at the end of the stems. It requires some humidity and will not tolerate intense heat or frost. It is grown from cuttings or seed.

Natural habitat: Brazil

LOPHOCEREUS

There is some debate over whether there are several species of this genus, or several varieties of one species. The southernmost plants are smaller, more densely branched and branch higher on the stems. The flowers are similar, varying from white to dark red. The genus is found from extreme southern Arizona (USA), into mainland Mexico and Baja California (Mexico).

△ *Lophocereus schottii*

Branching from the base, the stems grow 12cm/4½in wide and up to 6m/20ft tall. Tan bristles cover the mature tips of the stems. These tips bear pink 3cm/1¼in wide flowers, in the summer. It tolerates intense heat and sun, but will be damaged by extended periods of frost. It is grown from seed or cuttings.

Natural habitat: Mexico, the south of Arizona, Baja California (Mexico)

◁ *Lophocereus schottii monstrose*

This naturally occurring mutation is unique in that, despite being sterile, it continues to exist in the wild. When the stems break off or topple over, they root along the sides. There are at least two forms of this mutation from different locations: fma. *obesa* (pictured here) and fma. *mieckleyanus*, which is thinner, with less pronounced tubercles that are often arranged spirally. It is grown from cuttings, and requires a minimum of 21°C/70°F to root and thereafter high temperatures. It will tolerate −4°C/25°F, briefly, but the stem tips should be covered.

Natural habitat: Baja California (Mexico)

83

MAMMILLARIA

One of the largest genera, with about 250 species, this is, under-standably, one of the most common in cultivation. The species vary from dwarf species no more than 2cm/¾in in size to massive clusters more than a metre/yard across. While many of the species are somewhat tender, others will tolerate heavy frost and a few thrive in full sun. The flowers, although small, are often borne in rings around the crowns of the stems for several weeks. There are many species that are easy to cultivate as well as those of interest to the advanced collector and they range from the south-western USA into Mexico.

△ *Mammillaria bocasana*

△ *Mammillaria bombycina*

△ *Mammillaria duwei*

Often sold as the "powder puff" cactus, this species gets its common name from the white, hair-like spines that often hide the stiff radial spines and hooked central spine. The 6cm/2½in wide stems can form a 25cm/10in wide, flattened cluster. Its pinkish-yellow flowers are produced during the summer. A woollier form, *M. bocasana* fma. *multilanata*, is also commonly available. *M. bocasana* is somewhat prone to rot, particularly in larger plants. It tolerates temperatures of −7°C/20°F for short periods and it is propagated from seed.

Natural habitat: Mexico

Its attractive spination and many pink spring flowers have made this species very popular. The 6cm/2½in wide stems can make clusters to 30cm/12in or more. It has no special requirements but will not withstand long periods below −4°C/25°F. It is grown from seed.

Natural habitat: Mexico

Often considered a form of *M. nana*, this species has dense, pubescent radial spines and occasionally produces pubescent hooked central spines. The 4cm/1½in wide stems can form a small cluster with age. The small yellow flowers are produced for many weeks in the spring. It can tolerate temperatures down to −7°C/20°F, but will not put up with excess moisture during the winter. It is propagated from seed.

Natural habitat: Mexico

△ *Mammillaria candida*

Generally solitary, the 10cm/4in wide stems of this species will occasionally cluster with age. When grown in adequate light, the dense, white spines completely hide the stem. Light pink flowers are borne in rings in late spring. It will tolerate temperatures of –7°C/20°F, for short periods. It is grown from seed.

Natural habitat: Mexico

△ *Mammillaria carmenae*

Rediscovered in the 1970s, this choice species has become quite common. Although dwarf and mostly solitary in its habitat, the stems will grow to 5cm/2in and make 15cm/6in wide clusters in cultivation. It will tolerate some frost, but is particularly rot-prone if kept too wet in cool weather. It is, primarily, grown from seed.

Natural habitat: Mexico

◁ *Mammillaria geminispina*

Clumping to form plants up to 40cm/16in across, this species is commonly available in two fairly distinct forms. Known as *M. geminispina nobilis*, this is the more recent introduction and has thinner stems than the older form, 7cm/2¾in wide as opposed to 10cm/4in wide; it can have central spines up to 5cm/2in long. Both forms produce rings of 7mm/⅓in wide, dark pink flowers in the spring and make good landscape plants in areas where the temperature doesn't drop below –7°C/20°F, or stay below freezing for more than 24 hours. Outstanding clones of this species are propagated from offsets, but it is generally grown from seed.

Natural habitat: Mexico

MAMMILLARIA

△ *Mammillaria glassii*

There are several varieties of this species and they vary in the size of the stems, 2–4cm/¾–1½in wide, and the size and colour of the flowers. All form dense, flat cushions of stems up to 17cm/6½in wide. They flower freely but are somewhat rot-prone. They will tolerate –4°C/25°F briefly, and are grown from seed or offsets.

Natural habitat: Mexico

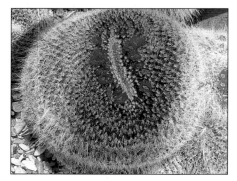

△ *Mammillaria hahniana*

A favourite plant of beginners, it has 8cm/3¼in wide stems, which form clusters up to 25cm/10in across. The length and thickness of the white hair varies. In early spring, concentric rings of dark pink flowers are produced, around the tips of the stems. It will tolerate –4°C/25°F, briefly. It is grown from seed.

Natural habitat: Mexico

△ *Mammillaria guelzowiana*

The flattened, 4cm/1½in wide stems of this problematic species are densely covered in white, hair-like spines, as well as having stiff, tan, radial spines and a hooked central spine. The plant can make a cluster up to 20cm/8in or more, but should always be kept in a shallow pot to prevent root rot, particularly with larger clusters. If adequate summer heat, without very harsh sunlight, is provided, it will produce some of the showiest flowers in the genus; they are bright pink, with a light, spicy scent, and up to 7cm/2¾in across. Kept dry in the winter, this species will tolerate a temperature down to –7°C/20°F, for short periods. It is grown from seed.

Natural habitat: Mexico

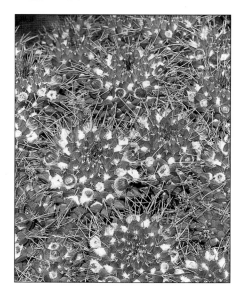

◁ *Mammillaria compressa*

Although the individual stems only grow to 10cm/4in wide, the mature clusters become some of the largest in the genus, growing to more than 1m/1yd wide. It is variable in spine colour (yellow to red) and length (up to 7cm/2¾in long). It will tolerate –7°C/20°F, briefly, and can tolerate full sunlight in a landscape. It is grown from seed or offsets.

Natural habitat: Mexico

△ *Mammillaria lauii* fma. *subducta*

Several forms of this species come from the same mountain but from different altitudes. The form pictured here is from the lowest altitude and it differs in its yellow spines: fma. *lauii* is white-spined, and fma. *dasyacantha*, from the highest altitude, is smaller and has soft white spines. It is one of the earliest species of *Mammillaria* to flower, in the spring, sometimes in midwinter. The stems of this variety grow to 7cm/2¾in across, making small clusters to 15cm/6in across. It is rot-prone, will tolerate −7°C/20°F briefly, and is grown from cuttings and from seed.

Natural habitat: Mexico

△ *Mammillaria huitzilopochtli*

This is a club-shaped, solitary species. Most plants only have radial spines, but about five per cent have 2cm/¾in long, black, central spines. In early spring, several rings of pink flowers encircle the stems, several centimetres down from the tips. It will not tolerate prolonged frost, and is grown from seed.

Natural habitat: Mexico

◁ *Mammillaria (Cochemiea) maritima*

From the subgenus *Cochemiea*, the flowers of this species are 2cm/¾in wide, 4cm/1½in long and bright red, typical for that group of plants. The 5cm/2in thick stems cluster from the base and, in its habitat, can form clusters 50cm/20in tall and 1m/1yd across. Thriving at high temperatures, it will not tolerate frost. It is grown from seed or offsets.

Natural habitat: Baja California (Mexico)

MAMMILLARIA

△ *Mammillaria microhelia*

The stems of this species will grow to 25cm/10in tall but are sparingly branched. The combination of golden and brown spines is quite attractive, particularly in spring, when it flowers. The flowers are 1cm/½in across and can vary from yellow to pink. It is rot-prone, especially when mature. A shallow pot and coarse compost (potting soil) are recommended. It will take cold down to −4°C/25°F, for short periods, and it is grown from seed.

Natural habitat: Mexico

△ *Mammillaria pectinifera*

Occasionally found listed under its old name, *Solisia pectinata*, this rare dwarf is still sought after and prized. The 4cm/1½in wide stem is solitary but can cluster in age. The flowers are 1.5cm/⅝in across, white, and are borne in a ring around the side of the plant. Slow-growing and rot-prone, it does better underpotted with a coarse compost (potting soil). It is hardy down to −7°C/20°F; it is grown from seed and, occasionally, grafted.

Natural habitat: Mexico

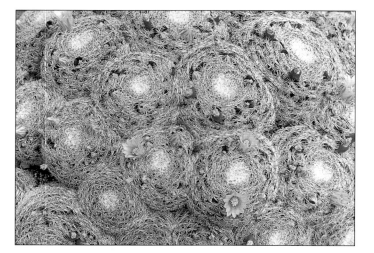

◁ *Mammillaria microthele*

The minute, white spines densely cover this flat, clustering species. It can branch dichotomously (one branch dividing into two at the growing tip) or by offsetting, the 6cm/2½in wide stems forming a cluster 30cm/12in across. In spring, the 5mm/¼in wide flowers emerge from the spines for several weeks but rarely make complete rings of flowers. It will tolerate temperatures down to −10°C/15°F, for short periods.

Natural habitat: Mexico

△ *Mammillaria nivosa*

Covered with stiff 1cm/½in long, golden spines, the stems grow to 4cm/1½in across, making 15cm/6in wide clusters. The yellow flowers, borne in spring, are not too apparent among the similarly coloured spines; the flowers give rise to dark red fruit late in the summer. This species will not tolerate frost. It is grown from seed.

Natural habitat: Cuba

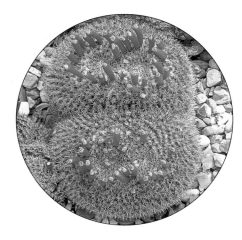

△ *Mammillaria perbella* fma. *pseudoperbella*

Closely related to *M. microthele*, this species only branches dichotomously, with each head splitting into one or more 7cm/2¾in wide heads and forming a low, rounded cluster, up to 30cm/12in across. The 7mm/⅛in wide, pink flowers are never borne in great profusion, but they open on and off all summer. The long, red fruit are often more attractive than the flowers. It is grown from seed and will tolerate −10°C/15°F, briefly.

Natural habitat: Mexico

△ *Mammillaria plumosa*

This species has 5cm/2in wide stems, which form dense, white mounds up to 30cm/12in wide. In the spring the small, light yellow flowers poke through the feather-like spines; although not showy, their strong, sweet fragrance often betrays their presence. It is rot-prone, particularly if water is trapped under the spines. It can tolerate −10°C/15°F, briefly. It is grown from seed.

Natural habitat: Mexico

▷ *Mammillaria perezdelarosae*

Introduced in the early 1990s, this species is closely related to *M. bombycina*. In its habitat, it is small and solitary; in cultivation, it can grow to 6cm/2⅓in broad and 10cm/4in tall, sometimes offsetting. If grown in inadequate light, the stem tends to etiolate, becoming thin and pointed. It is also somewhat rot-prone. It will tolerate −4°C/25°F for brief periods, and it is grown from seed.

Natural habitat: Mexico

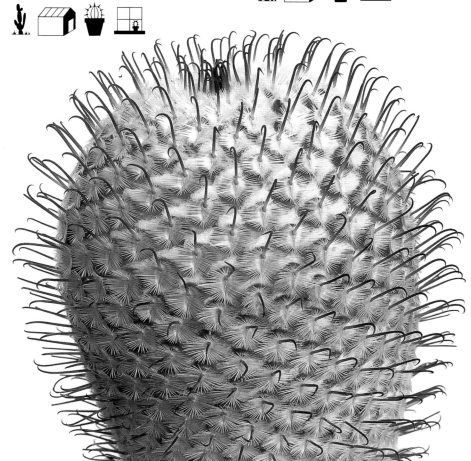

MAMMILLARIA

△ *Mammillaria zeilmanniana*

Despite coming from a remarkably small range in the wild, this has become one of the most common *Mammillaria*. It is also one of the most prolific bloomers, producing rings of dark pink or, occasionally, white flowers continuously, for several months. It is a very soft-bodied plant, and care should taken not to overwater it. If kept dry, it is hardy to −7°C/20°F, for short periods. It is grown from seed.

Natural habitat: Mexico

△ *Mammillaria prolifera*

As the name suggests, this species clusters heavily. The 2.5cm/1in wide heads spread to fill shallow pots up to 25cm/10in wide. Although the small yellow flowers are not very noticeable, they are often followed by bright red fruit that last for weeks. It is hardy down to −4°C/25°F for short periods. It is grown from offsets or seed.

Natural habitat: Mexico

◁ *Mammillaria saboae* var. *haudeana*

Of the three varieties of this marvellous dwarf species, this is the fastest and easiest to grow. The stems grow to 2cm/¾in wide and, by offsetting heavily, form a low mat up to 15cm/6in across in cultivation. The flowers are quite large for the genus, 2.5cm/1in wide on the end of a long tube. It is fairly rot-prone. Like other closely related species, the fruit ripen internally. In the plant's habitat, the fruit are released slowly as it expands and shrinks with the seasons. In cultivation, it is generally retained in the plant, since they are not subjected to drought (commercial growers pollinate stock plants intensively and, literally, throw them into a blender to obtain the seeds). The variety will tolerate bright, indirect light and brief periods down to −4°C/25°F, if kept dry. It is occasionally grown from seed but generally from offsets.

Natural habitat: Mexico

◁ *Mammillaria schumannii*

The old name for this species is *Bartschella schumanni* but it is now considered a *Mammillaria*. The attractively odd, bluish stems grow to 3cm/1¼in wide and 10cm/4in long, making clusters 13cm/5½in across. During the summer, the 3cm/1¼in wide, pink flowers are borne on the tips of the stems. It will tolerate intense heat and sunlight, but not frost. It is rot-prone, and is propagated from seed or cuttings.

Natural habitat: Baja California

◁ *Mammillaria pringlei*

Though the species is often considered a form of *M. rhodantha*, the stems of this cactus grow to 12cm/4½in wide and 20cm/8in tall and are covered in dense, golden spines. In summer, rings of bright pink flowers are borne from the crown. It is a fast and easy species to grow and is hardy down to −4°C/25°F, briefly. It is grown from seed.

Natural habitat: Mexico

△ *Mammillaria supertexta*

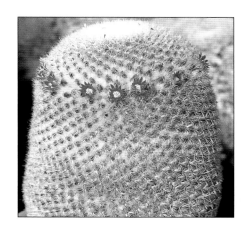

This slow-growing, attractive species forms a single stem, 5cm/2in across and 12cm/4½in tall. If it is grown hard – with high amounts of light and a minimum of water and fertilizer – the stem is completely hidden in fine, white spines. In the spring, several consecutive rings of minute, deep red flowers encircle the stem. It will tolerate some frost, and is grown from seed.

Natural habitat: Mexico

▷ *Mammillaria solisioides*

Only occasionally available, this solitary species is rare in its natural habitat and heavily protected. The slow-growing, solitary stem will eventually reach 7cm/2¾in wide and tall. In spring, this bears 2cm/¾in wide, yellow flowers around the crown. It is exceptionally rot-prone, and will tolerate some light frost. It is grown from seed.

Natural habitat: Mexico

MATUCANA

This Peruvian genus is sometimes united with *Borzicactus* because of floral similarities. The species can be solitary or clustering, and spherical to, eventually, columnar. Many of the species will not tolerate much cold, but those from a high elevation can endure some frost. The flowers are generally zygomorphic (bilaterally symmetrical) and can be white, yellow, orange, pink or red. Most *Matucana* have no other special requirements than to be kept warm in the winter; they tend to lose their roots if kept cold and wet.

△ *Matucana aureiflora*

Unusual in this genus because of its actinomorphic (radially symmetrical) flowers, the lightly spined body is flattened and can grow to 12cm/4½in across. In the spring, the 4cm/1½in wide, bright yellow flowers are produced in several flushes. It should be protected from frost or intense sunlight. It is grown from seed.

Natural habitat: Peru

▷ *Matucana formosa*

This species forms a solitary, barrel-shaped body, 17cm/6½in broad and tall. During the summer, it produces several flushes of 3cm/1¼in wide, 5cm/2in long, orange-red flowers. It will not tolerate a heavy frost or intense sunlight. It is grown from seed.

Natural habitat: Peru

◁ *Matucana intertexta*

The shiny, green, solitary stems of this species grow to 15cm/6in broad and 30cm/12in tall. In the summer, it bears 5cm/2in long, 3cm/1¼in wide, light orange flowers, with darker highlights along the edges of the petals. It will not tolerate a heavy frost or intense sunlight. It is grown from seed.

Natural habitat: Peru

△ *Matucana madisoniorum*

The rough, grey-green body of this plant has quite variable spination. Seedlings of the species are all quite heavily spined. Seedlings from plants occurring at lower altitudes are generally spineless at maturity whereas those from higher altitudes retain their 4cm/1½in long, curving spines. The orange flowers are typical of the genus, 3.5cm/1⅜in wide and 5cm/2in long. The flowers are produced several times through the summer. The plant will not tolerate frost and it is grown from seed.

Natural habitat: Peru

MYRTILLOCACTUS

A genus with only about three species, it is generally tree-like in its habitat, the largest plants growing up to 5m/16½ft tall. In the summer, there are often two or three small, white flowers per areole, followed by small, purple berries, which are edible. Cuttings should be taken in mid-summer, when the night temperature is high, or they will not root. Their care is simple and they grow quite quickly. The genus is found from mainland Mexico into Baja California.

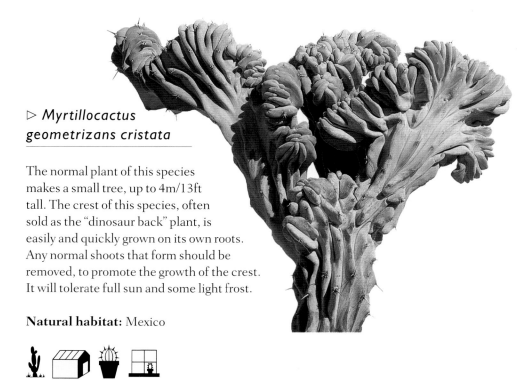

▷ ***Myrtillocactus geometrizans cristata***

The normal plant of this species makes a small tree, up to 4m/13ft tall. The crest of this species, often sold as the "dinosaur back" plant, is easily and quickly grown on its own roots. Any normal shoots that form should be removed, to promote the growth of the crest. It will tolerate full sun and some light frost.

Natural habitat: Mexico

OBREGONIA

This monotypic (having only one species) genus comes from a small area in Tamaulipas, Mexico. Although highly protected, it still exists as sometimes dense colonies of single-stemmed plants. It is closely related to *Ariocarpus* and *Lophophora*. Once uncommon in cultivation, this is now a popular species.

▷ ***Obregonia denegri***

The solitary stems can grow to 13cm/5in wide and 9cm/3½in tall. From the woolly crown emerge 2.5cm/1in wide, white flowers; they appear sporadically throughout the summer. Provided with a coarse compost (potting soil), warmth and bright, but not intense, light, it can grow to flowering size in three or four years. If kept dry, it will tolerate −7°C/20°F, briefly. It is grown from seed but can be grafted to accelerate growth.

Natural habitat: Mexico

OPUNTIA

Ranging from Canada to southern Argentina, this large genus has species ranging from dwarf plants only a few centimetres tall to tree-like species 30m/100ft tall. Two features separate this genus from many of the others. First, the growth habit is generally in joints or segments. Often, the genus is separated into at least two groups. The *Platyopuntia* have round, flattened joints, called pads; they are commonly called "prickly pears", as they have spiny, often edible, fruit.

The *Cylindropuntia* have long, cylindrical joints, and are commonly called "chollas". The second distinctive feature of *Opuntia*, which is shared by only a few other genera, is the glochids – specialized small, barbed spines, which are borne at the base of the large spines. These can be very irritating if not handled with care. In some species, these become airborne when the plants are handled. Misting the plants with water will reduce this problem.

△ *Opuntia fulgida* var. *fulgida*

△ *Opuntia invicta*

△ *Opuntia lindheimeri*

Commonly called the "jumping cholla" or "chainfruit cholla", this has purple flowers that produce sterile fruit, from which other flowers are borne, sporadically, in the summer. Chains eight fruit long are common. Since no seed is produced, the plant propagates itself by dropping its joints. These detach readily at the slightest vibration and are distributed by native fauna and tourists. It forms small bushes to 2.5m/8ft tall. It will tolerate −10°C/15°F briefly, and is grown from cuttings.

Natural habitat: Arizona (USA), Mexico

Fiercely armed, this species forms mounds 2m/6½ft broad and 45cm/18in tall. When the spines are new, they are an attractive pink. The 5cm/2in wide, bright yellow flowers are produced in the summer. It will tolerate −7°C/20°F, briefly. It is grown from seed or cuttings.

Natural habitat: Baja California (Mexico)

Producing shrubby to tree-like growth, this species ranges from 2–4m/6½–13ft tall. The flowers, varying from yellow to red, are produced in late spring, and form 3cm/1¼in wide fruit, ripening to a dark purple in late summer. Also commonly available is the "cow's tongue", *O. lindheimeri* var. *linguiformis*, with yellow flowers and long, tongue-shaped pads. It will tolerate temperatures down to −12°C/10°F, for brief periods. It can be grown from seed but is more commonly grown from cuttings.

Natural habitat: Texas (USA)

OPUNTIA

96

△ ▷ *Opuntia microdasys* var. *alba* and *Opuntia microdasys monstrosus*

There are several varieties of this species, which are commonly called "bunny ears". This plant is spineless and, despite its tame appearance, is covered with tufts of thousands of barbed glochids, which can be very irritating. Var. *alba* is the smallest of the varieties and only grows to 45cm/18in tall; other varieties can grow to 60cm/2ft tall and 2m/6½ft across. The flowers are, typically, lemon yellow and 3–5cm/1¼–2in wide. The *monstrosus* form, sometimes sold as "funny bunny", is popular because of its thicker, distorted growth and occasional crested flowers. It will tolerate temperatures down to –7°C/20°F, for short periods. It can be grown from seed but, in practice, is almost entirely raised from cuttings. It is advisable to mist the plant

with water prior to making cuttings, to keep the dislodged glochids from becoming airborne.

Natural habitat: Mexico

△ *Opuntia tunicata*

A smaller species of "cholla", this plant forms a small bush, up to 45cm/18in tall. The small, yellow flowers are produced in early summer. It will tolerate –4°C/25°F, briefly. It is generally grown from cuttings.

Natural habitat: Mexico

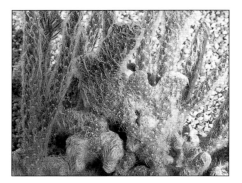

△ *Opuntia vestita*

Unusual because of the white hair covering its stems, this South American species also has thin, white spines hidden amongst the hair. The crested form, as seen in some of the stems of the plant pictured here, is fairly common in cultivation. The 3cm/1¼in wide, red flowers are discreetly produced in the summer. It has a tendency to rot. It is generally grown from cuttings and will tolerate some frost.

Natural habitat: Bolivia

OREOCEREUS

Commonly referred to as the "old man of the Andes", this high-altitude genus is readily available in cultivation. From prostrate clusters to erect plants over 3m/10ft tall, this genus is characterized by long, hair-like spines. Additionally, the plants are armed with stout yellow to red spines, which extend beyond the white hair. It is thought that the white spines provide cold protection as well as a shield from the intense ultraviolet light these plants grow under. While these plants need bright light to produce dense spination, they will not tolerate this in combination with high temperatures. The genus ranges from Peru to Bolivia and Argentina.

△ *Oreocereus celsianus*

One of the heaviest-bodied species in the genus, with stems that can grow to over 11cm/4¼in thick and over 2.5m/8ft tall, this is not as densely hairy as other species, but is armed with thick reddish spines. It will tolerate temperatures down to -7°C/20°F, for short periods, but take care to prevent rot by not overwatering in the winter. It is grown from seed.

Natural habitat: Bolivia, Argentina

◁ *Oreocereus henricksenianus*
var. *densilanatus*

More freely flowering than its relatives, this species has stems that grow to 8cm/3¼in in diameter and 3m/10ft tall, branching from the base. In the early summer, the long 3cm/1¼in wide, dark red flowers poke through the hair on the sides of the plant near the top. If kept dry, it will tolerate temperatures to −7°C/20°F for short periods. It is grown from seed.

Natural habitat: Peru

97

OROYA

Now considered to contain just two species, this small genus has solitary stems that are, initially, flattened and, later, shortly columnar. The flowers are unusual and vary from yellow to pink. They are not very common, and are particularly difficult to grow. Like many genera, the lower sides get a brown, woody appearance with age.

◁ *Oroya peruviana*

Now considered synonyms of this species are *O. gibbosa*, *O. laxiareolata*, *O. neoperuviana* and *O. subocculata*. The flattened, solitary stem will grow up to 20cm/8in in diameter and more than 30cm/12in tall. The short flowers open in early summer, sometimes in a ring around the centre of the plant. The flowers are pink at the base and lighter pink at the tips of the petals. It will tolerate −7°C/20°F, briefly. It is grown from seed.

Natural habitat: Peru

98

ORTEGOCACTUS

This Mexican genus is monotypic and thought to be a link between *Mammillaria* and *Coryphantha*. It is slow-growing and still relatively uncommon in cultivation.

▷ *Ortegocactus macdougallii*

The odd, bluish, 3cm/1¼in wide stems of this unusual species can form a cluster up to 10cm/4in across. In the spring, the bright yellow flowers are produced from the tips of the stems. It tends to have an orange or reddish discoloration near the base of the stems, which can sometimes cover the entire plant, but bright light and good air movement can keep this under control. It is quite rot-prone and does well in very shallow pots with a coarse compost (potting soil). If on a hardy stock or on its own roots, it will tolerate −7°C/20°F, briefly. It is grown from seed, cuttings, or on a graft.

Natural habitat: Mexico

△ *Parodia magnifica*

One of the larger species in the genus, the spherical to shortly columnar, blue stems grow 15cm/6in wide and form clusters 30cm/12in wide. The lemon-yellow flowers are borne for a couple of weeks in the late spring. It has a tendency to split if overwatered but, otherwise, is not difficult to grow. It will tolerate –7°C/20°F, briefly. It is grown from seed.

Natural habitat: Brazil

△ *Parodia microsperma*

△ *Parodia mairanana*

This species is solitary, growing to 5cm/2in or more wide and, eventually, as tall. The flowers, borne in the spring, are 3.5cm/1⅜in wide and rich orange to orange-red in colour. It will tolerate only brief frost. It is grown from seed.

Natural habitat: Bolivia

△ *Parodia punea*

This solitary species grows to 7cm/2¾in wide and 8cm/3¼in tall. In the spring, the 2cm/¾in orange flowers are produced from the crown. It will only tolerate frost briefly and it is grown from seed.

Natural habitat: Bolivia

The list of synonyms for this variable species is too long to list here. Over its range, the body size, spine colour and length, and flower colour vary so widely that it was originally described as more than a dozen different species. The solitary stem grows to 9cm/3½in wide and 18cm/7in tall; the 4cm/1½in wide flower can vary from yellow to red. It will tolerate brief periods of frost. Although the dust-fine seeds germinate quickly, the seedlings remain quite small for a year or more, requiring patience and a stable environment during that time.

Natural habitat: Argentina

PARODIA

◁ *Parodia tephracanthus*

This species is the combination of all the species originally in the genus *Malacocarpus* (later known as *Wigginsia*). The body is solitary or, occasionally, clustering, and up to 15cm/6in wide and tall. In the spring, woolly brown buds appear in the woolly white crown, producing light yellow flowers. Although easy to grow, the stem turns brown with age. It will tolerate temperatures down to −4°C/25°F, for short periods. It is grown from seed.

Natural habitat: Brazil, Uruguay, Argentina

◁ *Parodia uebelmanniana*

A popular species, the solitary, low body grows to more than 10cm/4in wide and tall. The flowers are 3cm/1¼in broad and of a rich purple. There is a yellow-flowered form, which is distinguishable only when in flower. It is hardy to −7°C/20°F, for brief periods. It is grown from seed.

Natural habitat: Brazil

PEDIOCACTUS

This small, North American genus includes some of the most difficult species to cultivate on their own roots. In habitat, they are subjected to hot, dry summers and extended periods below freezing. Most of the growth occurs in the spring. Most species have a small distribution in the wild. In cultivation, seedlings or offsets of the species are generally grafted, and grow rapidly.

▷ *Pediocactus simpsonii* var. *minor*

One of the several varieties in this most widespread species, it is more easily grown than the rest of the genus. It is generally low-growing and, sometimes, solitary, growing to 8cm/3¼in wide; but it can form clumps up to 20cm/8in. The buds form in the winter, swelling and opening in the spring and producing 2cm/¾in light pink flowers. It will tolerate extended periods below −18°C/0°F,

especially if covered with snow. It can be grafted, but grows well from seed or cuttings on its own roots.

Natural habitat: Arizona, New Mexico, Colorado, Utah, Oregon and Washington (USA)

PELECYPHORA

This genus contains two species, which are both as sought-after as they are slow-growing: a 1cm/¹/₂in wide plant may be five to seven years old. Both are restricted in their natural habitat and are highly protected. The flowers are uniform in both species: dark purple and 2.5cm/1in wide, they are borne several times from late spring through summer, and produce a small, dry fruit, which is hidden among the tubercles. Instead of collecting the seed, many growers will let the seed trickle down from the plant and harvest the seedlings that germinate around the parent.

△ *Pelecyphora asseliformis*

Named the "hatchet cactus", for the shape of the tubercles, this species forms clusters flat with the ground in its habitat. It is rot-prone and should be grown in a small pot with a coarse compost (potting soil). The plant pictured is at least 40 years old. The fastest method of producing large specimens is to graft small seedlings or offsets, grow them on for several years, de-graft them, and re-root the mature plant. It will tolerate temperatures to −7°C/20°F, for brief periods.

Natural habitat: Mexico

△ *Pelecyphora strobiliformis*

Previously in the monotypic genus *Encephalocarpus*, this plant differs from the asseliformis species in having scale-like tubercles and by generally being solitary; otherwise, the flowers and fruit are almost identical. Rot-prone and slow-growing, it is often grafted to speed its growth and ensure its long-term survival. The unusual, clustering specimen pictured is at least 40 years old. It will tolerate brief periods to −7°C/20°F.

Natural habitat: Mexico

PERESKIA

Often referred to as "primitive cacti", these plants probably resemble the ancestral cacti: spiny shrubs and trees, with flowers borne singly or in clusters. The species of *Pereskia* range from tuberous shrublets 1m/1yd tall to proper trees more than 11m/36ft tall. The flowers vary from white or yellow to pink, red or purple.

◁ *Pereskia weberiana*

Forming a shrub 1–3m/1yd–10ft tall, this species has a thickened rootstock and can be trained as a succulent bonsai. It bears 1cm/½in wide, white flowers, sporadically, from spring to late summer. It will not tolerate frost without some tip damage but, with the two other Peruvian species, is hardier than the rest of the genus. It is grown from seed or cuttings.

Natural habitat: Peru

104

PILOSOCEREUS

The species, found from Mexico south to Brazil, are generally upright; they branch with relatively thin stems and, upon maturity, develop more wool in the flowering zone on the stem, superficially resembling a cephalium. Because there is no great modification of the stem in this area – for example, the development of a groove in which the flowers form – however, the genus is termed a pseudocephalium. Many of the species are seen in cultivation, particularly those from Brazil, because of their attractive coloration and adaptability to pot culture.

▷ *Pilosocereus alensis*

The bluish-green stems grow to 7cm/2¾in thick and 6m/20ft tall, branching from the base. The short spines are tan but, near the top of the flowering stems, are obscured by white to yellowish wool. The light purple flowers open to 3–4cm/1¼–1½in wide. This species is hardier than most and will tolerate some brief frost. It is grown from seed.

Natural habitat: Mexico

QUIABENTIA

This genus is a member of the subfamily that contains the *Opuntia*. The shrubby plants bear large, fleshy leaves during the growing season. They range from shrubs 2m/6½ft tall to trees 15m/50ft high and are found from Bolivia to Argentina.

▷ *Quiabentia chacoensis*

Forming a small, shrubby plant up to 3m/10ft tall, the glossy, green leaves are shorter than the 5cm/2in long, barbed spines. It is relatively fast-growing and will not tolerate much frost. It is generally grown from cuttings.

Natural habitat: Argentina

REBUTIA

This genus has become commonly available because of its freely flowering nature and small size. The species bear a wide range of flower colours: white, yellow, orange, pink, red and purple. *Rebutia* has recently been amplified by the inclusion of the genera *Sulcorebutia* and *Weingartia*. While the original members of the genus can tolerate frost and grow well in cooler, lower light levels than most cacti, they do, however, suffer when exposed to intense light and high temperatures. Former members of *Sulcorebutia* will not tolerate as much cold, can endure higher temperatures and more sunlight, but tend to be tuberous-rooted and more rot-prone. Former *Weingartia* members form larger plants, which tolerate little frost but endure hot indirect light and are not particularly rot-prone. Often solitary in their habitat, which ranges from Bolivia to Argentina, they can form large clusters in cultivation.

△ **Rebutia albissima**

△ **Rebutia arenacea**

△ **Rebutia graciliflora** var. **borealis**

Although this former *Sulcorebutia* was named for its white spines, there are brown-spined forms as well. The flattened stems grow to 5cm/2in broad and cluster to 11cm/4¼in. The purple flowers open to 3cm/1¼in wide. It will take brief periods of –4°C/25°F and is grown from seed or cuttings.

The spines of this former *Sulcorebutia* are short. Often solitary, the 5cm/2in thick stems can form a 15cm/6in wide cluster. In the spring, red buds form low on the sides of the plant and open into orangy-yellow, 2.5cm/1in wide flowers. It will tolerate –4°C/25°F, briefly. It is grown from seed or offsets, or grafted.

The stems of this recently introduced species grow 3cm/1¼in wide and 6cm/2½in long, in a cluster. In late spring, the buds form on or near the base of the stems, and produce a flush of 2.5cm/1in wide orange flowers for a couple of weeks. It will tolerate –7°C/20°F, briefly. It is grown from seed or offsets.

Natural habitat: Bolivia

Natural habitat: Bolivia

Natural habitat: Bolivia

△ *Rebutia heliosa* var. *condorensis*

One of three varieties of this species, the 3cm/1¼in wide stems are covered with dense, soft, grey spines. The stems make 12cm/4½in wide clusters, which produce a profusion of 2.5cm/1in wide, orange-red flowers in the spring. Like the other varieties of this species, it is quite rot-prone, and prefers a shallow pot with a coarse compost (potting soil). It will tolerate brief periods at −7°C/20°F. It is grown from seed or offsets.

Natural habitat: Bolivia

◁ *Rebutia mentosa*

Chestnut-coloured spines cover the flattened stems of this species, typical of several formerly in *Sulcorebutia*. The heads can grow to 9cm/3½in wide and cluster up to 15cm/6in across. In the spring it bears 2.5cm/1in wide, pink flowers. It will tolerate −7°C/20°F, briefly. It is propagated from seed or by grafting.

Natural habitat: Bolivia

REBUTIA

△ *Rebutia marsoneri*

The flat, 5cm/2in wide stems will produce a 10cm/4in wide cluster. In the spring, 3.5cm/1⅜in wide bright yellow (or, occasionally, red) flowers emerge from the lower sides of the plant. It will tolerate −10°C/15°F, briefly. It is grown from seed or offsets.

Natural habitat: Argentina

△ *Rebutia narvaecensis*

Also known as *R. espinosae*, the flattened stems of this species grow to 4cm/1½in in diameter, forming clusters to 12cm/4½in across. In spring, delicate pink, 3cm/1¼in wide flowers ring the stems. It is somewhat rot-prone. It will tolerate −7°C/20°F, briefly.

Natural habitat: Bolivia

△ *Rebutia muscula*

The 3cm/1¼in wide stems grow taller than they are broad. The clusters grow to 12cm/4½in across and, in spring, produce many light orange flowers. It will tolerate a temperature of −7°C/20°F, briefly. It is grown from seed or offsets.

Natural habitat: Bolivia

◁ *Rebutia wessneriana* var. *krainziana*

Also sold as *R. krainziana*, the lightly spined stems will grow to 5cm/2in wide and 7cm/2¾in tall, and form clumps 10cm/4in wide. The flowers are 3.5cm/1⅜in wide, and can be orange-red or yellow. It will tolerate −7°C/20°F, briefly. It is grown from seed or offsets.

Natural habitat: Bolivia

△ *Rebutia steinbachii* fma. bicolor

The stems of this former *Sulcorebutia* will grow to 5cm/2in broad and form a flattened cushion, with erect brown spines. The flower colour is so variable that a half-dozen varieties have been named. These are largely disregarded, since a single population may vary from yellow, through orange to scarlet or magenta. It will tolerate –4°C/25°F, briefly. It is grown from seed or, to maintain the flower colour, from offsets of known plants.

Natural habitat: Bolivia

△ *Rebutia neocummingii*

Originally in the genus *Weingartia*, this species grows larger than the traditional *Rebutia*, with stems 9cm/3½in wide, forming clusters up to 25cm/10in across. The green buds produced on the shoulder of the stems are often borne two or three per areole and open into 2cm/¾in wide, yellowish-orange flowers. It will not tolerate more than brief exposure to frost without being damaged, but will put up with considerably more sun and heat than the typical species of *Rebutia*. It is propagated from seed.

Natural habitat: Bolivia

△ *Rebutia rauschii*

A beautiful and difficult dwarf species, formerly *Sulcorebutia*, it was introduced in the 1970s in several different forms: purple-bodied with black spines, green-bodied with black spines and purple-bodied with golden spines. Legend has it that these were all forms collected from the same population, on the same expedition. In any case, the stems of this species grow to 3cm/1¼in wide and will cluster to 9cm/3½in. In the spring, 3cm/1¼in wide magenta flowers emerge randomly from the cluster of stems. It is often seen grafted, since it is quite rot-prone. It will tolerate –7°C/20°F, briefly. It is now being grown from seed but the original material is still available, propagated from offsets or by grafting.

Natural habitat: Bolivia

◁ *Rebutia miniscula* fma. *senilis*

This species has several varieties, which vary in spination and flower colour. Pictured is the plant originally named *R. senilis*, with dense, long, white spines and a 3cm/1¼in wide, dark red flower. The 5cm/2in wide heads produce a clump 12cm/4½in across. It is a little more rot-prone than the average *Rebutia*. It will tolerate –10°C/15°F, briefly.

Natural habitat: Argentina

STENOCACTUS

Also sold under the name *Echinofossulocactus*, these are closely related to *Ferocactus* and *Thelocactus*. The genus is generally characterized by its many thin, wavy ribs. These plants rarely make individual stems larger than 12cm/4½in, but often cluster with age.

▷ *Stenocactus coptonogonus*

This species is not typical of the genus, more closely resembling a *Ferocactus*. The solitary head grows to 10cm/4in wide and tall. The pink and white flowers are 3cm/1¼in across. It will tolerate −10°C/15°F briefly, and is grown from seed.

Natural habitat: Mexico

STENOCEREUS

This genus consists of low, bushy, rambling species, and large many-branched, columnar species. The flowers are nocturnal or diurnal and range from white to red. In recent years, *Stenocereus* has been amplified by the inclusion of species of *Hertichocereus*, *Isolatocereus*, *Lemaireocereus*, *Mariginatocereus*, *Marshallocereus*, *Pachycereus* and *Ritterocereus*. A few of the species are used in landscapes in frost-free areas, and most can tolerate a great deal of intense light and heat. They range from extreme southern Arizona, well into Mexico.

◁ *Stenocereus thurberi*

Although often called the "Arizona organ pipe" cactus, only the very northern tip of its range extends into Arizona. The red-spined stems grow to 12cm/4½in thick, more than 3m/10ft tall, and cluster from the base, making a clump 3m/10ft or more wide. The 7cm/2¾in wide, pink flowers open on summer days. Mature plants will tolerate heavy frost with only tip damage, but thin seedlings can be frozen to the ground, which will generally kill them. It is grown from seed.

Natural habitat: Arizona (USA), Mexico

STETSONIA

This hardy monotypic genus is becoming a popular landscape plant in areas that do not stay below freezing for more than 24 hours. Because of the long spines, it is not recommended for high traffic areas. Its natural habitat is Argentina.

▷ Stetsonia coryne

The grey-blue stems of this species branch off a main trunk, eventually forming a plant up to 3m/10ft wide and 8m/26ft tall. Called the "Argentine toothpick", its spines can exceed 15cm/6in in length. Intense sunlight and exposure to frost will promote heavier branching, and tend to produce a bushy plant as wide as it is tall. It will tolerate −7°C/20°F briefly, as a larger plant. It is grown from seed.

Natural habitat: Argentina

TEPHROCACTUS

These relatives of *Opuntia* are often included in that genus. All have the typical jointed habit of growth as well as barbed glochids. There are several species occurring at altitudes of more than 3,500m/11,480ft in the Andes, that make flattened cushions, covered with white hairs, and are humorously referred to as "vegetable sheep". They are fine additions to cactus gardens that don't have very severe weather. They range from southern Argentina, to northern Peru, on both sides of the Andes.

▷ Tephrocactus articulatus

A variable species, which has been sold under several names. Depending on the clone, the joints can range from 4cm/1½in to 15cm/6in long, they can be devoid of spines, bearing only glochids, or bearing white to brown, flattened spines from 4cm/1½in to 15cm/6in long. It will tolerate −10°C/15°F briefly, but, if freezing temperatures persist, the joints separate at the union and fall to the ground. These pieces can be planted in the spring and will root relatively easily. Occasionally grown from seed, it is most often grown from cuttings of selected clones.

Natural habitat: Argentina

THELOCACTUS

Close relatives of *Ferocactus*, these plants generally have tubercles instead of ribs or, occasionally, tuberculation ribs. They can tolerate fairly cold temperatures and harsh light and heat. The flowers are generally large and showy and are borne intermittently throughout the summer. Many of the species are solitary, but a few are clustering. The habitat is from Texas (USA) south into Mexico.

△ *Thelocactus bicolor* var. *bolansis*

This large variety of *T. bicolor* is often densely covered in white spines, though their spine colour can, occasionally, be pink or red. The stems can grow to 6cm/2⅓in broad and 25cm/10in tall, forming 30cm/12in wide clusters in extreme age. The flower is smaller than typical for this genus, only 5cm/2in broad, and tends to be a uniform light pink. It will tolerate −7°C/20°F, briefly. It is grown from seed.

Natural habitat: Mexico

△ *Thelocactus bicolor* var. *bicolor*

The more common variety of this species, the body is generally solitary, growing to 6cm/2⅓in broad and 12cm/4⅓in tall. There are several other varieties of this species (besides *T. bicolor* var. *bolanis*), which vary in spine colour, length, and density. The plant pictured is typical, with the bicoloured flower up to 7cm/2¾in wide. This species blooms periodically throughout the summer. It will tolerate −7°C/20°F, briefly. It is grown from seed.

Natural habitat: Texas (USA), Mexico

△ *Thelocactus macdowellii*

Generally seen as a solitary stem, 10cm/4in wide and up to 15cm/6in tall, this species occasionally makes beautiful clusters. In the late spring, bright pink flowers emerge from the dense, white spines, opening to 4cm/1½in. This species seems to be a little more rot-prone than the other species of *Thelocactus*. It will tolerate −7°C/20°F, briefly. It is grown from seed.

Natural habitat: Mexico

113

△ *Thelocactus rinconensis*

The flat-stemmed species is solitary and can easily grow to 18cm/7in wide in cultivation. It is quite variable in the number and length of the spines; the stems can be green to grey, and the flower, while typically yellowish white, is dark pink from certain locations. It is not very fast-growing, but will tolerate intense sun and temperatures down to −7°C/20°F, briefly. It is grown from seed.

Natural habitat: Mexico

△ *Thelocactus setispinus*

Formerly of the now defunct genus *Hamatocactus*, it is often still sold under that name. One of the more common cacti, it will flower at a year old from seed, producing its 4cm/1½in wide, red-throated, yellow flowers, from spring until early autumn (fall). It often sets bright red fruit, which persist on top of the plant. It will tolerate −7°C/20°F, briefly. It is grown from seed.

Natural habitat: Texas (USA), Mexico

◁ *Thelocactus hexaedrophorus* var. *lloydii*

An odd, soft-bodied species, the solitary grey stem of which can grow to 12cm/4½in wide and 10cm/4in tall. The 5cm/2in wide, silky white flowers are borne early in the summer. This species is not as variable as *T. bicolor*, although there are several named varieties, and they differ more or less only in the length of spines and mature size of the plant. *T. hexaedrophorus* var. *lloydii* is the westernmost variety, being somewhat smaller in body and less variable in spination. It will tolerate −7°C/20°F, briefly. It is grown from seed.

Natural habitat: Mexico

TURBINICARPUS

This genus of slow-growing, dwarf species has been sought after by collectors for decades. All are highly protected in their habitat and many originate from incredibly small, isolated populations. All of the species tend to be rot-prone and are often grafted but, as grafted plants, they grow quickly and can produce quantities of seed. The flowers range from 1–3cm/½–1¼in wide, and can be white, yellow, pink, or purple.

△ *Turbinicarpus lophophoroides*

Named for its resemblance to the genus *Lophophora*, it has a solitary, often club-shaped stem, 5cm/2in wide and up to 10cm/4in tall. Several times in the summer, light pink, 3cm/1¼in wide flowers cover its crown. It is rot-prone and requires warm nights for summer growth. It will tolerate −7°C/20°F, briefly. It is grown from seed or grafted.

Natural habitat: Mexico

△ *Turbinicarpus schmeidickianus* var. *flaviflorus*

One of the smaller varieties of this species, the club-shaped solitary stem can grow to 3cm/1¼in wide and 9cm/3½in tall. The 1.5cm/⅝in, yellow flowers are produced in the early summer. Rot-prone, it does well underpotted (kept rootbound in a small pot), and can remain in a small pot for the life of the plant. It will tolerate −4°C/25°F, briefly. It is grown from seed or grafted.

Natural habitat: Mexico

△ *Turbinicarpus pseudomacrochele* var. *krainzianus*

Unlike many of the others in this genus, this species tends to offset heavily. The 3cm/1¼in wide stems can form clusters up to 15cm/6in across, and produce flushes of 1.5cm/⅝in, light yellow flowers several times during the summer. It is rot-prone and requires a coarse compost (potting soil). It will tolerate -4°C/25°F, briefly. It is grown from seed and occasionally grafted.

Natural habitat: Mexico

◁ *Turbinicarpus schmeidickianus* var. *schwarzii*

Also sold as *Turbinicarpus polaskii*, it is generally solitary in nature but, in cultivation, can make clusters up to 13cm/5in across, in a few decades. The flat stems bear 3cm/1¼in wide, pink flowers several times in the late spring and summer. It has a thick taproot and is prone to rot. It will tolerate −7°C/20°F, briefly. It is grown from seed or grafted.

Natural habitat: Mexico

UEBELMANNIA

Described in 1973, this unique genus has about six species. These tropical plants appreciate warmth and some humidity. They will do well under normal care, provided that the environment is not too hot and dry, but are often grafted to prevent them from losing their roots in the winter. Perfectly clean specimens are rare since they tend to develop round purple blotches on the sides, scarring the plant. All of the genus is from Minas Geraes, Brazil.

△ *Uebelmannia buiningii*

The smallest member of the genus, its purple body grows to 8cm/3¼in wide and a little taller. The 1.5cm/⅝in wide flowers are produced for several weeks in the spring and again, intermittently, in the summer. It is very rot-prone and will not tolerate frost. It is grown from seed and often grafted.

Natural habitat: Brazil

△ *Uebelmannia flavispina*

Often considered to be a form of *U. pectinifera* (the mature plants are quite similar but, as a juvenile, *U. flavispina* has a dark green body with yellow spines, whereas *U. pectinifera* is dark purple with black spines), this species bears golden spines on an olive green body, growing to 12cm/4½in wide and 30cm/12in tall. It will not tolerate any frost. It is grown from seed and occasionally grafted.

Natural habitat: Brazil

▽ *Uebelmannia pectinifera*

Popular since its introduction, this species will grow to 15cm/6in wide and 50cm/20in tall. The 5mm/¼in wide flowers emerge sporadically from the woolly crown, from spring through summer. It will not tolerate frost. It is grown from seed and occasionally grafted.

Natural habitat: Brazil

PLANT DIRECTORY
succulents

This directory provides a full photographic reference to the vast range of different succulent plants. These include the unusual Stone plants (*Lithops* and *Conophytum*), the small and large, succulent-leafed members of the *Crassula* family, climbing vines like the Wax flower (*Hoya*), the large rosettes of the *Agave* and *Aloe*, as well as the globular to tall-growing, spiny Spurges (*Euphorbia*).

◁ *Species of* Aloe *range from tiny bulbs to large trees, as here.*

ABROMEITIELLA (*Bromeliaceae*)

These dwarf members of the pineapple family form mounds or mats, made of many small rosettes. The leaves vary from grey-green to green. They are fairly slow-growing but will tolerate low humidity, temperatures down to 2°C/35°F and some sun.

▷ *Abromeitiella brevifolia*

The dark green, spiny rosettes of this most common species grow to only 3cm/1¼in in diameter. Over a decade or more, they will cluster to form a rounded mound up to 1m/1yd across. The flowers are green, and 3cm/1¼in long. If lightly shaded, this species will tolerate heat and some light frost. It is grown from seed or cuttings.

Natural habitat: Argentina, Bolivia

ADENIA (*Passifloraceae*)

A popular genus of caudiciforms (succulents with a "caudex", or swollen base, formed from a thickened root, or stem, or both), many form huge trunks with vining branches. Although in the passion-flower family, this large genus is not grown for its flowers, which are rather inconspicuous, unisexual, and borne on separate plants. While a few of the species have some spiny armature, most are armed with poisonous sap, and care should be taken when pruning them. Many of the species are relatively fast-growing, if warm conditions and adequate water and fertilizer are provided. Those that produce leaves are winter-deciduous. All can be grown from cuttings but they generally do not produce a normal caudex. Cuttings from mature plants, oddly enough, tend to flower more freely, and are used for seed production. *Adenia* prefer a minimum temperature of 7°C/45°F. They occur in Africa and Madagascar.

△ *Adenia spinosa*

This forms a round, squat caudex more than 1.5m/1½yds wide and 40cm/16in tall. The caudex is topped with thin, spiny branches with slightly lobed, deciduous leaves. It will tolerate hot, bright light, but not frost. It is grown from seed.

Natural habitat: South Africa

◁ *Adenia globosa*

Both this species and the larger and less common *A. ballyi* share this growth form; a large, round, bumpy caudex surmounted by thick, spiny branches. The trunk grows to 1m/1yd high and thick, with branches more than 1m/1yd long. It is grown from seed or cuttings, but the latter seldom develop a typical caudex. It will tolerate hot, bright light, but not frost.

Natural habitat: Tanzania

△ *Adenia venenata*

Faster-growing than *A. glauca*, this species produces thicker vines. The lobed leaves have extra-floral nectaries, which secrete a sweet but caustic nectar (which is very attractive to ants). The caudex is green or purplish in strong light and grows more than 1.5m/1½yds tall and 15cm/6in thick, topped with vines. The vines can grow several metres in a season, gripping for support with numerous tendrils. In its habitat, the vines often cascade from the tops of the mature plants. It will not tolerate frost but can be acclimatized to full sun outdoors for the summer. It is grown from cuttings or seed, forming a better caudex from seed.

Natural habitat: Eastern Africa

△ *Adenia aculeata*

Growing to more than 1m/1yd tall, this has a caudex and square vining stems that are randomly studded with black prickles. The leaves vary from slightly lobed to deeply dissected. Propagated from seed or cuttings, it can be grown in bright light, if the caudex is somewhat shaded, but it will not tolerate any frost.

Natural habitat: Somalia

△ *Adenia glauca*

The large caudex of this common species forms on top of thickened roots and narrows into long, vining stems, with light green leaves. Cream-coloured flowers are borne in spring. Female plants produce few, seeded yellow fruit. It seems susceptible to chlorosis, or yellowing of the leaves, and prefers slightly acid conditions. In its habitat, it grows in the shade of shrubs; in cultivation, the caudex prefers shade and the vines sun. It will not tolerate frost and is grown from seed.

Natural habitat: South Africa

ADENIUM (*Apocynaceae*)

In the early 1970s, small plants of *A. obesum*, the most common species, were rare and expensive. Now all but one of the species are available, and reasonably priced. In addition to the pure species, many new hybrids are being bred, with larger, more intensely coloured flowers that are borne for more of the year. In tropical climates, they are fast becoming popular landscape plants, with prodigious trunks and masses of flowers. The flowers resemble the common oleander, a close relative. Like oleander, all species of *Adenium* are poisonous, the degree varying from species to species; *A. boehmianum* is still used as an arrow poison.

The genus occurs mostly in Africa, with one species in Arabia and one on the Isle of Socotra (an island in the Indian Ocean). In cultivation, they prefer bright light, some humidity, a well-drained compost (potting soil), and plenty of water and fertilizer during the growing season. They perform well in bonsai-type pots. While these plants will survive as houseplants, they perform best if they can be moved outside for the summer. In winter, they are partially to completely deciduous and should be kept fairly dry. They prefer to stay above 7°C/45°F, although they can tolerate 4°C/40°F, briefly, provided the daytime temperature is above 15°C/60°F or higher. Overwatering in the winter can quickly rot the roots. *Adenium* are grown from seed or cuttings.

△ *Adenium x (A. crispum x A. somalense)*

While considered by some to be a variety of *A. somalense*, *A. crispum* is much slower in growing, forming a shorter, thicker subterranean caudex. This hybrid of the two combines the finer appearance of *A. crispum* with the fast growth of *A. somalense*. Its flowering season is longer than that of either parent, flushing in the spring and again in late summer or autumn (fall).

◁ *Adenium boehmianum*

Still relatively uncommon, this species is grown more for its flowers than the caudex. Multiple thin stems arise to 1m/1yd or more, from an underground caudex, which can be raised for effect. The leaves are wide and rounded, greyish green and pubescent. The flowers are 4cm/1½in broad, pink to lavender, with a darker, solidly coloured throat. This species tends to have the longest dormant season, being completely deciduous for three to five months. It will not tolerate any frost or long periods at or below 7°C/45°F. It is grown from seed.

Natural habitat: Africa

◁ *Adenium obesum*

Occurring over a large range, this plant varies in the size and intensity of its flowers. In its natural habitat, it is generally found as a small bush with a large, underground caudex. The average flower of a wild plant is 4cm/1½in broad, with white petals with dark red edges and a yellow throat. This species is being bred to increase the size and number of the flowers, and to extend the flowering season. The caudex can be raised for effect but grows more quickly if it is left buried, being raised after several years rather than pulled up incrementally each season. The large root makes this species particularly susceptible to rot in the winter; it should be kept quite dry unless high daytime temperatures can be provided. It is grown from seed or cuttings.

Natural habitat: Africa

ADENIUM

△ *Adenium x 'Crimson Star'*

A cross of *A. obesum* and *A. swazicum*, this is one of the most popular hybrids available. Given the right conditions, it will flower for nine months of the year. Because it is only grown from cuttings, the caudex consists of twisted, finger-like roots, which thicken with time and can be raised for effect. Occasional pruning is recommended, as this cultivar can be somewhat leggy, particularly if grown in bright light. It will tolerate 4°C/40°F, briefly, but prefers higher temperatures. It is grown exclusively from cuttings.

△ *Adenium somalense*

This species can grow to over 3m/10ft tall in its habitat; in cultivation, it can grow to 1m/1yd tall in a couple of seasons, under the right conditions. The leaves are long and sharply pointed, with pronounced white venation (veining). The flowers are 3cm/1¼in broad, with dark red edges and nectar guides (prominent lines running down the throat). While the seedlings are, initially, tall and spindly, they will thicken with time, producing most of the caudex above ground. This species will tolerate sun for half the day. It will not tolerate any frost or long periods at or below 7°C/45°F. It is generally grown from seed.

Natural habitat: Somalia

ADROMISCHUS
(*Crassulaceae*)

This South African genus has become fairly common and popular in the last decade. While a few species can grow to 10–15cm/4–6in tall, most form small clumps of succulent leaves, often with a tuberous root or small caudex. The plants can be propagated from seed although, more commonly, individual leaves are used, which easily root and produce plantlets from the base. Certain species are highly variable; choice clones, with intense markings or unique textures, are eagerly sought after. Since the plants have a tendency to shatter when roughly handled, mail order companies sometimes offer leaves rather than whole plants. The small flowers vary from white to red and are generally borne on solitary spikes. Most of this genus will tolerate some frost, but not prolonged periods below freezing. They occur in south-west Africa.

△ *Adromischus cooperi*

This species is sometimes sold under the name *A. festivus*, and has 3–4cm/1¼–1½in long leaves that are round in cross-section, with a flattened, sometimes wavy, blunt tip. The leaves have a mottled colour, particularly in bright light, and form a small, clumping plant to 6cm/2½in across. The plant is grown from leaves or from seed. It will tolerate brief periods at −7°C/20°F.

Natural habitat: South Africa

◁ *Adromishcus cristatus*

This species forms small clumps of 5cm/2in long, green, pubescent leaves, whose ends are quite wavy. More than most species, this produces great quantities of red aerial roots, which cover the stems. It is grown from leaves or seed and it will tolerate temperatures down to −4°C/25°F, for a short time.

Natural habitat: South Africa

123

AGAVE (*Agavaceae*)

A large genus of rosette-forming succulents, these are generally short-stemmed, although a few will form stems up to a 1m/1yd tall. *Agaves* vary, from dwarf species only 12cm/4½in wide to huge plants almost 3m/10ft in diameter. Most *Agave* are monocarpic, each stem flowering only once and then dying. The flowering process can take almost a year, with the flowering rosette putting all of its stored energy into the effort. Some flower stalks reach 10m/30ft or more tall. If it is successfully pollinated, one plant can produce tens of thousands of seeds; however, the time from seed to flowering is 10–30 years and because of this, species grown from seed seem to be available in either small numbers or by the thousands. Ranging from the south-western USA to south of Mexico, species of *Agave* can be selected for a wide range of conditions and make excellent landscape plants.

◁ △ *Agave americana* and *A. americana* 'Medio-picta alba'

The standard form of this species makes huge landscape plants, suitable for warmer climates. The rosettes grow to 2.5m/8ft wide and 2m/6½ft tall, offsetting more or less freely from the base, although runners can emerge from the ground several metres/yards away from the parent plant. In addition to the normal form, four different variegated cultivars are commonly grown. *A. americana marginata* fma. *alba* and fma. *aurea* have white or yellow variegation on the leaf margins. *A. americana* 'Medio-picta alba' fma. *aurea* have white or yellow bands down the middle of the leaves. The variegated forms grow half or two-thirds of the size of the normal form. *A. americana* will tolerate frost but can be damaged at −7°C/20°F. The normal form is propagated by seed or offsets; the variegated forms by offsets only.

Natural habitat: Mexico

◁ *Agave colorata*

The wide, blue, toothed leaves of this popular species form a loose rosette, up to 1.2m/4ft across. It suckers sparingly from the base and, in age, will tend to lean to one side. Although it originated in a fairly tropical climate, it will tolerate cold down to −7°C/20°F, briefly. It is grown from seed or offsets.

Natural habitat: Mexico

◁ *Agave angustifolia* var. *marginata*

Growing to 1m/1yd wide and up 40cm/16in tall, with stems generally branching from the base and forming clusters up to 3m/10ft wide, this is one of the few *agaves* that forms much of a stem. Fairly tropical, it grows quickly, but will not tolerate much frost. In order to maintain the variegated leaf margins, it must be propagated from cuttings.

Natural habitat: Costa Rica to Mexico

AGAVE

△ *Agave parryi* var. *hauchucensis*

The range of this species extends over hundreds of kilometres, consisting of isolated populations on various mountain ranges from Arizona into Mexico. Because of this, several varieties have evolved, many of which were once considered separate species. Occurring around the Hoecake Mountains in south-eastern Arizona, this variety is quite variable. The plant pictured is the most desirable form, with wide, densely overlapping leaves, although many plants have considerably thinner leaves and more open rosettes. It grows to 1.5m/ 1½yds wide, offsetting sparingly. It is grown, predominantly, from seed. It will tolerate −12°C/10°F for brief periods.

Natural habitat: Arizona

▷ *Agave palmeri*

Its dark blue leaves are 3–5cm/1¼–2in wide and grow to 1m/1yd long, forming a dense rosette up to 1.5m/1½yds across. Over its range, it can vary in size, with a few western populations consisting of individuals only 40cm/16in across. It will tolerate −12°C/10°F, briefly.

Natural habitat: south-east Arizona, New Mexico (USA)

◁ *Agave macroacantha*

The thin, blue leaves will form a rosette more than 40cm/16in wide, eventually clustering. It will tolerate intense sun and heat, but not heavy frost. It is grown from seed; particularly handsome clones – selected for their robustness and thick, black spines – are grown from offsets.

Natural habitat: Mexico

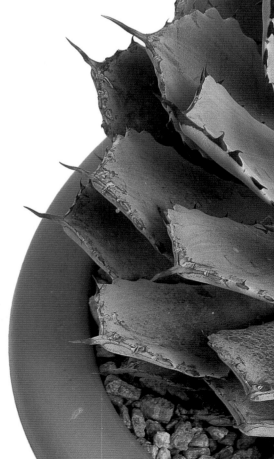

126

◁ *Agave parryi var. truncata*

This southern variety is one of the most beautiful, although not nearly as hardy as some of the northern varieties. The dense rosettes grow to 1m/1yd wide, sending up suckers up to 1m/1yd away. The plant pictured is the clone originally collected by Gentry, author of *Agaves of North America*; this work is still the definitive publication on the genus. This clone is the most beautiful available, having wider and bluer leaves than most seed-grown plants. It is grown from seed but selected clones are grown from suckers. It will tolerate temperatures of −4°C/25°F, for short periods.

Natural habitat: Mexico

△ *Agave ferox*

This large species is fairly common in landscapes in areas that receive little frost. The leaves are dark green, growing to 35cm/14in wide and over 1m/1yd long. Offsetting sparingly, it sometimes forms several-headed clusters. It will flower at 10–15 years old, producing a stalk up to 10m/30ft tall. It will tolerate fairly hot sun and −4°C/25°F, briefly.

Natural habitat: Mexico

127

◁ *Agave potatorum*

A quite variable species, plants available commercially vary from dwarf clones 30cm/12in across, to clones that reach more than a 1m/1yd in diameter. Equally variable are the leaf shape and the teeth on the margins. None of the variations will tolerate heavy frost without some damage and, depending on the clone, some are sensitive to intense heat as well. Occasionally grown from seed, truly outstanding clones are propagated from offsets.

Natural habitat: Mexico

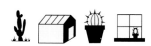

AGAVE

▷ *Agave victoria-reginae*

When mature, this species is one of the most attractive *agaves*, forming a tight, spherical rosette. The standard variety grows to 60cm/2ft in diameter and is solitary, but a common small variety, *A. victoria-reginae* var. *compacta*, offsets heavily but reaches only 35cm/14in in diameter. It is grown from seed and/or offsets, depending on the variety. Small plants need some protection from intense sun, but mature specimens can be acclimatized to full exposure. The species will tolerate −7°C/20°F, for brief periods.

Natural habitat: Mexico

◁ *Agave* x 'Leopoldii'

An attractive hybrid of *A. filifera* x *A. schidigera*, this offsets readily. The rosettes will grow to 18cm/7in wide, forming clusters up to 40cm/16in wide. It will tolerate prolonged exposure to temperatures down to −7°C/20°F and makes an excellent landscape or pot plant. It is propagated by offsets.

ALBUCA
(*Asphodeliaceae*)

This genus of succulent bulbs is just gaining popularity, with only a few species now available. Some are highly reduced, producing only a single leaf in a season from a bulb little more than a 1cm/½in across. This genus is not particularly difficult to grow, so long as the plants are kept fairly dry when dormant. It is South African.

▷ *Albuca spiralis*

Quite uncommon a few years ago, this unusual species will doubtless take its place among hobbyists' favourites in the near future. Its leaves are tightly spiralled, particularly when grown in bright light. The fleshy bulb can grow to more than 5cm/2in in diameter and will cluster with time. In late summer, the flower stalk, an unbranched spike, will grow to 15cm/6in, bearing small pendulous, greenish flowers. It should be kept fairly dry when it is dormant and it will not tolerate frost.

Natural habitat: south-west Africa

ALLUADIA (*Didiereaceae*)

This genus forms part of the thorn-shrub forest in Madagascar. Most species of *Alluadia* have a juvenile growth form of a branched shrub a few metres/yards high, eventually forming a single-trunked tree, branching well above the ground. Some can grow to 15m/50ft tall. All but one species produce deciduous leaves, borne from the same nodes year after year. While these plants are often confused with members of the genus *Fouquieria*, they are actually closely related to the Cactaceae. They are dioecious (having flowers which are either male or female on separate plants in the same species), bearing many small, mostly whitish flowers on mature plants. They will not tolerate prolonged frost but make excellent full-sun patio plants, until they grow too large to be moved indoors. Most are easily propagated from cuttings; they are not often grown from seed as it is rarely available.

△ *Alluadia dumosa*

Forming a shrub as a juvenile, this species will grow to more than 10m/30ft at maturity. The leaves are reduced to inconspicuous scales. Generally grown from cuttings, these plants will tolerate only the lightest of frost, and prefer warmer, more tropical conditions for rapid growth.

Natural habitat: Madagascar

◁ △ *Alluadia procera*

This species is typical for the genus, forming a small shrub with basal branches and, like the plant pictured here, eventually sending up a main trunk. At maturity, this forms a tree to 15m/50ft tall, with a few upper branches. This species can flower at 3m/10ft tall. It will not tolerate any frost and is generally grown from cuttings.

Natural habitat: Madagascar

ALOE (*Asphodeliaceae*)

This large and very popular genus occurs from Africa to Madagascar. The most common growth form is that of a rosette of thickened leaves, either with or without a stem; however, they range from small bulbs with grass-like leaves to massive trees 10m/30ft tall. The flowers range from white to red and are often borne in profusion. The small oval berries are green. Some of the dwarf species and their hybrids make fine pot plants, suitable for the patio or windowsill, while most of the genus is better planted as landscape plants in areas that receive little or no frost. Most larger-growing species will tolerate at least half a day of sun, whereas smaller ones need shade; a few are dormant in summer. Few species survive a hard frost without some damage. They are propagated from seed or offsets.

△ *Aloe barbadensis*

Still known to much of the world as aloe vera, the "healing aloe", it is distributed from grower to grower as much as it is sold in any number of retail outlets. Hybrids of this species are fairly common but the true species is equally widely available. It grows 20cm/8in wide, upright rosettes, which offset freely. The leaves are 5cm/2in wide, unmarked and dull green. Yellow flowers are produced on unbranched spikes about 1m/1yd tall in early summer. The sap of this plant is widely used for its curative property, but care should be taken to be sure of its identity. If this plant is being grown for its sap, it is best to keep it well hydrated, as the sap from a drought-stressed plant will be particularly viscous and strong-smelling. It grows well in a half day of sun and will tolerate light frost without much damage. It is occasionally grown from seed, but most commonly from offsets.

Natural habitat: Cape Verde Islands, Canary Islands

◁ *Aloe dichotoma*

One of the largest members of the genus, it forms a tree up to 10m/30ft tall, with a thick trunk and peeling bark. The individual rosettes are 30cm/12in wide, with dull green leaves that are 5cm/2in wide and taper to 20cm/8in long. Despite its size, the flowers of this aloe are unremarkable: they are yellow and borne on a few unbranched spikes 30cm/12in long. In warmer climates, this is a more-or-less winter-growing species and is best transplanted in the autumn (fall). A well-drained compost (potting soil) or location is recommended, as the trunk is rot-prone. It will tolerate intense sun and high temperatures, as well as some brief frost but, if temperatures below −2°C/28°F are expected, the trunk should be wrapped up; or the thin stems below the rosettes will freeze before the leaves will. It is grown from seed.

Natural habitat: Namibia, South Africa

ALOE

 Aloe distans

This prostrate species forms rosettes 12cm/4½in wide that branch from the base, sometimes growing to more than 1m/1yd long. The plant pictured is a particularly attractive clone, with bright yellow teeth. Scarlet flowers are borne densely on branched spikes 40cm/16in long. It will tolerate light frost and prefers some shade. While it is grown from seed, certain clones are propagated from cuttings.

Natural habitat: South Africa

△ *Aloe harlanii*

An attractive and common species, this is ideal as a houseplant, its white and green leaves forming rosettes 18cm/7in in diameter. In spring, it produces spikes of light pink flowers, 35cm/14in tall. It will tolerate bright, indirect light and intense heat, but no frost. It is propagated from seed or cuttings.

Natural habitat: Africa

△ *Aloe humilis*

Among the hardier of the small aloes, this species will eventually cluster into a low mound more than 30cm/12in wide. The red flowers are borne on unbranched spikes, to 35cm/14in tall, in the spring. This species will tolerate a temperature down to –4°C/25°F, for brief periods, and half a day of sun.

Natural habitat: South Africa

▽ *Aloe* x 'Doran Black'

Over the last decade, many fine aloe hybrids have appeared on the market. The dwarf hybrids are the most popular, requiring little space and infrequent care. *Aloe* x 'Doran Black', like many of these, does well as a windowsill plant, flowering in an 8cm/3¼in pot. The fat leaves make rosettes 8cm/3¼in wide, offsetting from the base. Throughout the summer, it produces 25cm/10in tall, thin, unbranched spikes, with light red flowers. Many of the dwarf aloe hybrids have parents from Madagascar and do not tolerate full sun or frost. This commercial hybrid is grown only from offsets.

ALOE

◁ *Aloe ramosissima*

This and *A. dichotoma* are sometimes considered the same species, *A. ramosissima* being the smaller, coastal form. The unbranched spikes of yellow flowers are nearly identical to *A. dichotoma*, but the plant is more heavily branched, growing only to 2m/6½ft tall. The leaves are also narrower and shorter than those of *A. dichotoma*. This species is more of a winter-grower, preferring to be transplanted in the autumn (fall). It will not tolerate much frost and prefers some shade in the heat of the day. It is grown from cuttings, occasionally, but more generally from seed.

Natural habitat: South Africa

ANACAMPSEROS
(*Portulacaceae*)

In 1994, this genus was split into three smaller genera: *Anacampseros*, *Avonia*, and *Grahamia*. The remaining members are all from South Africa, having rosettes of smooth or hairy leaves that occasionally form a tuberous root or small caudex. The flowers range from white to pink, open for a short time in the afternoon and are often self-fertile; the seeds are borne in a cup made of upright filaments and are thrown from the plant in the wind. While a few are slow-growing and extremely dwarf, the majority of species are easy to grow and make good pot plants. They will not tolerate frost but can survive half a day of sun and fairly intense heat.

△ *Anacampseros rufescens* 'Sunrise'

This cultivar is now relatively common. The leaves vary from green at the base to pink and yellow at the tips; the brighter the light, the more intense the colour. It comes true from seed and will, eventually, make clusters of rosettes 10cm/4in across. Pink flowers open to 2cm/¾in in mid to late afternoon on hot days. It will not tolerate frost or hot, all-day sun.

ARGYRODERMA

Named for their silvery skin, these plants are an extremely succulent and almost stemless species. These South African miniatures have paired, succulent leaves, either singly or in clusters, with flowers in yellow or purple. A very well-drained compost (potting soil) is required to prevent it from rotting.

◁ *Argyroderma ringens*

This clustering species has 5mm/¼in purple flowers in late summer. It will tolerate low temperatures, if kept dry, but should not be subjected to freezing temperatures. Propagation is generally from seed, but heads can be removed from clusters and rooted.

Natural habitat: Cape Province (South Africa)

AVONIA (*Portulacaceae*)

In 1994, this genus was split off from *Anacampseros*. All species have a thin, papery scale that covers the much-reduced leaves. The stems form clusters from a fibrous or, in some species, tuberous root. They require a particularly well-drained compost (potting soil). They will tolerate fairly hot, bright light, but no frost. The genus occurs in north-east, east and southern Africa.

▷ *Avonia papyracea*

Fairly common, this species grows several 1cm/½in thick stems from a stout taproot. The small, white flower is borne from the tip of the stem in summer on hot afternoons. Since the flower is open for such a short time, and is the same colour as the leaf scales, the hobbyist is often aware only after the fact, when the small fruit emerges from the end of the stem. It prefers heat during the growing season, and will not tolerate frost.

Natural habitat: South Africa

BRACHYCHITON (*Sterculiaceae*)

Sold as "Australian bottle trees", several species of this genus have become common landscape trees in areas that do not experience prolonged periods below freezing. The leaves vary from large and slightly lobed to thin and digitate. All of the species form a more or less thickened trunk and are quite drought-hardy, tolerating dry soil without wilting. Only a few species are used for succulent bonsai (for example, *B. gregoryi*, *B. rupestris*), and these form thickened roots, which can be raised for effect. The flexible stems are easily bent and trained. All species will tolerate intensely hot sun, given adequate water, and some frost.

▷ *Brachychiton rupestris*

In its habitat, this species forms a tree 8m/26ft tall with a bottle-shaped trunk, 1.5m/1½yds in diameter. As a pot plant, its roots develop far more quickly than the trunk, and are often raised for effect. This is probably the most drought-tolerant of the genus and it will not wilt even after being dry for a couple of days; it defoliates after continued drought, rather than dying. The leaves are single in mature plants, 7.5mm/³⁄₁₆in wide and 7–10cm/2¾–4in long, but in young plants are four- or five-lobed. It will tolerate full, intense sun and brief periods down to −7°C/20°F, making it one of the few "hardy" caudiciform trees. It is grown from seed.

Natural habitat: Australia

BURSERA (*Burseraceae*)

This New World genus is among the finest for succulent bonsai. While some tropical species are typically shrubs and small trees, many of the species have thickened trunks, often with peeling or colourful bark. The leaves vary from solitary to compound, with thin leaflets, and most species are deciduous. The flowers are quite small and nondescript, giving rise to a single seed. Most *Bursera* have terpenes in the sap. These aromatic chemicals give each a distinctive odour when pruned or otherwise damaged. Additionally, many produce a resinous sap, which is collected by indigenous people and burned, earning them the name "incense trees". This is not surprising, since frankincense and myrrh come from *Boswellia* and *Commiphora*, closely related genera. They are grown from seed or cuttings. Most species will tolerate hot, bright sun, given adequate water, but will be damaged or killed by heavy frost. They should be kept fairly dry while they are dormant. The genus ranges just into the USA, but is mostly native to Mexico.

△ *Bursera fagaroides*

In habitat, this common species forms a thick-trunked tree 5m/16½ft tall; also, in part of its range it occurs as a natural bonsai. Mature trees are often no more than 20cm/8in tall, pruned by wind or frost. This form can be reproduced in cultivated plants with adequate water, fertilizer, and judicious pruning. The compound leaves are glossy green and deciduous, occasionally turning bright yellow in the autumn (fall). The bark on mature stems is tan and peels away in layers. It will tolerate hot, bright sun but should be protected from frost. It is generally grown from seed.

Natural habitat: Mexico

△ *Bursera hindsiana*

Forming a tree 3m/10ft tall, this species has red bark and light green, pubescent leaves. White flowers are borne in clusters near the ends of the branches. While mostly deciduous, often some leaves are retained throughout the winter. It will tolerate hot, bright sun but not frost. It is grown from seed or cuttings.

Natural habitat: Baja California (Mexico)

△ *Bursera microphylla*

Growing to 5–10m/16½–30ft tall, the sap of this species is particularly aromatic, and the resin is used as incense. The deciduous, compound leaves are a dark, glossy green, reduced to thin leaflets. Small plants tend to develop thick roots long before the trunk thickens. At maturity, the trunk is white, with peeling bark. Wild plants exposed to wind and frost become beautiful, natural bonsais. It will tolerate full, hot sun, but should be protected from frost. It is grown from seed or cuttings.

Natural habitat: Mexico north into Arizona, California (USA)

Bursera

◁ *Bursera schlectendahlii*

This Mexican species develops peeling, reddish bark, when mature. The deciduous leaves are single or compound, with three leaflets, and they often develop a waxy coating. Plants will tolerate hot, bright sun but any frost will kill them. They are propagated from seed or cuttings.

Natural habitat: Mexico

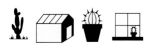

138

CALIBANUS
(*Agavaceae*)

This monotypic genus forms a large, rounded caudex, topped with thin, grass-like leaves. It is closely related to the genus *Nolina*, varying principally in its floral characteristics.

▷ *Calibanus hookeri*

Although plants of this species are not impressive as seedlings, once the caudex reaches several centimetres/inches in diameter, it can be raised for effect. When mature, the hemispherical caudex can be more than 40cm/16in across. This dioecious species bears small, pink flowers on a slightly pendulous stalk, 30cm/12in long. It can easily tolerate −10°C/15°F for short periods. It is grown from seed.

Natural habitat: Mexico

CARALLUMA (*Asclepiadaceae*)

This genus ranges from Africa to eastern India and contains some of the foulest-smelling flowers in this group of succulents. In the wild, flies are the pollinators and are attracted in great numbers to a plant in full flower. Generally borne in late summer, the flowers are the typical starfish shape of the stapeliads (the general term for the members of the *Asclepiadaceae* with succulent stems, like the genus *Stapelia*). The flowers range from less than 1cm/½in to 5cm/2in or more across in various colours; yellow, tan, pink and, more commonly, maroon to dark brown. The plants vary from thin, prostrate stems less than 1cm/½in thick to 3cm/1¼in thick, upright clumps, 20cm/8in tall. Most species will tolerate hot, bright, indirect light, but no frost, and should be kept quite dry in the winter. Many are easily grown from cuttings, or can be grown from seed.

△ *Caralluma socotrana*

The species forms a whitish-green, coral-like clump of upright stems up to 15cm/6in tall and 25cm/10in wide. In the autumn (fall), maroon flowers are borne. It is grown from seed or cuttings.

Natural habitat: Socotra (an island in the Indian Ocean)

CEPHALOPENTANDRA (*Cucurbitaceae*)

This monotypic genus will doubtless be a favourite plant in years to come. It produces a large and interesting caudex, but not the copious quantities of vines that are typical of other succulent members of the cucurbit family – as well as of the more familiar, edible family members, such as cucumbers and squashes – and which can so easily overpower nearby plants.

▷ ▷ *Cephalopentandra ecirrhosa*

The seedlings of this newly introduced, vining caudiciform begin life as a rosette of light green leaves, on top of a small caudex. With ample root run, warmth and water in the summer, the seedlings produce vines with long, grey-green leaves. Eventually, the caudex becomes conical, more than 30cm/12in in diameter. The dioecious flowers are cream-coloured, 4cm/1½in wide. When ripe, the fruit turns a bright orange. It will tolerate sun for half the day but no frost. It is propagated from seed.

Natural habitat: Ethiopia, Kenya, Uganda

CERARIA (*Portulacaceae*)

This small genus from south-west Africa consists of small-leaved, succulent shrubs. They vary from 20cm/8in to more than 1.5m/1½yds tall, having thickened trunks. The dioecious flowers are pink or white, borne near the ends of the branches and less than 5mm/¼in in diameter. Grown from seed or cuttings, all species are excellent for succulent bonsai. They will tolerate hot, bright light, but no frost. They should be kept fairly dry in the winter.

△ *Ceraria pygmeae*

As the name suggests, this is a dwarf species, growing to 20cm/8in tall and a little wider. Eventually forming a large, thickened trunk and roots, it is very good for succulent bonsai. Not as fast as the other species, it grows about 10cm/4in per year. It will tolerate hot, bright light, requires a well-drained compost (potting soil), and does not tolerate frost. It is grown from seed or cuttings.

Natural habitat: South Africa

◁ *Ceraria fruticulosa*

This forms a small shrub in its habitat; in cultivation, individual shoots can easily grow more than 20cm/8in in a season. The leaves vary between clones growing up to 5mm/¼in wide and 1.5cm/⅝in long, but are often only a quarter of that. In early summer, five-petalled, pink flowers 3mm/⅛in wide open along the ends of the branches. Roots thicken in time and can be raised for effect. Both the mature roots and stems will develop red bark. The plant pictured is 22cm/8¾in tall and over 12 years old. It will tolerate hot, bright light but no frost. It grows well from cuttings or seed.

Natural habitat: South Africa

CEROPEGIA (*Asclepiadaceae*)

This large and diverse genus can be found in Africa, eastern India and the Canary Islands. Many species form underground tubers, with perennial or annual above-ground vines or upright stems. Other species lack any underground storage organs, forming thickened, upright or vining stems. The unscented flowers have a long tube that widens at the base. Down-pointing hairs in the floral tube guide the pollinating insect into the flower and only wilt and release the fly after pollination has taken place. In many of the species, the petals are joined at the tips. While leaves are present in all species, in some they are reduced to small scales. Plants in this genus require some shade and warmth; and a particularly well-drained compost (potting soil) should be provided for species with large tubers if they are to be grown successfully.

△ *Ceropegia stapeliiformis*

Similar to *C. devechii*, the 1.5cm/⅝in thick vines grow to 1.5m/1½yds long. The white and purplish-brown flowers are 5cm/2in long and 3cm/1¼in wide. In the right conditions, it will flower from spring to autumn (fall). It will not tolerate full sun, nor frost. It is propagated by seed or from cuttings.

Natural habitat: South Africa

△ *Ceropegia devechii*

The mottled, grey-green vines of this species are 1cm/½in wide and grow to more than 1m/1yd long. Produced in the summer, the flowers are 4cm/1½in long and 5cm/2in wide. It prefers bright, indirect light, and will not tolerate any frost. If winter warmth cannot be provided, it should be kept fairly dry. It is propagated by seed or cuttings.

Natural habitat: Africa

CHEIRIDOPSIS (*Mesembryanthemaceae*)

Most species of this large genus have a unique growth pattern, producing two differently shaped pairs of leaves, one appearing as a short sheath around the inner, larger pair. Many species will form larger clusters in time and are good rock-garden plants for areas with light frost. The flowers, often more than 5cm/2in across, are usually yellow and are borne in the spring.

△ *Cheiridopsis peculiaris*

This "peculiar" species has an even more exaggerated growth habit than is typical of the genus. The first pair of leaves lies flat on the ground, while the second is upright. This species is generally solitary and requires a longer, drier rest in the winter than some of the more easily grown species. It is propagated from seed.

Natural habitat: Cape Province (South Africa)

◁ *Cheiridopsis vanzijlii*

Forming cushions of rounded stems resembling pebbles in its natural habitat, this species lacks the typical growth form and all leaves are of a similar size. The yellow flowers are 6cm/2½in across. It will tolerate temperatures of −4°C/25°F for brief periods. It is grown from seed.

Natural habitat: Cape Province (South Africa)

CISSUS (*Vitaceae*)

This large genus in the grape family has been split in the last decade or so, with the largest caudiciform species placed in the genus *Cyphostemma*. The remaining species are vining plants, some very succulent and others not. Of interest to the succulent collector are the species with succulent vines, or annual vines that die back to the caudex, or tuberous roots. The flowers are unremarkable, minute and green, but they do produce small, red, inedible grapes. Most of the succulent species will tolerate a half-day of sun, but few will survive any frost. The genus occurs from the New World into Asia, but the bulk of the succulent species are African.

▷ Cissus tuberosus

As a mature plant, this species is quite attractive, but can be a nuisance. In the spring, vines with 3cm/1¼in wide, dissected, green leaves grow from the lumpy green caudex. Wherever the nodes of these vines touch moist soil, they will root, forming another small caudex during that season. If allowed to grow freely in an outdoor bed for the summer, one small plant can take over several square metres/yards. It will tolerate intense sun and heat, and the caudex can tolerate brief periods of frost.

Natural habitat: Mexico

◁ Cissus saundersii

Similar to several related species, this forms an annual vine of thickened leaves from a tuberous root. The slightly pubescent, compound leaves are 8cm/3¼in across, with five leaflets. During a season, several metres/yards of vines can be produced, climbing upwards with the help of tendrils. Eventually, a thickened, above-ground trunk is formed but the branched, tuberous roots can be raised at any time. The vines will tolerate intensely hot sun, but the exposed roots should be shaded. It will not tolerate frost, and should be kept fairly dry while it is dormant. It is propagated from seed and, occasionally, from cuttings.

Natural habitat: Africa

COMMIPHORA (*Burseraceae*)

Mostly from Africa and Madagascar, this genus holds the promise of many fine species, perfect for succulent bonsai. Although one species produces the incense myrrh from its aromatic resinous sap, many species have little or no fragrance. The leaf size and shape vary enormously in the genus, as do the size and growth habit of the plants. In their habitat, they range from dwarf, windswept natural bonsais to thick-trunked bushes and trees. Most are deciduous and should be kept fairly dry during the winter. The flowers are generally small, producing a single, seeded fruit about 5mm/¼in across. If provided with adequate water during the growing season, they will tolerate intensely hot sun, but they will not survive frost. They are grown from cuttings or seed.

▷ *Commiphora glandulosa*

This fast-growing species is likely to become common, because of its rapidly growing and easy-to-cultivate properties. The plant pictured is a two-year-old seedling that was bedded out for one summer, and it has already developed a thickened trunk and peeling bark. The deciduous leaves are three-lobed and light green. Unlike many other Commiphora, this species produces spiny, short branches among the foliage. It will tolerate hot, intense sun but no frost. It is easily grown from cuttings or seed.

Natural habitat: Africa

CONOPHYTUM *(Mesembryanthemaceae)*

This large and varied genus of small and difficult plants is not as popular now as it doubtless will be in the future. Because of the often minute size of this plant, it is possible to house a large number of species in a fairly small space. Recently, a monograph was written on the genus by Steven Hammer. This comprehensive work does much to reduce the confusion surrounding the taxonomy of these species. The genus now also includes the members of the former genus *Opthalmophyllum. Conophytum* are winter-growers, requiring only shade and occasional misting in the summer. In late spring, the heads start to shrivel and, by midsummer, they have dried, covering and protecting the new leaves within. In the autumn (fall), the new leaves burst through the dried remains. Like *Lithops*, they consist of one to many pairs of leaves, but some species, in extreme age, will form a short stem. The individual heads range from 2mm/less than ⅛in to 3cm/1½in wide, in a large variety of shapes and colours. The flowers are also quite variable within the genus, nocturnal to diurnal, white or pink to purple, or yellow to orange. They occur in South Africa.

△ **Conophytum friedrichiae**

△ **Conophytum limpidum**

△ **Conophytum verrucosum**

Originally an *Opthalmophyllum*, this species has the appearance of a soft-bodied *Lithops*. The body is solitary or, rarely, clustering to two to three heads, to 2cm/¾in wide and 3cm/1¼in tall, purplish with rounded green windows. It is more easily grown than the more typical *Conophytum*, tolerating some moisture when dormant, but should be protected from frost. It is grown from seed.

Natural habitat: South Africa

Also originally an *Opthalmophyllum*, this species forms clumps, often with more than 50 heads. The bodies are green, topped with rounded, glassy windows, to 2.5cm/1in wide and slightly taller. The flowers are produced in the autumn (fall); they are occasionally white, but normally pink, and often scented. The plant needs bright, indirect light and moderate warmth; it will tolerate some summer watering and must be protected from frost. It is grown from seed.

Natural habitat: South Africa

This warty species is often solitary, but occasionally forms clusters of several heads. The leaves are variable both in the degree of roughness and the colour. They range from reddish brown to olive. The flowers are produced in the autumn (fall) and are 2–3cm/¾–1¼in wide, white to pale pink. It requires bright, indirect light and protection from intense heat, but will tolerate light frost. It is grown from seed.

Natural habitat: South Africa

COTYLEDON (*Crassulaceae*)

A few years ago, many species were split off from this genus and reclassified as *Tylecodon*. The remaining species are small, ever-green shrubs, with succulent leaves and slightly thickened stems. The flowers are generally orange to red. Many of the species will tolerate half a day of sun and some frost. They range from South Africa to Arabia.

▷ *Cotyledon undulata*

This common and beautiful species is named for its wavy-leaved margins. The shrubby growth can be up to 50cm/20in tall. The new growth has a coating of white, waxy bloom that is gradually washed off by watering. Five-petalled, red flowers are borne in the summer. It grows well from seed or cuttings, looking best in large plantings. It will tolerate hot sun for half the day and brief periods of frost.

Natural habitat: Africa

146

CRASSULA (*Crassulaceae*)

This large genus contains the main species of succulents that are now common houseplants, *Crassula portulacea*, the "jade tree", being the most common. Most are leaf succulents, although several develop thick trunks in time. Most are easily grown, generally being propagated from stem cuttings. While they occur outside Africa, only the species from South Africa are generally of interest to collectors.

△ *Crassula* x 'Morgan's Pink'

◁ *Crassula muscosa*

Known for years as *C. lycopodioides*, this common species has many different forms. The stems grow to 5cm/2in wide, forming a shrublet more than 25cm/10in tall. Occasionally, minute flowers are produced in the summer. It can withstand high temperatures and intense light, but no frost. It is easily rooted from cuttings and grows well as a houseplant.

Natural habitat: South Africa

This hybrid of *C. falcata* x *C. mesembryanthemopsis* forms a compact plant up to 5cm/2in wide, with a short stalk of pink flowers. It is among the many hybrids produced in the 1970s and 1980s. Many are easily grown and make attractive windowsill plants, requiring only occasional pruning as they become leggy. Although very popular a decade ago, they have fallen out of favour, but are sure to have a resurgence one day. It will not tolerate any frost. It is grown from stem or leaf cuttings.

CYPHOSTEMMA (*Vitaceae*)

This genus was split from *Cissus* a few years ago. It consists of caudi-ciform species from Africa and Madagascar. The forms range from vines with underground caudices to vining or non-vining species with huge, sometimes tree-like, above-ground caudices, more than 2m/6½ft tall. Most species are deciduous, dropping all leaves and much of the vines produced in the previous season's growth. In late summer, small, red, inedible grapes are produced. The larger tree-forming species can tolerate intensely hot sun and, when mature, some brief, light frost. Their growth increases markedly if they are given plenty of root run. In temperate climates, species like *C. juttae* can be bedded out in a well-drained compost (potting soil) for the summer. As autumn (fall) approaches, they are dug up and stored bare-rooted through the winter, to be planted the next summer. They occur in South Africa and Madagascar.

△ ***Cyphostemma montagnacii***

This species forms compound leaves, 4cm/1½in wide and 6cm/2½ in long, on thin vines arising from large, under-ground roots. In its habitat, the single, large root grows to more than 10cm/4in thick and 30cm/12in long; in cultivation, however, the roots often tend to branch. The roots can be raised for effect, but should be sheltered from hot, direct sun. It will tolerate a fairly hot, bright exposure, but will not tolerate frost. It is propagated from seed or, occasionally, from cuttings.

Natural habitat: Madagascar

△ ***Cyphostemma juttae***

Probably the most common of the genus, this forms a thick, conical caudex in its habitat, more than 1m/1yd tall. The leaves grow to 20cm/8in long, are grey-green and, in full sun, fold upwards from the sides. If given plenty of heat, water and root run in the summer, it is a fairly fast grower. If kept in a small pot, its annual growth can be negligible. It is grown from seed.

Natural habitat: Namibia

◁ ***Cyphostemma glabra***

Still often listed under the genus *Cissus*, this species is quite similar to *Cissus saundersii*. However, the leaves are larger and not at all pubescent. It can produce several metres/yards of vines each summer; these are mostly dropped in the winter. Forming a thick, main stem to 50cm/20in tall, it also has large underground roots, which can be raised for effect, but care should be taken to shade these from intensely hot sun. It will not tolerate frost and should be kept fairly dry when dormant. It is grown from cuttings, occasionally, but mostly from seed.

Natural habitat: South Africa

147

DASYLIRION (*Agavaceae*)

Although some species develop a thickened trunk, most are not succulents as much as they are xerophytes. All bear long, thin leaves, often arranged as ball-shaped rosettes. The hundreds of tan-to-yellow flowers are borne on a long spike.

▷ *Dasylirion longissimum*

This species has thin leaves, 1–2m/1yd–6½ft long, and top stems that can reach more than 2m/6½ft tall. It is becoming a more common landscape plant in areas that do not experience temperatures below –10°C/15°F. Acceptable – but rarely used – in containers, it is propagated by seed.

Natural habitat: Mexico

148

DINTERANTHUS (*Mesembryanthemaceae*)

From the Cape Province in South Africa, this genus is closely related to *Lithops*. The plants are stemless, forming clusters of paired, generally whitish leaves. The yellow flowers are produced from late autumn (fall) to spring. It grows mostly in the winter, requiring only occasional watering in the summer.

▷ *Dinteranthus microspermus* ssp. *puberulus*

The individual heads are 2.5cm/1in wide and 3.5cm/1⅜in long, forming 8cm/3¼in wide clusters. In the autumn (fall), yellow flowers emerge from the centre of each head. It will tolerate intense heat as well as brief periods down to –4°C/25°F. It is grown from dust-fine seed, which needs a temperature of around 38°C/100°F to germinate. Otherwise, its care is the same as for *Lithops*.

Natural habitat: South Africa

DIOSCOREA (*Dioscoreaceae*)

From Africa and extending from Mexico south into South America, this large genus of vining caudiciforms includes the common yam. While a few of the species have large, above-ground caudices, most are completely subterranean, from thumb-sized tubers to those weighing more than 50kg/110lb. The genus contains both winter-and summer-growers.

▷ *Dioscorea elephantipes*

The most common species among collectors, the caudex grows to 1m/1yd in diameter and height in its habitat. It is a winter-grower but, in some climates, grows mostly in the spring and autumn (fall). As a seedling, the caudex forms below ground, growing much faster if left buried for the first couple of years. It will not tolerate any frost. It is grown from seed.

Natural habitat: southern Africa

149

DORSTENIA (*Moraceae*)

This large, tropical genus is a member of the fig family, occurring both in the New and Old Worlds. Varying from herbs to shrubs, succulent or not, their small flowers are borne as an aggregate on a disc called a hypanthodium. This flowering structure is generally flattened, but can be cup-shaped, round or elliptical, and often has long, thin bracts on the margin. When a seed is ripe, the cell below swells until a membrane over the seed ruptures, expelling it several feet. Often, the best-growing *Dorstenia* in a collection are the ones that self seed in another pot quite by accident. There are still new species and forms appearing on the market, including *D. gigas*, a large, caudiciform species from Socotra (an island in the Indian Ocean). All require warmth and adequate water when growing, but should be kept fairly dry when leafless. The bulk of the interesting succulent species is from Africa.

△ *Dorstenia foetida*

There are a multitude of forms, both in leaf and stem, in what is referred to as the "*Dorstenia crispa/foetida* complex". Plants in this group can grow to 20cm/8in tall. The hypanthodia are produced throughout the growing season, and are self-fertile. This species prefers some shade, warmth, adequate water when in growth and a well-drained compost (potting soil). It will not tolerate cold. It is grown from seed.

Natural habitat: north-east Africa

DUVALIA (*Asclepiadaceae*)

These smaller-growing stapeliads have short-jointed, generally prostrate stems. The flowers often have narrow petals and range from tan to black. They need warmth and will not tolerate cool moisture. When propagated from seed, the joints often root on the underside as they grow, making them very easy to propagate. They occur in southern Africa.

△ *Duvalia parviflora*

▷ Duvalia radiata x D. sulcata

In any plant family, hybrids are inevitable, whether they are produced intentionally or occur naturally. Like the plant pictured, most have traits of both parents. This species is not remarkable but some intergeneric hybrids in this family are quite stunning.

This species is typical of the genus, with short, rounded joints 1cm/½in wide and 4cm/1½in long. The tan flowers open to 1.5cm/⅝in in late summer. It prefers warmth and some shade, often growing well as a joint placed in the pot of some large-growing caudiciform. It is propagated from cuttings or seed.

Natural habitat: Cape Province (South Africa)

150

DYCKIA (*Bromeliaceae*)

These relatives of the pineapple are easily grown and becoming quite common. New Brazilian species are still being described. The leaves are more or less fleshy, and smooth or densely covered in silvery-white scales. The rosettes grow from 10–40cm/4–16in in diameter, forming clumps or mats. They do not require such high humidity as many of the members of the family but they do need some shade.

◁ Dyckia marnier-lapostollei

The silvery rosettes of this pretty species grow to 15cm/6in, forming clusters to 30cm/12in or more. The leaf margins are densely lined with short, recurved (curling back on themselves, like a cat's claws) teeth. *D. marnier-lapostollei* looks best when grown in bright conditions but, if the heat is excessive, the leaf-ends start to shrivel. It is quick-growing, given adequate warmth and light, but will not tolerate frost. It is grown from seed or from offsets.

Natural habitat: Brazil

ECHEVERIA (*Crassulaceae*)

This large genus of leaf succulents extends from Mexico south to north-western South America. The rosettes vary from tight and short-stemmed to loose, on upright or hanging stems. Individual rosettes vary from 3cm/1¼in to more than 20cm/8in wide. The leaves vary widely, from thin to thick, and smooth to pubescent, and come in many colours, including soft pastel shades of blue, pink, purple and red. In addi-tion to the natural forms of this genus, many hybrids have been made, bred for their large, colourful leaves, which are sometimes wavy or carbuncled. In their habitat, most species grow in shade and many tolerate some frost. The large, showy hybrids tolerate a much narrower range of exposure, suffering both from high and low temperatures. They can be propagated from seed, offsets or individual leaves.

△ *Echeveria agavoides*

This slow-growing species forms stemless rosettes to 18cm/7in, sometimes offsetting from the base. The thick leaves are edged with red. The yellow and red flowers are borne on a spike up to 50cm/20in tall. It will tolerate more sun than many species, and brief periods of frost. It is propagated from seed.

Natural habitat: Mexico

△ *Echeveria lilacina*

Grey rosettes of the thin, fleshy leaves of this species can grow to 12cm/4½in across, and branch sparingly. In late spring, several spikes of reddish flowers grow to 16cm/6¼in tall. This species will take a fair amount of heat, if shaded, and will tolerate brief periods to −7°C/20°F. It offsets sparingly and is mainly propagated from leaves and seeds.

Natural habitat: Mexico

ECHEVERIA

△ *Echeveria* x 'Topsy Turvy'

◁ *Echeveria purpusorum*

This small species is somewhat difficult, but quite attractive and worth the effort. The rosettes of thick, pointed leaves grow only to 6cm/2⅜in or so and, in the right light, take on a purplish cast. In the late spring, the flower spikes emerge, bearing yellow flowers. This species prefers bright, cool light; it may bleach out in intense sun. It needs a well-drained compost (potting soil) and will tolerate some frost. It is propagated from seed.

Natural habitat: Mexico

This cultivar has unusual blue-green leaves that are thick and folded sharply down, and cristate (crested) rosettes often appear. Late in the growing season, short spikes of distorted, red flowers are produced. It is easily grown from leaves or offsets and will tolerate hot, indirect light as well as brief periods down to −7°C/20°F.

152

EDITHCOLEA
(*Asclepiadaceae*)

This small genus contains odd-looking stapeliads with spiny, greenish-brown, often lifeless-looking stems. In their habitat, as do some other stapeliads, these form mounds that eventually die from the centre outwards, forming "fairy rings" in the same way that fungi do. The flowers have a brownish-yellow background, with varying amounts of red-brown spots.

▷ *Edithcolea grandis*

Commonly called the "Persian carpet flower", this plant with spiny 1.5cm/⅝in thick stems does best in a hanging basket. The flowers are produced from the newest growth and are borne singly. They open to 8cm/3¼in or more, the dark reddish spots on the petals varying considerably from clone to clone. Some select clones appear almost all black. Typically for this family, they do have a fetid odour, but it is not overpowering. This species is notorious for rotting and old plants are seldom seen; when a large specimen rots, though, many cuttings are produced. It prefers a minimum of 27°C/80°F to root from cuttings and will not tolerate prolonged cool, wet roots. Also, an exceptionally well-drained compost (potting soil) is recommended. It will not tolerate any frost.

Natural habitat: north-eastern Africa

EULOPHIA (*Orchidaceae*)

A large genus of terrestrial orchids, of which only a few are of interest to the succulent collector. The flowers of the most xerophytic species are rather small and not highly coloured, but they are borne on tall stocks, some to 2m/6½ft. A handful of species is being produced and distributed commercially to succulent collectors. These have somewhat thick, often stiff, leaves on top of thick, green pseudobulbs. The beauty of these species lies in their ability to flourish under the same conditions required by *Adeniums*, *Pachypodiums* and other succulents and caudiciforms. They will not tolerate frost but, if given some shade, will endure high temperatures and low humidity. The succulent members of this genus are from South Africa.

▷ **Eulophia pettersii**

The leaves of this durable species are very stiff, somewhat like an agave, 14cm/5½in long on top of a fluted pseudobulb, 3.5cm/1⅜in wide and 8cm/3¼in tall. The brownish-yellow flowers are 3cm/1¼in wide and borne on a stock that is more than 1m/1yd tall. In the spring, the new growth emerges from the ground around the periphery of the cluster. Plants with six pseudobulbs are large enough to flower. The potting compost (potting mix) should be loose and well drained. This species will tolerate temperatures down to 4°C/40°F, for brief periods, and dry heat, if provided with some shade.

Natural habitat: southern Africa

153

EUPHORBIA (*Euphorbiaceae*)

From non-succulent weeds to trees, to succulent miniatures and gi-ants, this genus of around 2,000 species contains more succulent members than any other single genus. The bulk of the succulent species occurs in Africa and Madagascar, but a few come from the Canary Islands, the island of Socotra, India and the Americas.

A fairly uniform floral structure unites these diverse species. The flowers are highly reduced and unisexual, borne within a cup-shaped inflorescence called a cyathium. The cyathia can be monoecious – with both sexes of flowers – or dioecious, strictly male or female. A monoecious cyathia will have many male flowers but only one female flower and these often emerge from the cyathia before the males, to prevent self-fertilization. The attractive portions of flowering *Euphorbia* are, firstly, the five glands that ring the cyathia and are often mistaken for small petals; secondly, the paired cyathial bracts attached below the glands – which can be brightly coloured – and, thirdly, the brightly coloured leaves that appear occasionally, as with E. *pulcherrima*, the common poinsettia.

The fruit has a three-celled ovary which, when ripe, cracks open, often audibly, throwing the seeds up to several metres/yards. Although many species bear an array of spiny armaments, quite a few are appar-ently defenceless. However, these and their armed relatives have as sap a sticky, white latex which ranges from benign through irritating to quite toxic, with the potential to blister skin and even cause blindness. In some species, the sap is under considerable pressure and can spray out when the plant is damaged. Using neoprene gloves and eye protection when handling most poisonous species is recommended. Rubbing alcohol is good for removing *Euphorbia* sap from skin, as soap and water merely spread the sap around.

Since this genus occurs over such a wide variety of conditions, there can be no generalizations about care. *Euphorbia* are propagated from seed, cuttings, rhizomes, offsets, occasionally from leaves and by grafting.

△ *Euphorbia abdelkuri*

This bizarre species is among other unusual species in several families from the island of Socotra. The spineless grey stems have the appearance of being made from melted wax. Another odd feature is the latex, which is yellowish and fairly poisonous. In habitat, this will form a rounded bush, 2m/6½ft tall. Because of its nativity and slow-growing nature, it is only now becoming widely available. It will tolerate intense indirect light and heat, but it is extremely slow-growing if heat is not available and it will not tolerate any frost or long periods of having wet, cold roots. This monoecious species is grown from seed occasionally, but more often by cuttings or grafting.

Natural habitat: Socotra (an island in the Indian Ocean)

△ *Euphorbia aeruginosa*

A beautiful species, this is now widely available. It forms clumps of 1cm/⅓in thick stems, 30cm/12in wide and 18cm/7in tall. In late spring, yellow cyathia form on the upper portions of the stems, standing out nicely from the blue stems and reddish spines. It will not tolerate any frost. It is easily grown from cuttings but take care when doing this, as the sap is particularly irritating.

Natural habitat: South Africa

△ *Euphorbia balsamifera*

While not uncommon, nice specimens of this are somewhat rare. In its habitat, it grows as a shrub to 2m/6½ft tall, but can also form a beautiful natural bonsai as a windblown short tree. In cultivation, it requires fairly intensive training to achieve this look. It is more or less a winter-grower, although that varies with the latitude. It prefers bright light but not intense heat and will not tolerate frost.

Natural habitat: Somalia, Morocco, Canary Islands

△ *Euphorbia albipollenifera*

This species in the "Medusa's head" group forms a main stem 6cm/2½in or more wide, on a thickened root. The branches are quite thin and 10cm/4in long. The monoecious cyathia have white glands that are attractive up close. It will tolerate hot, indirect light but no frost. It is grown from seed.

Natural habitat: South Africa

◁ *Euphorbia ambovombensis*

Part of a group of related species from southern Madagascar, this one has the added bonus of an enlarged base, which can be raised for effect. Its crinkled, brownish leaves are 7mm/⅓in wide and 2cm/¾in long, forming small rosettes on the end of the stems. The monoecious cyathia are nondescript, covered with two olive-drab bracts. This species, like its close relatives, is ant-pollinated; the cyathia are borne pointing down at nearly ground level. It will not tolerate hot, intense sun, nor will it flourish in cold, wet conditions. It is propagated from seed and cuttings.

Natural habitat: Madagascar

EUPHORBIA

△ *Euphorbia cap-saintmariensis*

Related to *E. ambovombensis*, this is faster-growing, with a smoother, white trunk. It forms an underground caudex and, in cultivation, a spreading, short canopy to 30cm/12in, making it an ideal subject for succulent bonsai. The cyathia are small and tan. It prefers a moist, well-drained compost (potting soil), warmth and bright, indirect light. It will not tolerate any frost or long periods of moist cold. It can be grown from seed, leaves or cuttings.

Natural habitat: Madagascar

△ *Euphorbia clavarioides* var. *truncata*

The main trunk of this variety is hidden under a dense mat of 1.5cm/⅝in wide, light green stems. In its habitat, it will form a flat pad of stems to 30cm/12in across. The cyathia are yellow and are produced in early summer. It will tolerate dry heat, but prefers some shade, a well-drained compost (potting soil) and protection from frost. It is grown from seed.

Natural habitat: South Africa

△ *Euphorbia francoisii*

A relative of *E. ambovombensis*, this species is well suited for succulent bonsai. The leaves are quite variable, both in their width and coloration. The leaves generally have two shades of green, withered veins and a varying amount of white. The 2cm/⅜in thick stems and large roots are white. It is monoecious, bearing small green cyathia. It prefers warmth and bright, indirect light, to bring out the best colour in the leaves. It will not tolerate frost or long periods of cool moisture. It is grown from seed; particularly attractive clones can be propagated from leaves or stem cuttings.

Natural habitat: Madagascar

◁ *Euphorbia columnaris*

Nearly extinct in the wild, this solitary species grows to more than 1m/1yd tall. In spring, 3mm/⅛in wide, yellow, dioecious cyathia are borne in clusters above the curved, paired spines. Because of the small number of clones in cultivation, seed production is low; however, it grows well from offsets produced by grafted plants. It will tolerate a bright, hot exposure, but no frost. It is generally available as grafted plants or rooted cuttings.

Natural habitat: Somalia

△ *Euphorbia cylindrifolia* var. *tuberifera*

Related to *E. ambovombensis*, this variety forms around a flattened caudex topped with thin, white branches. The caudex can grow to 15cm/6in, and the canopy of prostrate stems to 25cm/10in wide. The grey-green leaves resemble those of its close relatives, looking as if they have been rolled, leaving a groove on the upper surface. The monoecious cyathia are not particularly notable. It will not tolerate intensely hot sun, preferring some shade and warmth, nor any frost. It is grown from cuttings or seed, although seedlings form the most typical caudex.

Natural habitat: Madagascar

157

◁ *Euphorbia bupleurifolia*

The brownish stem, topped with long, green leaves, is reminiscent of a pineapple fruit. In cultivation, the trunk can grow to 6cm/2½in in diameter and 15cm/6in tall, clustering from the base. The dioecious cyathia are borne singly, on stocks arising from the crown, bearing two bracts, the same colour as the leaves. It is somewhat difficult to look after, rotting if kept too wet but languishing if water is withheld; it prefers warmth and some shade. It is grown from seed.

Natural habitat: South Africa

EUPHORBIA

△ *Euphorbia horrida* var. *striata*

One of the hardier species, this can be used in landscapes in hot areas that get limited amounts of frost. Its stems are variable in the size and colour, ranging from blue-green to whitish, growing to 15cm/6in across, and forming clumps up to 1m/1yd tall. It will tolerate half a day of sun and –4°C/25°F, briefly. It is grown from seed or cuttings.

Natural habitat: South Africa

▷ *Euphorbia fruticosa*

The specimen pictured here is often sold as the "large blue form". In habitat, it can grow to 50cm/20in tall, as a rounded, spiny shrub. In addition to the attractive, blue-green body and dark brown spines, in early summer, many bright yellow monoecious cyathia are borne on the ribs on the upper portions of the stems. It grows quite quickly from cuttings, and makes an attractive and long-lived grafting stock. It will tolerate hot, bright light but will not survive any frost.

Natural habitat: Yemen

◁ *Euphorbia gorgonis*

Named appropriately after the mythical Gorgon, Medusa, the round main "head" is topped with tapering, snake-like shoots. The main trunk grows to 10cm/4in or more, and the arms to 12cm/4½in. The green, monoecious cyathia are borne from the tips of the branches. It will tolerate intense heat, but needs some shade in the afternoon; it will not tolerate any frost. It is generally grown from seed since, like its relatives, when an arm is rooted, it generally forms just a long arm and not the typical main stem with arms.

Natural habitat: South Africa

158

△ *Euphorbia inermis*

The section of the genus *Euphorbia* called Medusae includes many species all with a more or less round central stem bearing long arms. The name of one species, *E. caput-medusae*, literally means "Medusa's head". *E. inermis* is one of the larger medusoid species but this forms a caudex more than 10cm/4in thick, arising from a large root. The arms can grow to 2.5cm/1in thick, and a mature plant may have a spread more than 50cm/20in across. The monoecious cyathia are yellow or white, showy when borne in profusion in the summer, and have a pleasant fragrance detectable several metres/yards away. It will tolerate morning sun, but not frost, and requires some shade. It is grown from seed.

Natural habitat: South Africa

△ *Euphorbia milii* **var. bojeri**

Euphorbia milii has over 20 varieties. In cultivation, they are all semi-deciduous but, in habitat, all are totally deciduous. They form shrubs 30cm–1m/12in–1yd tall. The cyathial bracts are brightly coloured, varying in wild varieties from yellow to red. Some plants can flower almost all the year round. Hybridization has increased the range of flower colour. None will tolerate hot, dry sun, or frost. They are grown from seed or cuttings.

Natural habitat: Madagascar

◁ *Euphorbia lactea variegata cristata*

One of the most common species, the normal plant forms a much-branched shrub to 2m/6½ft tall, with three or four angled, dark green stems with a paler band in the centre. Several different variegates and cristates (crested forms) are available. None of these cultivars is difficult to grow, although the highly variegated forms like 'Grey Ghost' and its crest can be slow-growing and less tolerant of intense sun. It will tolerate morning sun, but no frost. It is generally propagated from cuttings, although extreme forms are sometimes grafted.

Natural habitat: India

159

EUPHORBIA

△ *Euphorbia piscidermis*

△ △ *Euphorbia obesa* and *E. obesa cristata*

This choice species is still uncommon in cultivation, but should be more available in the years to come. In its habitat, it forms a solitary stem 5cm/2in in diameter and up to 8cm/3¼in tall. In the spring, the minute green cyathia emerge from between the scales. In cultivation, it is most often seen grafted, where it can make a beautiful cluster if put on a large and vigorous stock. When grown from seed, it spends its first year or two as a tiny, sticky ball, encrusted with bits of the potting material, which keeps the small seedling from dehydrating. It will tolerate a few hours of morning sun, but must be kept from frost. Grown on its own roots, it is quite rot-prone.

Natural habitat: Ethiopia, Somalia

Ironically, one of the most popular and interesting of *Euphorbia*, this species is almost extinct in the wild, through continued collection. It is quite common in cultivation, due to its relative ease of culture and rapid growth to flowering size, often in only two years from seed. This species grows 8–10cm/3¼–4in in diameter and eventually to over 20cm/8in tall. As it ages, the bottom portion of the stem becomes brown. The green dioecious cyathia are borne on the tips of the plants, most heavily in the spring. The crested form of the species is generally available grafted, although seedlings will crest from time to time and

are then maintained on their own roots. If cuttings are to be made from a crested plant, the whole plant must be processed, as the cut portion tends to dry excessively, eventually killing the entire crest. Normal plants of *E. obesa*, as well as its hybrids, make good grafting stock for this species and others that have an antipathy for *E. fruticosa* as a stock. It will tolerate morning sun and brief, light frost.

Natural habitat: South Africa

◁ *Euphorbia persistens*

Related to *E. tortirama*, this species bears four angled stems on top of a thickened root. Akin to the growth form of the medusoid species, this group of *Euphorbia* have a single main trunk, which produces spreading arms. A mature plant can have a spread of 30cm/12in. It will tolerate intense heat if given some afternoon shade, but will not tolerate any frost. It is grown from seed.

Natural habitat: South Africa

△ *Euphorbia poisonii*

This species is still uncommon in collections, along with its close relatives, *E. sudanica* and *E. unispina*. In its habitat, it forms a branched shrub more than 1.5m/1½yds tall. The deciduous leaves are light green, 5cm/2in wide and 12cm/4⅓in broad. Despite its moderate size at maturity, it is quite slow-growing, only producing around 10cm/4in of stem growth per year. The nondescript green cyathia are borne while the plant is out of leaf. It will tolerate hot, bright light during the growing season if watered well, but requires warmth during the winter. It will tolerate cooler temperatures if it is kept dry while dormant.

Natural habitat: Ghana, Nigeria

△ *Euphorbia royleana*

Originating in the foothills of the Himalayas in India, this is among the most cold-hardy of the tree-like *Euphorbia*. The stems are 4cm/1⅝in wide, with short spines, and eventually form a small tree 6–8m/20–26ft tall. During the summer, the new growth bears thick green leaves, 3cm/1¼in wide and 10cm/4in long. It will tolerate intense heat and sun, with adequate water, as well as brief periods to –4°C/25°F. It is grown from seed or cuttings.

Natural habitat: eastern India

EUPHORBIA

△ *Euphorbia suzannae*

In its habitat, this species forms solitary stems to 10cm/4in tall or compact clusters about 12cm/4⅓in wide; however, in cultivation, it can grow much larger, forming mounds upwards of 35cm/14in across. In the spring, it bears many nondescript green cyathia. There are also cristate (crested) forms of this species in cultivation, both green and variegated. It will tolerate bright, indirect light and fairly intense heat. It will not tolerate frost. It is easily grown from seed or cuttings, although plants from seed have more compact growth and a more attractive appearance.

Natural habitat: South Africa

△ *Euphorbia symmetrica*

Although this plant closely resembles *E. obesa*, it is quite distinct in several aspects. At maturity, it does not become columnar but can form a round stem up to 15cm/6in in diameter, which offsets sparingly. Also, the dioecious cyathia on mature plants are borne three across, rather than singly, and it has a thicker taproot. It will tolerate morning sun and hot dryness, as well as brief frost, but not cold, wet roots. It is grown from seed.

Natural habitat: South Africa

△ *Euphorbia tortirama*

Even as small seedlings, plants of this species bear distinctive, twisted branches. At maturity, the arms grow to 3.5cm/1⅜in thick and more than 25cm/10in long. The trunk will grow to 20cm/8in high on top of the stout taproot that can be raised for effect. As the branches age, they naturally turn brown from the base, and are often removed to improve the appearance. In the spring, the plain green cyathia are borne on the ends of the branches: they are monoecious. Because of the tuberous root, a particularly well-drained compost (potting soil) is recommended, but the plant is not otherwise difficult to grow. It tolerates morning sun and dry heat, but will not put up with frost. Plants grown from seed rather than cuttings are recommended.

Natural habitat: South Africa

◁ *Euphorbia virosa*

This attractive species has gained a
well earned reputation for being quite
poisonous, although it is no more so
than the common, tree-forming species
E. cooperi or *E. tirucalli*. The 8cm/3¼in
thick stems form large clumps and will
tolerate intense hot sun for half a day. It
will not tolerate any frost. It is grown
from seed.

Natural habitat: South Africa

◁ *Euphorbia trapifolia cristata*

While the normal plant of this species
is somewhat uncommon, the cristate
(crested) form is more prevalent in
cultivation. During the summer, the
newest growth bears thick, wavy-
edged leaves 2cm/¾in wide and
3cm/1¼in long. These are mostly
shed in the winter. Although it can be
grown on its own roots, grafted plants,
such as the one pictured, are faster
and easier to grow. This is grafted on a
short stock of *E. fruticosa* and is just
over three years old, from a 4cm/1½in
wide piece. It requires bright light
and will tolerate heat and dryness,
but no frost.

Natural habitat: Sudan

FENESTRARIA (*Mesembryanthemaceae*)

A monotypic genus, it previously contained two species, of which *F. aurantiaca* is now considered a subspecies. The leaves are club-shaped, with a windowed tip. In cultivation, they form many-headed clusters, more than 10cm/4in broad.

▷ *Fenestraria rhopalophylla*

This species is commonly known as "baby toes". In its habitat, the leaftips grow flush with the soil, and all of the light the plant receives filters through the transparent windows. The flowers vary from white to yellow, with long, thin petals, open to 3–4cm/1¼–1½in wide. It is particularly rot-prone, requiring bright light and good air movement, and will tolerate –4°C/25°F, briefly. It is generally grown from seed, but clusters can be divided and rooted.

Natural habitat: Namibia

FICUS (*Moraceae*)

M any common plants are members of this genus including the edible fig. They originate mostly in western Mexico and Baja California. They survive drought by defoliating, waiting for the next wet period. The leaves of these xeric (adapted to a dry climate) species are generally heart-shaped, and the bark varies from white to brown.

▷ *Ficus palmeri*

This species is closely related to *F. petiolaris*. Its caudex grows faster, forming a thicker, squat plant. This and other *ficus* are easily trained over rocks, and are some of the only caudiciforms which will grip the rock tightly with their roots, making it an ideal subject for succulent bonsai. It will tolerate deep shade to full sun but, if it is kept too dry, readily defoliates. It cannot tolerate any frost and is grown from seed.

Natural habitat: Mexico

FOCKEA *(Asclepiadaceae)*

Although there are only about ten species in this genus, one or two are generally found in every collection of caudiciforms. These are vining plants with small green to white flowers and a basal caudex that, in its habitat, is partially or totally underground. These are "understory" plants, an expression that generally refers to species that grow under the canopy of larger trees and shrubs. In this case, however, as with many species of vining caudiciforms, the trunk grows in the shade of the adjacent shrubs, and uses them as support for its vines, flowers and fruit. While the leaves and vines will tolerate intense sun and heat, therefore, the caudex should be shaded. They are rot-prone, particularly in the winter, and should be kept warm in a well-drained compost (potting soil). Somewhat contrary to this, in the right conditions, the caudices will grow much more rapidly if buried in deep, large pots. After attaining a more robust size, the caudices can be raised for effect. They occur from South Africa to east Africa.

◁ **Fockea edulis**

This species and *F. crispa* are the two most common in the genus, although *F. crispa* may now be considered a synonym of *F. edulis*. The leaves are dark green, 1cm/½in wide and 3–4cm/1¼–1½in long, with wavy edges. The vines can grow more than 30cm/12in in a season, but respond well to pruning. The warty, white caudex can develop a variety of shapes, from short and squat, to gnarled, obese and prostrate. In the summer, the 1.5cm/⅝in wide, green flowers are borne on the older portions of the vines. These can be pollinated by fruit flies, resulting in single greyish pods 8cm/3¼in long. The caudex should be shaded from intense sun and it will not tolerate any frost or long periods of wet cold. It is propagated from seed.

Natural habitat: southern Africa

FOUQUIERIA (*Fouquieriaceae*)

This small genus is restricted to mainland Mexico and Baja California, with one species occurring in the south-western USA. They are spiny shrubs, with deciduous leaves that drop as soon as moisture is short; they come into leaf just as quickly when there is a good rain. These are summer-growing species and are deciduous in winter. The flowers are borne at the ends of the mature branches and range from white to yellow to red. A few species will tolerate some frost and all will do well in intensely hot sun, provided they have adequate moisture.

◁ *Fouquieria diguetii*

This species forms a much branched shrub to 4m/13ft tall, with a slightly thickened base. The leaves are greyish-green and pubescent, 1cm/½in wide by 3.5cm/1⅜in long. In the hyper-arid inland portions of its range, it grows very slowly, and plants 1.5m/1½yds tall can be more than 100 years old. It bears red flowers but is not grown for these. In contrast to its growth in its habitat, it can grow exceptionally fast in cultivation, given root run, heat and plenty of water and fertilizer, growing 1m/1yd in the first two years. It will tolerate full sun and heat, but only light frost. It grows well from seed or cuttings.

Natural habitat: Baja California (Mexico)

◁ *Fouquieria fasciculata*

Among the two most sought-after species in this genus (*F. purpusii* being the other one), this forms a conical caudex, with either single or multiple trunks, up to 5m/16½ft tall. The attractive combination of dark green bark and leaves and reddish-brown spines makes this a worthwhile plant, even as a seedling. The small, white flowers are produced in short clusters at the branch ends in winter. This species will tolerate full sun and heat and a temperature down to −4°C/25°F, for short periods. It is grown from seed or cuttings.

Natural habitat: Mexico

△ *Fouquieria macdougallii*

This does not form a very large caudex, but is the species in the genus most easily persuaded to flower. Producing a couple of flushes of bright red flowers during the spring and summer, it can grow to flowering size from seed in three or four years. It will tolerate full sun and light frost. It is grown from seed or cuttings.

Natural habitat: Mexico

167

▷ *Fouquieria splendens*

This species generally branches from the base, forming more than a dozen canes 3cm/1¼in thick and up to 3.5m/11ft tall. The thin, light green leaves are produced after a good rain, and often dropped after several weeks without further rain. In late spring, spikes of flowers, usually red, are borne from each mature stem, often when the plant is totally leafless. There are also white- and yellow- flowered populations, but these are rare in cultivation. It will tolerate moderate periods down to −7°C/20°F. It is generally grown from seed.

Natural habitat: south-west USA, Mexico

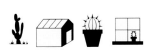

FRITHIA (*Mesembryanthemaceae*)

While this monotypic genus superficially resembles *Fenestraria*, it is different in other aspects.

▷ *Frithia pulchra*

The leaves of this small species are rough to the touch, flexible, club-shaped, 1cm/½in wide and 2.5cm/1in long, with a windowed tip. They can form a cluster of stemless rosettes up to 6cm/2½in wide, with 3–5cm/1¼–2in wide, individual rosettes. In the summer, the flowers (pink with a white centre) are borne in the centre of the rosette and have no stock, and by midday they open to 2.5cm/1in. It will tolerate bright, indirect light and moderate heat. It likes a very well-drained compost (potting soil) with good air movement. It is grown from seed.

Natural habitat: South Africa

168

GASTERIA (*Asphodeliaceae*)

Oddly enough, this genus is named for the flower, as its shape is reminiscent of a stomach. Varying very little between species, the flowers are pink or red and white, and are borne on a solitary or branched spike, from late winter through early summer. Most species are very easily grown and have become common houseplants, tolerating low light levels. They also do well in hot, bright, indirect light. Most species offset, some profusely, and are also easily grown from rooting single leaves, which often produce several plants from the base. *Gasteria* interbreed easily in cultivation, and many of the plants in the trade are of questionable background. There are several named hybrids that are quite attractive and relatively common. They occur in South Africa.

△ *Gasteria armstrongii*

This popular species is shown here with both juvenile and mature characteristics. The leaves are long and grooved like a mature plant, but they have not begun to form a rosette. In the spring 2cm/¾in long, red flowers are borne It will take hot, indirect light, but no frost. It is grown from seed, offsets or leaves.

Natural habitat: South Africa

▷ *Gasteria armstrongii* hybrid *variegata*

One of the many hybrids found in collections, offsets can grade from completely green to completely yellow, and the more yellow they have, the slower their growth. Solid yellow offsets are short-lived, perishing from lack of nourishment. Like most variegates, it will tolerate less intense sun than a normal plant, but develops better colour when grown in as bright a light as it will tolerate.

169

GIBBAEUM (*Mesembryanthemaceae*)

Notorious for its difficulty in cultivation, this South African genus contains several interesting species. It forms clusters with one or two leaf pairs on each short stem. Many are winter-growers and the flowers range from white to pink, purple and magenta. They will tolerate hot, indirect light, and will survive light frost, but not long periods of cool dampness.

▷ *Gibbaeum heathii*

The leaf-pairs of this clustering species form roughly spherical heads 2–3cm/¾–1¼in high. The white flowers, sometimes with a blush of pink, open in the spring. Largely a winter-grower, this species needs shade and a minimum of water in the summer. It will tolerate light frost. It is grown from seed.

Natural habitat: South Africa

GRAHAMIA (*Portulacaceae*)

Recently split off from *Anacampseros*, the few species in this genus are widely separated, occurring in New Mexico and western Texas, Mexico, Bolivia and Argentina, and Australia. These range from small herbaceous plants with tuberous roots to short shrubs. The flowers are pink or white. As in *Anacampseros* the seed is often produced in quantities, resulting in many seedlings appearing near to the parent plant.

▷ *Grahamia coahuilense*

This species is easily grown, perhaps even becoming a pest as it self-seeds in other pots. It forms limp, 10cm/4in long stems, with succulent leaves emerging from a cluster of thickened roots. Under optimum conditions, 2cm/¾in wide, pink flowers are borne throughout the summer. It has a tendency to become limp and wrinkled if underwatered, but it revives quickly and is quite resilient. It will tolerate hot morning sun, but should be protected from frost. It is grown from seed or cuttings.

Natural habitat: Mexico

GRAPTOPETALUM (*Crassulaceae*)

Native mostly to Mexico, one or two species stray north into Arizona. They bear fleshy leaves in rosettes, stemless to long-stemmed. The flowers are not more than 1.5cm/⅝in across, and are borne upright, early in the summer, on many-branched stalks. They are usually white, often with red markings on the petals. These species are generally very easy to grow, often tolerating hot morning sun and some frost. They can be grown from seed, cuttings and leaves.

◁ *Graptopetalum bellum*

Still sold under the older generic name *Tacitus*, this relatively new species is now mass-produced and widely available. It forms flat rosettes, which cluster with age, forming clumps to 12cm/4½in across. On mature plants, each rosette is capable of producing several flower stalks in early summer. Rather than being a solitary spike, each inflorescence is branched, producing a cluster of flowers at the same height. Growing to 10cm/4in tall, the spikes bear bright pink flowers for several weeks. This species needs more shade than most, but will tolerate brief periods of frost, down to −7°C/20°F. It is propagated from seed or offsets.

Natural habitat: Mexico

◁ *Graptopetalum superbum*

Popular but still not common, this beautiful species forms a flat-topped, 10cm/4in, purple rosette on a stalk. It will tolerate half a day of sun, but suffers if exposed to intense heat in the summer. It will survive light frost. It is grown from seed, cuttings or leaves.

Natural habitat: Mexico

GRAPTOVERIA (*Crassulaceae*)

This hybrid genus comes from crossing a *Graptopetalum* with an *Echeveria*. Since *Graptopetalum* generally tolerate more sun and heat than *Echeveria*, hybrids of the two are both hardy and beautiful, although their flowers are unremarkable. They are propagated from cuttings and leaves.

◁ x *Graptoveria* 'Silver Star'

Widely available, this hybrid of *Graptopetalum filiferum* forms low, offsetting rosettes of dense, pale green leaves. The offsets grow to 8cm/3¼in wide, clustering to 12cm/4½in. It will only tolerate a few hours of sun, but takes brief periods to –4°C/25°F. It is grown from offsets.

△ x *Graptoveria amethorum*

This small hybrid forms a 5cm/2in wide rosette of fat, green leaves. In bright light, the tips are slightly purple. It will tolerate some morning sun and fairly intense heat and brief periods to –4°C/25°F. It is grown from leaves or offsets.

HAWORTHIA (*Asphodeliaceae*)

This large genus of dwarf succulents seems to change yearly, the names and numbers of species being endlessly shuffled. From South Africa and south-west Africa, many of these species are quite variable, leading to much of the nomenclatural confusion. Some authors have suggested that this is due to the ease of hybridization within the genus, but most species offset readily and were, historically, propagated asexually. Until recently, many of the plants in cultivation were propagules from clones collected long ago, their lineage long lost.

The plants form rosettes, a few with long grass-like leaves but most with succulent leaves; some are very thick with windowed upper surfaces. Many have thick contractile roots, which pull the plants into the earth, so that only the upper, windowed leaf surface is exposed. The flowers, mostly small and white, are borne on single or branched spikes to 30cm/12in long. In their habitat, they grow in rock crevices and among bushes, out of the direct sun. All but the most difficult species make good houseplants, surviving, if not thriving, even in conditions of very low light. Most species, as well as many named hybrids and variegates, are widely available. They are grown from seed, offsets and leaves.

◁ *Haworthia bolusii* var. *bolusii*

The stemless rosettes of this uncommon species grow to 10cm/4in across. They grow mostly in the autumn (fall) and spring. During the summer, the oldest leaves die, forming a sheath of dry, outer leaves, and watering should be reduced. In the autumn (fall), the rosettes open, with new, green growth. This plant will offset sparingly with age. It tolerates bright light but not excessive heat, nor any frost. It is grown from seed.

Natural habitat: South Africa

△ *Haworthia viscosa* var. *caespitosa*

The pointed, dark green leaves of this species form 2.5cm/1in, triangular stems, which grow 10cm/4in tall. Within this species, there is some variation; more compact forms than the specimen pictured offset less freely. It grows well in low light, but forms a tighter, more attractive shape in a bright, warm situation. It is easily grown from cuttings, offsets or seed.

Natural habitat: South Africa

△ *Haworthia cooperi*

The form of this popular species pictured is from Bolo Reserve. It is smaller than the typical plants found in cultivation, the rosettes only growing 3–4cm/1¼–1½in wide. Offsetting readily but not excessively, it is fairly easy to grow. It requires shade from hot sun but will tolerate warm, bright light and must be protected from frost. It is grown from seed or offsets.

Natural habitat: South Africa

△ *Haworthia limifolia*

This is among the most common species in cultivation. It forms rosettes 8cm/3¼in across and clusters up to 20cm/8in wide. It can tolerate low light but looks best in a bright, warm exposure. It is grown from seed, offsets or leaves.

Natural habitat: South Africa

◁ *Haworthia comptoniana*

Quite rare only a few years ago, this beautiful species is now readily available. The triangular leaves can grow to 2.5cm/1in wide and long, the upper surface windowed, varying from green with white veins to almost solid, glassy white. It has a dormant period in summer, particularly when exposed to intense heat. During this time it should be watered sparingly. It is propagated by seed or from leaves.

Natural habitat: South Africa

△ *Haworthia cuspidata variegata*

H. cuspidata is considered a hybrid rather than a valid species. The leaves are 2.5cm/1in wide, forming loose rosettes 9cm/3½in across. The degree of variegation varies greatly, and plants that are solid yellow, or almost so, are very difficult to keep alive, if separated from the original plant. *H. cuspidata* cannot tolerate hot, bright light or frost, and its variegates require more shade.

Natural habitat: South Africa

173

HAWORTHIA

△ *Haworthia koelmanniorum*

Closely related to *H. limifolia*, this species forms open rosettes of long, brownish leaves up to 13cm/5in across. It will not tolerate frost. It grows quickly from seed, cuttings or leaves and develops its best colour if grown in brighter light.

Natural habitat: South Africa

△ *Haworthia truncata*

With flat-topped, windowed leaves looking as though they had been cut, this species has contractile roots that pull the plant into the ground, leaving only the windows to take in sunlight. The leaves form a line rather than a rosette and, clustering from the base, can form 15cm/6in wide clumps. The average form of this species has a clear, milky window with smooth edges, but there exist many variations and some collectors specializing in this species have scores of different clones. During the heat of summer, reduce watering, as the thickened roots or basal leaves can rot. This species grows well in bright, warm light, but will not tolerate any frost. It is grown from seed, offsets or leaves.

Natural habitat: South Africa

◁ *Haworthia reinwardtii* var. *chalumnensis*

This is the largest of several attractive varieties of *H. reinwardtii*. All of the varieties bear raised white markings, arranged in rows. It forms 6m/20ft wide rosettes, which become prostrate in time, offsetting from the base and forming 20cm/8in wide clumps. It is easily grown, tolerating low light, but looks best if grown in a brighter-than-average situation, where the rosettes will grow more tightly and take on a reddish colour. It grows well from cuttings, offsets or seed.

Natural habitat: South Africa

174

HOODIA (*Asclepiadaceae*)

This genus has perhaps a dozen species, but only a few are available in cultivation and there is some confusion about the true identity of these. *Hoodia* are some of the largest and hardiest of the stapeliads, the upright, spiny stems forming clumps 30cm/12in high and wide. The flowers have the typical five petals and are large and disc-shaped, in colours ranging from off-white to rust. Large plants in full flower are as impressive-looking as they are unpleasant-smelling, attracting hordes of flies. They will tolerate a bright, hot exposure and light frost, but should be kept fairly dry during the winter. They occur in south-western Africa.

△ **Hoodia macrantha**

This species is one of the three most commonly available, along with *H. bainii* and *H. currori*. It forms clumps of greyish-green stems, 4cm/1½in thick and up to 50cm/20in tall. The rust-red flowers open in mid-summer, to 8cm/3¼in. It will tolerate morning sun, intense heat and very light frost. It can be grown from cuttings but will make a mature plant in three to four years.

Natural habitat: southwest Africa

175

HOYA (*Asclepiadaceae*)

This large genus of tropical vines occurs from India and China to Australia. Not all of the species are succulent, and some require conditions suitable for tropical orchids, but many only need warm shade and protection from intense heat or prolonged cold. The flowers are borne in umbels along the vine.

▷ **Hoya imperialis**

This large-growing species also has among the largest flowers in the genus. The stems can grow to over 5m/16 ½ft long, with leaves more than 15cm/6in long. In the summer, the light purple flowers open to 7.5cm/3in wide. This species requires plenty of room and does well in high humidity. It requires warmth and bright, indirect light with no frost. It is grown mostly from cuttings.

Natural habitat: India

HUERNIA (*Asclepiadaceae*)

Unlike most of the related genera, the flowers of this large genus have no scent, either foul or fragrant. The stems vary from short, rounded joints on 2cm/¾in long stems to upright stems 13cm/5in tall. The flowers range from off-white to maroon, often banded or striped. In some species, there is a raised, fleshy circle in the centre of the flower, resembling a lifebelt (life-saver). The flowers are borne from early summer to autumn (fall), depending on the species. The root systems are short and fibrous, so shallow pots are recommended. While a few species are slow-growing and fairly rot-prone, most only require warmth, bright, indirect light and protection from frost. They should be kept fairly dry in the winter.

△ *Huernia kennedyana*

A little more difficult than most, this species is slow-growing and rot-prone. The round joints grow to 2cm/¾in wide by 3cm/1¼in long, forming a low mat. In the autumn (fall) the flowers open to 2cm/¾in; they are yellow with maroon spots and have raised teeth in the throat. A particularly well-drained compost (potting soil) is recommended for this species. It will tolerate hot, indirect light, but no frost. It is grown from seed or cuttings.

Natural habitat: South Africa

△ *Huernia recondita*

Large-growing for the genus, the prostrate stems can exceed 20cm/8in in length. The flowers open rather flat, to 3.5cm/1⅜in, with red and yellow stripes. It needs warm, bright light and protection from frost. It is grown from seed or cuttings.

Natural habitat: Ethiopia

◁ *Huernia levyi*

The stems of this species are typical for the genus, growing 2.5cm/1in wide and 7cm/2¾in high. The flower, borne in the late summer and autumn (fall), is tubular, 1.5cm/⅝in wide and 3cm/1¼in long, and yellow, with red spots. This is not a difficult species to grow, and cuttings of a couple of stems taken in the spring will flower that year. It requires warm, bright light and protection from frost. It is grown from seed or cuttings.

Natural habitat: Zimbabwe

LITHOPS (*Mesembryanthemaceae*)

These highly succulent, South African plants are as popular as their appearance is unusual. Whereas many plants have evolved highly succulent stems devoid of leaves, *Lithops* species are stemless, consisting only of pairs of thick leaves. Their small size, cryptic coloration and tendency to grow flush with the surface of the ground allow them to escape detection by predators when in their habitat. When almost hidden below ground, all the light enters through the windowed tips of the leaves. The coloration of their leaf-faces varies considerably, even within a species. *Lithops* require watering only when the leaves start to shrivel (in the spring), and never when the soil is already moist. In the autumn (fall), white, yellow or, occasionally, peach flowers emerge from the cleft in the leaves, and at this time watering should be reduced. During the winter and spring, new leaves are formed within the old, and watering should be kept to a minimum or withheld altogether.

Lithops will tolerate intense heat and bright, indirect light as well as –4°C/25°F, briefly. They can be propagated by separating clumps of heads, but are predominantly grown from seed.

△ *Lithops aucampiae*

This species does not cluster heavily, having no more than six to ten heads, each growing to 3–4cm/1¼–1½in wide. There are several varieties, which vary in the patterns of the windows and in the colour, one variety being more olive green than brown. The flowers are yellow and 4cm/1½in wide. It is grown from seed.

Natural habitat: South Africa

△ *Lithops bromfieldii* var. *insularis* cvar. 'Sulphurea'

While the normal form of this common species has brown leaves with numerous red dots or lines, this cultivar is bright green. It can cluster heavily in cultivation, with old plants having up to 50 heads, each head being 1.5cm/⅝in across. The flowers are yellow, opening to 3cm/1¼in. It tolerates less intense light than its normal counterpart. Some of the oddly coloured sports of this species must be propagated from cuttings, but this one comes well from seed.

Natural habitat: South Africa

△ *Lithops bromfieldii* var. *menellii*

Growing slightly larger than the other varieties of this species, up to 18mm/¹¹⁄₁₆in wide, the windowed leaf-faces are less heavily marked and the form makes smaller clusters than var. *insularis*. The flowers are yellow, opening to 3cm/1¼in. It is grown from seed.

Natural habitat: South Africa

LITHOPS

△ *Lithops julii* 'Reticulate form'

This species is generally identifiable by the "lips", a darker line of coloration near the cleft in the leaves. In this attractive, highly coloured form, they are not as apparent but, in some individuals, they are the only dark pigment on the surface of the plant. *L. julii* does not form large clusters; often, plants that are 20–30 years old will still have only a pair of heads, each 2–3cm/¾–1¼in in diameter. The flower is white, opening to 3cm/1¼in. This variety is grown from seed.

Natural habitat: South Africa

◁ *Lithops werneri*

This dainty species grows to only 2cm/¾in wide, with round, slightly pebbled faces. In time, the heads will cluster to form plants 6–8cm/2½–3¼ in across. It is not particularly variable, with the markings more or less pronounced, depending on the individual. The flowers are yellow and open to 2–3cm/¾–1¼in. It is grown from seed.

Natural habitat: South Africa

△ *Lithops karasmontana* 'Mickbergensis'

Once considered a separate species, this is merely a form of a quite variable species, with fewer brown markings on the uneven, windowed surface of the leaves. Leaves of other forms range from having thick, dense, dark brown markings to rusty markings, or are entirely rust-coloured on the upper surface. The flowers are white, opening to 3cm/1¼in. This form is grown from seed.

Natural habitat: South Africa

△ x *Luckhoffia* (Asclepiadaceae)

Originally ascribed to the genus *Stapelia*, then considered a monotypic species in its own genus, *Luckhoffia* is now regarded as a natural hybrid between species of *Hoodia* and *Caralluma* x *L. beukmannii* and x *L. beukmannii cristata*. Both the normal and crested forms of this easily grown stapeliad are common in cultivation. The flexible, spiny stems are 2cm/¾in wide, upright at first and later becoming semi-prostrate. The foul-smelling, rust-coloured flowers are 4cm/1½in wide and borne sporadically throughout the growing season. This plant comes true from seed, which is produced if the species is visited by the right size of fly. This and the cristate (crested) form are easily grown from cuttings, as well. The number of cristate stapeliads available is steadily increasing but, so far, this is the fastest-growing and most stable. Both the normal and cristate forms will tolerate intense heat and bright, indirect light, but will not tolerate any frost or long periods of cold with wet roots.

Natural habitat: South Africa

LITHOPS (*Mesembryanthemaceae*)

These highly succulent, South African plants are as popular as their appearance is unusual. Whereas many plants have evolved highly succulent stems devoid of leaves, *Lithops* species are stemless, consisting only of pairs of thick leaves. Their small size, cryptic coloration and tendency to grow flush with the surface of the ground allow them to escape detection by predators when in their habitat. When almost hidden below ground, all the light enters through the windowed tips of the leaves. The coloration of their leaf-faces varies considerably, even within a species. *Lithops* require watering only when the leaves start to shrivel (in the spring), and never when the soil is already moist. In the autumn (fall), white, yellow or, occasionally, peach flowers emerge from the cleft in the leaves, and at this time watering should be reduced. During the winter and spring, new leaves are formed within the old, and watering should be kept to a minimum or withheld altogether.

Lithops will tolerate intense heat and bright, indirect light as well as –4°C/25°F, briefly. They can be propagated by separating clumps of heads, but are predominantly grown from seed.

△ *Lithops aucampiae*

This species does not cluster heavily, having no more than six to ten heads, each growing to 3–4cm/1¼–1½in wide. There are several varieties, which vary in the patterns of the windows and in the colour, one variety being more olive green than brown. The flowers are yellow and 4cm/1½in wide. It is grown from seed.

Natural habitat: South Africa

△ *Lithops bromfieldii* var. *insularis* cvar. 'Sulphurea'

While the normal form of this common species has brown leaves with numerous red dots or lines, this cultivar is bright green. It can cluster heavily in cultivation, with old plants having up to 50 heads, each head being 1.5cm/⅝in across. The flowers are yellow, opening to 3cm/1¼in. It tolerates less intense light than its normal counterpart. Some of the oddly coloured sports of this species must be propagated from cuttings, but this one comes well from seed.

Natural habitat: South Africa

△ *Lithops bromfieldii* var. *menellii*

Growing slightly larger than the other varieties of this species, up to 18mm/¹¹⁄₁₆in wide, the windowed leaf-faces are less heavily marked and the form makes smaller clusters than var. *insularis*. The flowers are yellow, opening to 3cm/1¼in. It is grown from seed.

Natural habitat: South Africa

LITHOPS

△ *Lithops julii* 'Reticulate form'

This species is generally identifiable by the "lips", a darker line of coloration near the cleft in the leaves. In this attractive, highly coloured form, they are not as apparent but, in some individuals, they are the only dark pigment on the surface of the plant. *L. julii* does not form large clusters; often, plants that are 20–30 years old will still have only a pair of heads, each 2–3cm/¾–1¼in in diameter. The flower is white, opening to 3cm/1¼in. This variety is grown from seed.

Natural habitat: South Africa

◁ *Lithops werneri*

This dainty species grows to only 2cm/¾in wide, with round, slightly pebbled faces. In time, the heads will cluster to form plants 6–8cm/2½–3¼ in across. It is not particularly variable, with the markings more or less pronounced, depending on the individual. The flowers are yellow and open to 2–3cm/¾–1¼in. It is grown from seed.

Natural habitat: South Africa

△ *Lithops karasmontana* 'Mickbergensis'

Once considered a separate species, this is merely a form of a quite variable species, with fewer brown markings on the uneven, windowed surface of the leaves. Leaves of other forms range from having thick, dense, dark brown markings to rusty markings, or are entirely rust-coloured on the upper surface. The flowers are white, opening to 3cm/1¼in. This form is grown from seed.

Natural habitat: South Africa

△ x *Luckhoffia* (Asclepiadaceae)

Originally ascribed to the genus *Stapelia*, then considered a monotypic species in its own genus, *Luckhoffia* is now regarded as a natural hybrid between species of *Hoodia* and *Caralluma* x *L. beukmannii* and x *L. beukmannii cristata*. Both the normal and crested forms of this easily grown stapeliad are common in cultivation. The flexible, spiny stems are 2cm/¾in wide, upright at first and later becoming semi-prostrate. The foul-smelling, rust-coloured flowers are 4cm/1½in wide and borne sporadically throughout the growing season. This plant comes true from seed, which is produced if the species is visited by the right size of fly. This and the cristate (crested) form are easily grown from cuttings, as well. The number of cristate stapeliads available is steadily increasing but, so far, this is the fastest-growing and most stable. Both the normal and cristate forms will tolerate intense heat and bright, indirect light, but will not tolerate any frost or long periods of cold with wet roots.

Natural habitat: South Africa

IBERVILLEA (*Cucurbitaceae*)

This small genus of caudiciforms occurs in Texas (USA), south into Mexico and west to Baja California. The thick, white-skinned caudices can be subterranean to partially exposed and produce annual vines. The leaves vary from lobed to heavily dissected and, in habitat, are hidden among the foliage of adjacent shrubs and trees. This genus grows well from seed, but is rot-prone when dormant.

▷ *Ibervillea tennuisecta*

In its habitat, this species forms a white-skinned, subterranean caudex, which can be buried 20cm/8in or more, and growing to more than 20cm/8in wide. The round leaves are often heavily dissected into thin leaflets. Ripening late in the summer and autumn (fall), the red fruit are round, bearing only a few seeds. While the caudex should be shaded, the vines will tolerate hot sun; however, they are killed by prolonged frost, and they die back in the winter. It is grown from seed and, occasionally, from cuttings.

Natural habitat: Texas (USA), Mexico

177

IDRIA (*Fouquieriaceae*)

This monotypic genus is sometimes included in *Fouquieria* and, while its status is in question, its uniqueness is not. In their habitat, these plants are most often a single stem rising high into the air. Although this species was thought to live in excess of 700 years, a recent study has shown that they may not live more than 100 years in their habitat. They are grown from seed and will survive intense heat and light frost.

▷ *Idria columnaris*

This is known as the "boojum tree". The chalky-white trunk can grow to 20m/66ft tall, with spiny, lateral branches that bear small, grey-green leaves in winter. It drops most of its leaves in the summer. Seedlings will stay in leaf and grow for the first two or three years, without going dormant. It does not take on a mature appearance for several years. At 2m/6½ft or more tall, straw-coloured flowers appear in the autumn (fall). It will tolerate intense sun, and −4°C/25°F, briefly. It is grown from seed.

Natural habitat: Baja California (Mexico), and a small area of mainland Mexico

JATROPHA (*Euphorbiaceae*)

A large genus of tropical and subtropical shrubs and herbaceous perennials, many species are excellent caudiciforms, suitable for succulent bonsai. Considered to be primitive relatives of *Euphorbia*, these plants do not share the same degree of flora-reduction. While the flowers are unisexual, *Jatropha* are monoecious, carrying both sexes on the same plant. When a cluster of flowers begins to open, the single female opens first, and has finished flowering before the multiple male flowers open. In addition, the flowers have petals, often brightly coloured, in shades of white, pink, orange and red. Many of the species will tolerate intense heat and sun and a few will survive frost, but their requirements are so varied that no general care instructions can be given for them. They range from Madagascar to Africa and South America, and north to the southern USA.

△ *Jatropha podagrica*

A popular species, this tropical shrub grows more than 1m/1yd tall, with a thickened base. The leaves are dark green, three-lobed and 12cm/4½in wide on 18cm/7in long petioles. During much of the growing season, the small, red flowers are produced sporadically. It will tolerate hot sun for half the day but will not survive any frost. It is grown from seed.

Natural habitat: Central America

△ *Jatropha cuneata*

Over part of its range, this species grows near the ocean and, whipped by the winds, forms beautiful natural bonsais, thick-trunked trees less than 30cm/12in tall. The deciduous leaves are three-lobed, light green and 2cm/¾in wide. The flowers are small and nondescript. It will tolerate heat and full sunlight but is frost-tender. It grows well from seed or cuttings.

Natural habitat: Baja California (Mexico)

◁ *Jatropha cordata*

This species follows the growth pattern of the North American *Jatropha* that respond to monsoonal moisture in the summer. Even when well watered and provided with adequate heat, it will not leaf out until early summer. The heart-shaped leaves are 3cm/1¼in wide, dark green and glossy. The white flowers are less than 5mm/¼in wide and are easily overlooked. Mature stems develop peeling, papery bark. The plant can be trained as succulent bonsai. It is grown from seed or cuttings.

Natural habitat: Mexico

KALANCHOE
(*Crassulaceae*)

The largest portion of this genus of interest to collectors is the species from Madagascar. These form small shrubs, with succulent leaves that have a variety of leaf-forms, from whole to serrated margins, smooth to densely pubescent and, in some cases, with plantlets borne on the margins. The flower colour is variable, most commonly pink or red, and the flowers are borne at the ends of the stems. The flowers are unusual, in that the parts are multiples of four (four sepals, four petals and eight stamens), rather than the multiples of five more typical of the family. They are often excellent houseplants, surviving in low light, although they prefer bright, indirect light and can tolerate intense heat. They will not tolerate any frost and may even be damaged by low temperatures above freezing, possibly up to 4°C/40°F.

△ *Kalanchoe thrysiflora*

This beautiful species will form clumps up to 60cm/2ft wide and tall, although the stems are often shorter and prostrate, branching from the base. In low light, the leaves are round and green, covered with a white bloom that is eventually washed off by rain or overhead watering. In brighter light, particularly in late summer, the leaves develop reddish margins. The flowers are 1.5cm/⅝in long and yellow. *K. thrysiflora* is able to tolerate morning sun and intense heat, but no frost. It is propagated from seed, cuttings or leaves.

Natural habitat: South Africa

◁ *Kalanchoe* aff. (related to) *marmorata*

Although attractive, this species can become a nuisance. The leaves bear many tiny plantlets along the margins, which are easily detached, rooting and forming plants in adjacent pots. Similar in leaf shape to the common *K. daigremontiana*, or "mother of thousands", the leaves are blue-green and grow to 5cm/2in wide and 15cm/6in long. It forms a single stem, up to 75cm/2½ft tall and, after flowering, dies, to be replaced by its hundreds of offspring. It will tolerate morning sun and intense heat, but no frost. It can be grown from seed, but is almost entirely propagated from plantlets.

Natural habitat: Madagascar

LAMPRANTHUS (*Mesembryanthemaceae*)

This is a fairly large genus of shrubby, South African succulents, which are cultivated for their flowers and relatively hardy nature. They will tolerate at least half a day of sun and some can endure short periods to −7°C/20°F. The flowers are borne in the summer and range from white to pink, red, orange and yellow.

▷ *Lampranthus haworthii*

Growing to 60cm/2ft tall, this species forms a densely branched shrub. The flowers open at noon to 7cm/2¾in wide, and are quite showy. It will tolerate intense sun, with adequate water, and brief periods of frost. It is grown from seed or cuttings.

Natural habitat: South Africa

LAPIDARIA (*Mesembryanthemaceae*)

As the name suggests, this monotypic genus looks as though the leaves have been carved from stone. It needs the same care as does *Lithops*.

▷ *Lapidaria margaretae*

This attractive miniature forms several, headed clumps, up to 8cm/3¼in in diameter. Unlike its close relative *Lithops*, it retains its leaves from the previous year, so that each head has two pairs of leaves. In the autumn (fall), bright yellow flowers emerge from each head, opening to 4cm/1½in wide in the afternoon, for several days. In midwinter or early spring, new leaves emerge and the oldest ones shrivel. It should be watered sparingly, if at all, in the winter, and does best if grown alongside cacti and watered as such in the summer, being allowed to dry between waterings. It will tolerate bright, indirect light and intense heat, and −4°C/25°F, briefly. It is grown from seed.

Natural habitat: Namibia

▷ *Lithops lesliei* var. *venteri* 'Maraisii'

Lithops lesliei is among the most common species and its varieties and forms can be found anywhere that *Lithops* are sold. All of the forms and varieties of the species have a similar general appearance, but the size of the windows and the general coloration can vary considerably. *L. lesliei* var. *venteri* has a grey upper surface, with many fine lines. 'Maraisii', pictured here, is an extreme form, in which the windows fill almost the entire leaf surface. The heads grow to 2.5–3.5cm/1–1⅜in across, forming small clumps. The white flower opens to 3cm/1¼in. It is grown from seed.

Natural habitat: South Africa

▷ *Lithops pseudotruncatella*

This harbinger of autumn (fall) is generally the first species to flower. The heads have a soft and bloated appearance, with a rounded window. There are several varieties and forms of this species and they range from white to tan on the sides, with a network of tan to dark brown markings on the faces. This is one of the larger species, with individual heads 4–5cm/1½–2in across; but they do not make many-headed clusters. As a seedling, it often does not form a complete fissure for several seasons, with only a small slit showing on the upper face. Yellow flowers open to 3–4cm/1¼–1½in. This variety is grown from seed.

Natural habitat: South Africa

183

MATELEA (*Asclepiadaceae*)

This Mexican genus of vines and small shrubs is rarely seen in cultivation, with one notable exception. The flowers are, typically, foul-smelling, drawing many flies as their chief pollinators.

▷ *Matelea (Gonolobus) cyclophylla*

One of the few New World caudiciforms in this family, this species has a caudex that can grow quite large, more than 30cm/12in across. It resembles a tan version of *Dioscorea*, the "turtle-back plant", but with soft, corky bark. Late in the spring or early summer, as the night temperatures exceed 18°C/65°F, one to several vines – bearing heart-shaped leaves up to 10cm/4in wide – grow from the apex of the conical trunk. The foul-smelling flowers can be borne several to every node; they are 2.5cm/1in wide and velvety dark green or purple in colour. If a flower is pollinated, generally, only a single seed horn is produced. In the autumn (fall), the vine dies back to the caudex and the fruit remains on the dead vine, ripening and opening late in the following spring. It will tolerate intense heat and bright light, when provided with adequate water. It is also fast-growing, if bedded out for the summer with plenty of root run in well-drained soil. During its very long dormant period, lasting up to five months, care should be taken not to overwater. It is not thought to tolerate frost. It is grown from seed.

Natural habitat: Mexico

MESTOKLEMA (*Mesembryanthemaceae*)

In this small genus of shrubby succulents, only a couple of species are of interest to the collector. Both *M. arboriforme* and *M. tuberosa* have tuberous roots and are excellent as succulent bonsai. The genus occurs in South Africa.

▷ *Mestoklema tuberosa*

The roots become long and thick with age, developing a dark red bark. While the above-ground stems are initially thin and limp, with judicious pruning specimens can easily be trained into the shape of a small tree 20cm/8in tall; they make excellent succulent bonsai. Throughout the summer, 7mm/⅓in wide, gold to orange flowers are borne in clusters at the tips of the stems. It will tolerate intense heat, half a day of sun, and –4°C/25°F, briefly. It is propagated by seed or cuttings.

Natural habitat: South Africa

MOMORDICA (*Cucurbitaceae*)

Of the more than 50 species in this vining genus, fewer than one dozen are of interest to collectors and fewer still are readily available. All are tropical, requiring protection from prolonged cold. They do well in hot, bright light, when provided with plenty of water.

▷ *Momordica rostrata*

This fast-growing relative of the cucumber will form an impressive, fluted caudex in a couple of seasons, with the right conditions. In the summer, this dioecious species produces masses of vines with dark, three-lobed leaves. Male plants bear quantities of yellow flowers, which are 2cm/¾in wide, with black spots at the bases of three of the petals. The flowers on female plants are few and solid yellow. The ripe fruit resemble small peppers; they are dark orange and 2cm/¾in wide by 6cm/2½in long. The caudex prefers some shade, but the vines thrive in full sun. It will not tolerate any frost. It is grown from seed.

Natural habitat: Africa

MONADENIUM
(*Euphorbiaceae*)

Plants in this genus of more than 50 species bear a strong resemblance to *Euphorbia*, to which they are closely related. The difference lies in the inflorescence: there is a single, ring-like gland surrounding the cyathia, rather than the five petal-like glands *Euphorbia* has. The cyathia are also borne facing laterally on the flower stalks. A pair of bracts are borne together above the cyathia; they are hood-like and, occasionally, brightly coloured. Often, a second series of cyathia will emerge from the bracts, forming a branched inflorescence. In species with brightly coloured inflorescences, this can be quite showy, lasting up to three weeks. The stems range from thin and annual ones, arising from underground tubers, to thick and perennial ones more than 1m/1yd long, forming small shrubs. The leaves are fleshy and annual, and vary considerably in colour and size, often bearing attractive markings. Many species will tolerate heavy shade but they look best in bright, indirect light. They will not tolerate any frost and should be kept fairly dry and warm during the winter. They occur widely in Africa.

△ *Monadenium rubellum*

Still known to many as *M. montanum* var. *rubellum*, this popular species is grown for its attractive inflorescence and tuberous root. The narrow, red, mottled leaves are borne on thin stems, arising from an irregular, branching, white, tuberous root. During much of the year, but particularly in the autumn (fall), many light pink inflorescences are borne from the stems. It is often displayed in bonsai pots, its tuberous root raised and its stems pruned and trained. It will tolerate bright, indirect light, but should be protected from long periods of intense heat. It is also rot-prone. It grows quickly from cuttings, producing a nice tuber in a couple of seasons; it is also grown from seed.

Natural habitat: Kenya

◁ *Monadenium ellenbeckii*

This forms a shrub to 1m/1yd tall, with few branches. The plain green leaves are borne for a very short time during the growing season and are 8mm/⁵⁄₁₆in wide and 1mm long. The inflorescence is small, yellowish-green and borne on short stalks, crowding the tip of the stem. It prefers bright, indirect light and warmth and will not tolerate frost or overly moist soil in the winter. It grows well from cuttings or seed.

Natural habitat: Ethiopia

△ *Monadenium ritchiei*

This species is quite common and often quite short-lived as a houseplant, rotting easily if overwatered in the winter. The green, tuberculate stems grow to 3cm/1¼in wide and cluster to form a plant 20cm/8in wide and tall. The leaves are roughly round and 3cm/1¼in across and are borne sparingly. If the plant lacks the right conditions, it will produce normal stem growth without bearing a single leaf. In the autumn (fall) and spring, small, light pink inflorescences are borne freely from the tips of the stems. It will tolerate intense heat and bright, indirect light, but should be kept quite dry during the winter and protected from frost. It grows well from cuttings or seed.

Natural habitat: Kenya

▷ *Monadenium coccineum*

This species is grown more for the inflorescence than for the form. The stems are semi-erect and grow to more than a 1m/1yd long. Light green leaves are 2cm/¾in wide and 3cm/1¼in long, with wavy edges. In the autumn (fall), branching, bright red inflorescences are borne several to each stem. These develop their best colour in bright light and persist for months. This species will tolerate bright, indirect light and intense heat, but no frost. It grows well from cuttings or seed and looks best when pruned occasionally, to increase branching.

Natural habitat: Africa

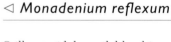

◁ *Monadenium reflexum*

Still not widely available, this attractive species is worth the effort of acquiring and growing it. It will form a branched plant with 3–6cm/1¼–2½in thick stems, which bear long, down-pointing tubercles. In seedlings, the leaves often have striking purple veins which, sadly, disappear as the plant matures. It is slow-growing and care should be taken not to overwater it in the winter. It will tolerate intense heat and bright, indirect light. It is generally grown from seed.

Natural habitat: Ethiopia

MONILARIA (*Mesembryanthemaceae*)

This is an odd genus, similar to *Mitrophyllum* and *Conophyllum*, all of which share the trait of having two different pairs of leaves each season. In *Monilaria*, the pair of "resting leaves" form a rounded body, protecting the second pair of leaves. During the growing season (winter), this second set bursts through the dried remains of the first. The leaves are generally long and green, often with many glassy cells densely covering the surface and giving a crystalline sheen. They prefer complete dryness when dormant and generous water when in active growth. The flowers range from white to pinkish and yellow. It is found in South Africa.

△ *Monilaria pisiforme*

Like many species of *Monilaria*, the stems become jointed, like a necklace. The flowers are white, with a reddish centre. It is generally grown from seed. It will tolerate moderate heat but must be protected from frost.

Natural habitat: South Africa

MONSONIA (*Geraniaceae*)

The genus *Sarcocaulon* has been discarded recently, moving all the species into the older genus *Monsonia*. These members of the geranium family are distinct from their close cousins in the genus *Pelargonium*, most notably by their actinomorphic flowers. That is to say, all five petals are of equal size and shape, and the flower can be divided in half in any direction, producing mirror images. The genus ranges through areas with summer or winter rainfall. Rather than treating the different species separately as summer- or winter-growers, it is wiser to provide them with water all year, keeping them in leaf even if not in active growth. Many hobbyists have let some of the very succulent species go dormant, then fail to be able to awaken them again. The leaves vary considerably, from glabrous to pubescent, whole to deeply incised. The flowers range from white to pink and yellow. They can be grown from cuttings but are mostly grown from seed. They occur from Namibia to South Africa.

△ *Monsonia vanderietiae*

Although this common species lacks the extremely thick stems of the very succulent *Monsonia*, it is much easier and faster to grow. The leaves are dark green, elliptical, and with a notch at the end. The plant forms a flat shrublet up to 30cm/12in wide. This flattened growth habit makes it ideal as succulent bonsai. Its pale pink flowers are 3cm/1¼in wide. It will tolerate intense heat and half a day of sun. It grows well from seed or cuttings.

Natural habitat: South Africa

MONSONIA

◁ *Monsonia penniculinum*

This amazing succulent occurs in an area which periodically receives no measurable rainfall for several years. During these dry periods, this species remains dormant inside its waxy skin, ready to produce a flush of incised, fuzzy leaves with the next rainfall. The thick stems form a small shrub 7cm/2¾in tall and, eventually, more than 15cm/6in wide. The flowers are light pink and 2cm/¾in wide. It will tolerate intense heat and half a day of sun, but no frost. It is grown from seed.

Natural habitat: Namibia

MORINGA
(*Moringaceae*)

This small, tropical genus includes several caudiciform trees from Africa and Madagascar. The deciduous, compound leaves are quite large and give the foliage a lacy appearance. Small, white flowers produce long pods, yielding large seeds.

▷ *Moringa droughardtii*

With a free root run and plenty of water, this species grows very quickly. The three-year-old plant pictured is 2m/6½ft tall. In its habitat, it forms a tree more than 8m/26ft tall, with a trunk more than 1m/1yd thick. The lacy, compound leaves are 20cm/8in wide and 30cm/12in long. It will tolerate full sun and intense heat, but no frost. It is grown from seed.

Natural habitat: Madagascar

NANANTHUS (*Mesembryanthemaceae*)

Often included in the genus *Aloinopsis*, these low-growing plants often form large, tuberous roots, which can be raised for effect. The flowers are borne in the autumn (fall); they are 2cm/¾in wide with yellow petals, sometimes with a reddish middle stripe. They will tolerate intense heat and bright, indirect light, as well as –4°C/25°F, briefly. This South African genus is grown from seed or cuttings.

▷ *Nananthus schooneesii*

Common and popular, this is generally the first species of *Nananthus* encountered by collectors. The leaves are 1cm/½in wide, forming a dense clump 7cm/2¾in or more wide. The tuberous root grows to 6cm/2½in wide at the crown and tapering to about as long. In the autumn (fall) it bears golden flowers, 2cm/¾in wide. It is prone to root rot. It will tolerate intense heat when protected from the full sun, and light frost. It is grown from seed.

Natural habitat: South Africa

OPERCULICARYA (*Anacardiaceae*)

Only one member of this genus of three species has become available in recent years, but it is quickly becoming quite popular. In habitat, *Operculicarya* can grow to 10m/30ft tall, forming a thick trunk and, in the case of *O. decaryi*, thickened roots. With adequate water, they will tolerate intense heat and sun, but they will not survive any exposure to frost. This genus is found only in south-western Madagascar.

▷ *Operculicarya decaryi*

This species has yet to make its mark as one of the best for succulent bonsai. The shiny green leaves are borne for most of the year, dropping for a short time in the winter, if at all. In intense sun, the leaves can take on a reddish cast. After a few years, the trunk will become thickened and warty. The roots thicken as well and may be raised for effect. It will not tolerate any frost but can take 4°C/40°F, for short periods. While seed is available, it is notorious for its poor germination, but cuttings will produce a normal-looking plant, quickly.

Natural habitat: Madagascar

ORBEOPSIS *(Asclepiadaceae)*

Most of the ten or so members of this genus originally belonged to *Caralluma*. They have light green,
prostrate stems, with foul-smelling flowers ranging from
yellow to dark purple. They require bright, indirect light
and warmth and are not difficult to grow.

▷ *Orbeopsis melanantha*

The foul-smelling flowers are dark purple, sometimes with a lighter
centre, and 3cm/1¼in broad, with fine, dark hairs on the margins of
the petals. The light green stems grow prostrate on the ground,
rooting on the underside. It will tolerate intense heat and bright,
indirect light, but no frost nor long periods with cold, wet roots. It
grows well from seed or cuttings.

Natural habitat: East Africa

190

OTHONNA *(Asteraceae)*

The plants in this South African
genus range from non-succu-
lent shrublets to short, thick, trunked, tree-like species; from more than
50cm/20in tall down to dwarf, tuberous species with only annual leaves
and flowers exposed above ground.
They are winter-growers requiring a
warm exposure, with plenty of water
and bright light, and a dry rest in the
summer. Relatives of the common
daisy, they have daisy-like flowers
that are, generally, yellow. They are
propagated from seed and cuttings.

△ *Othonna clavifolia*

Among the easiest of the *Othonna*, this
species forms a small shrub to 10cm/4in
or more tall and wide. The club-shaped
leaves are green in the growing season,
turning purple during the summer. The
yellow flowers are borne on long stalks in
the autumn (fall). It needs bright,
indirect light, but should be protected
from intense heat, and from frost. It is,
generally, grown from seed.

Natural habitat: South Africa

△ *Othonna herrei*

This is one of many very succulent and
more difficult *Othonna*. The 1.5cm/⅝in
wide stem grows to 7cm/2¾in tall and
has a knobbly shape from the persistent
leaf bases. The leaves are greyish with
wavy edges. The yellow flowers are
borne – several to a short stalk – in the
autumn (fall). It requires bright, indirect
light and protection from intense heat
and from frost. It is grown from seed.

Natural habitat: South Africa

PACHYCORMIS (*Anacardiaceae*)

This monotypic genus comes from Baja California, where it is called the "elephant tree". Several kilometres inland, these plants can grow more than 8m/26ft tall but, when exposed to the constant ocean breezes, their thick trunks hug the ground. In habitat, they are strictly winter-growers, shedding their leaves in late spring and bearing sprays of minute, pink flowers. As small plants, they can be seriously damaged by frost.

▷ *Pachycormis discolor*

Well adapted for succulent bonsai, this species is a winter-grower. While it can become huge in the wild, in cultivation, specimens a couple of metres/yards tall are more common. It is prone to rot from overwatering when dormant, so cut back on water when the leaves start to yellow and fall, in the late spring. In some extreme northern latitudes, it may act as if it were a summer-grower, so watch the plant's reaction to the seasons and adjust its care accordingly. It grows quickly from seed, forming a thick taproot and later a thickened above-ground stem.

Natural habitat: Baja California (Mexico)

PACHYPHYTUM (*Crassulaceae*)

Only a couple of species of this small, Mexican genus are generally available in cultivation. These plants are easily grown from their thick leaves, which are generally covered with a powdery bloom. They will tolerate higher temperatures than the closely related *Echeveria*, and can survive brief periods of exposure to −7°C/20°F. The flowers are often small and so generate little interest.

△ *Pachyphytum oviferum*

The most common of the genus in cultivation, this is generally what people think of when they consider *Pachyphytum*. The leaves are whitish and of a flattened egg-shape, 2cm/¾in wide and 2cm/¾in or more long. The intensely red flowers are borne in spring, on crook-shaped spikes. It prefers bright light and moderate warmth, tolerating more intense heat if shaded. It is generally grown from leaves or cuttings but occasionally from seed as well.

Natural habitat: Mexico

PACHYPODIUM (*Apocynaceae*)

The most common species in this genus, *P. lamerei*, the "Madagascar palm", can be found anywhere houseplants are sold. In many minds, this genus, together with *Adenium*, is synonymous with the concept of a caudiciform. The stems of *Pachypodium* range from large, underground roots with spindly stems, through flattened caudices, to middle-sized, thick-based caudiciforms and, ultimately, spiny, thickened, tree-like species. The flowers range in colour from white to pink and red and yellow. The fruit is, generally, a pair of horn-like pods with a groove running from the tip to the base, on the upper side. The sap of these *Pachypodium* is poisonous, but not caustic. They require bright light but heat tolerances vary from species to species. Some species will tolerate light frost, but most should be protected and kept at a minimum temperature of 4°C/40°F. They are grown from seed and occur in southern Africa and Madagascar.

△ *Pachypodium namaquanum*

This species is the slowest-growing of the tall *Pachypodium*, eventually reaching 3m/10ft but often taking more than a decade to reach only 50cm/20in tall. It produces much of its growth in the autumn (fall) and winter, only losing its leaves briefly in the spring. At 30cm/12in tall and six or more years of age, it can flower. The long, tubular flowers are borne at the crown of the plant and do not extend beyond the spines; they open only 1.5cm/⅝in wide, and have dark red petal tips. After flowering, the plant will produce another crown of leaves, 1.5cm/⅝in wide and 10cm/4in long, which are slightly fuzzy and with wavy edges. It will tolerate intense heat, half a day of sun, and light frost. It is grown from seed.

Natural habitat: Africa

△ *Pachypodium succulentum*

In its habitat, this species appears as a vining shrublet, with the large, turnip-shaped caudex completely under-ground. The caudex can be raised for effect. In the spring, the flowers are borne on the ends of the prostrate branches. They are 3cm/1¼in wide, white to pink, with a darker red middle stripe. The plant maintains some leaves all year; they are 5mm/¼in wide and

8cm/3¼in long. It will tolerate intense heat, but needs some shade, particularly if the root has been raised. It is prone to root rot. It should be protected from frost, but does not need high winter heat if it is kept fairly dry. It is grown from seed.

Natural habitat: Africa

△ *Pachypodium* x 'Arid Lands' (*P. namaquanum* x *P. succulentum*)

This was the first hybrid in this genus to be commercially offered, by Chuck Hansen of Arid Lands. While it does not produce the thick root of one parent or the thick stem of the other, its flowers are large, soft pink and borne for a very long time. With persistence and pruning, it can be trained into a short, tree-like bonsai. It tolerates intense heat but should be protected from frost.

◁ *Pachypodium saundersii*

This is the easiest of species with low thick bases to grow. It eventually forms a silvery, conical trunk 30cm/12in thick and more than 1m/1yd tall, with spiny branches 1–2cm/⅜–¾in thick. It is deciduous, dropping its leaves in the autumn (fall), just after flowering. The flowers are borne in clusters on the ends of the branches. They open to 4cm/1½in and are white, blushing with pink edges as they fade. At night, their spicy scent carries for several metres/yards, attracting the moths which pollinate them. It grows rapidly, particularly if it is bedded out and given a free root run. It also takes well to pruning, which helps to accentuate the developing caudex. It will tolerate intense heat, half a day of sun, and light frost, but should be kept fairly dry while leafless in winter. It is grown from seed.

Natural habitat: South Africa

◁ *Pachypodium geayi*

This species is generally known to most people only as a seedling or immature plant. At maturity, it grows to more than 5m/16½ft tall, forming a much-branched tree with a single, swollen, spiny trunk 3m/10ft or more tall. The flowers are white, 5cm/2in wide, and borne in clusters on 15cm/6in long stalks at the ends of the branches. In cultivation, plants have densely spined, single stems 10cm/4in or more in diameter, crowned with slightly fuzzy, dark green leaves. It will tolerate intense heat when provided with moving air and some shade. It should be protected from frost. It loses most of its leaves in the autumn (fall). It is grown from seed.

Natural habitat: Madagascar

PACHYVERIA (*Crassulaceae*)

The cultivars in this genus are the result of hybridization between Pachyphytum and Echeveria, tending to combine the thick leaves of the former and many-leaved rosettes of the latter.

▷ x *Pachyveria hybrid*

The plant pictured is one of the several, probably unnamed but common, hybrids that are commercially available. This particular hybrid will tolerate more heat and a brighter exposure than *Echeveria*, as well as temperatures of –4°C/25°F for brief periods. It is propagated from leaves and, eventually, forms clusters 10cm/4in wide.

194

PEDILANTHUS (*Euphorbiaceae*)

Closely resembling *Euphorbia*, this related genus differs in the cyathia, which face to the side and come to a point, like a bird's beak. The plants consist of thin, upright stems, with milky sap and short-lived leaves. There are only a few species, which are widely separated, occurring in Mexico and the West Indies.

▷ *Pedilanthus macrocarpus*

This species forms clumps of whitish, upright stems 1.5cm/⅝in thick, up to 1.5m/1½yds tall. The red cyathia are borne from the branch tips, resembling a bird's head. It tolerates lower light – the stems are not so erect as sun-grown plants and tend to become long and floppy – but is at its most attractive in full sun, remaining upright and developing a chalky-white colour. It will survive only light frost. It grows quickly from seed or cuttings.

Natural habitat: Baja California (Mexico)

PELARGONIUM (*Geraniaceae*)

This large genus contains many interesting succulent species, in addition to the common geranium. The bulk of the species of interest to succulent collectors occur in Africa. The forms range from subterranean tubers with annual, above-ground leaves to thick-stemmed shrublets. The zygomorphic (bilaterally symmetrical) flowers have five petals, borne in two pairs, one above the other, with the fifth petal below. The flowers of the highly succulent species are often quite small, less than 1cm/½in, but are occasionally brightly coloured or with fine lines or markings. They are winter-growing, requiring a fairly dry rest in the summer, particularly for the most succulent. They will tolerate bright, indirect light and should be protected from frost. They are grown from seed or cuttings.

△ *Pelargonium alternans*

△ *Pelargonium laxum*

△ *Pelargonium klinghardtense*

One of the most common species, this is fairly easy to grow. In its habitat, it forms a small, much-branched shrub, with 2–3cm/¾–1¼in thick stems, more than 60cm/2ft tall. In cultivation, the stems tend to be much thinner unless pruned and grown hard. The flowers are small and inconspicuous, borne in the autumn (fall).

Natural habitat: South Africa

The leaves of this species are grey-green, fleshy and heavily incised, and 3cm/1¼in wide by 8cm/3¼in long. Light watering in the summer will maintain a few leaves until growth begins in the autumn (fall). The branched stem grows to 30cm/12in tall and sits on top of thickened roots, which can be raised for effect. Small, pinkish flowers with a light, lemony scent are borne through much of the winter. It will tolerate bright light and intense heat, but no frost. It is grown from seed.

Natural habitat: South Africa

Growing to more than 40cm/16in tall, the thick, fleshy stem is smooth and light blue-green. The leaves are whole, 2cm/¾in wide by 4cm/1½in long and with wavy edges. The small, white flowers are borne in midwinter or spring. It develops the best appearance if grown a little more slowly and in bright light; if grown in low light with excessive fertilizer, the stem will be thin and spindly. It will tolerate hot, bright light but no frost. It is grown from seed.

Natural habitat: Namibia

PELARGONIUM

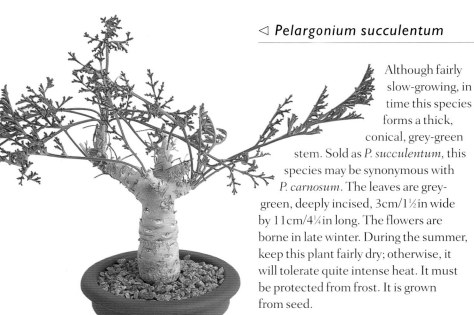

△ *Pelargonium reniforme*

◁ *Pelargonium succulentum*

Although fairly slow-growing, in time this species forms a thick, conical, grey-green stem. Sold as *P. succulentum,* this species may be synonymous with *P. carnosum.* The leaves are grey-green, deeply incised, 3cm/1½in wide by 11cm/4¼in long. The flowers are borne in late winter. During the summer, keep this plant fairly dry; otherwise, it will tolerate quite intense heat. It must be protected from frost. It is grown from seed.

Natural habitat: southern Africa

This species forms a small shrublet with thin branches from a tuberous root. The bright magenta flowers are 2cm/¾in wide and are borne throughout the autumn (fall) and winter. It will not tolerate frost and care should be taken not to overwater while it is dormant. It is generally grown from seed.

Natural habitat: South Africa

PIARANTHUS (*Asclepiadaceae*)

Similar to *Duvalia,* these small stapeliads generally have short, four-angled stems, forming low clusters. Free-flowering, flat-opening flowers are produced to 3cm/1¼in broad, varying from mostly light yellow to yellow densely covered with red dots or lines. The genus will tolerate high temperatures but prefers some shade and protection from frost. It comes from South Africa.

▷ *Piaranthus foetidus*

This species has stems 1cm/½in wide by 4cm/1½in long. The 2.5cm/1in wide flowers are borne in late summer and are yellow, with red lines. Tolerating lower light, it grows well with larger, upright caudiciforms, such as *Bursera, Adenium* and so on. It will not tolerate frost or prolonged cold, wet soil. It is grown from seed or cuttings.

Natural habitat: South Africa

PLEIOSPILOS (*Mesembryanthemaceae*)

More than 20 species are in this genus. They have thick, green leaves with darker green spots – some have just one pair; some have large clusters. The light-to-golden-yellow flowers (up to 8cm/3¼in wide), often coconut-scented, are borne in the autumn (fall).

▷ *Pleiospilos bolusii*

One of the two most common species and, initially, solitary, this can form a couple of pairs of leaves in time. The leaves grow to 3.5cm/1⅜in wide and 7cm/2¾in long; each "head" can produce several flowers. Do not overwater. It will tolerate intense heat, bright, indirect light and light frost. It is grown from seed.

Natural habitat: South Africa

PORTULACA (*Portulacaceae*)

Widely distributed, this genus has several common annual and perennial species. *P. oleracea* (purslane) is a common weed; originally Old World in origin, it is now a pest in nurseries and farms through much of the world. *P. grandiflora*, commonly sold as "moss rose", is cultivated for its large flowers and hardy nature as an annual in flower gardens. The flowers are white, yellow, orange, pink or red. Depending on the species, plants are grown from seed or from cuttings.

▷ *Portulaca molokaiensis*

This species is rare in the wild, but is becoming quite common in cultivation. It forms a small shrublet, with thick stems and round, fleshy leaves. It tolerates bright light and intense heat, but not frost. It grows well from seed or cuttings.

Natural habitat: Isle of Molokai (Hawaii)

PORTULACARIA
(*Portulacaceae*)

Perhaps now a monotypic genus, this is commonly available and forms a thick-stemmed shrub with succulent green leaves. It can be propagated from seed but, in practice, it is almost entirely grown from cuttings.

▷ *Portulacaria afra*

This succulent shrub grows more than a 1m/1yd tall, the trunk becoming thick and grey. The new stems are reddish-brown, bearing round, succulent leaves 1cm/½in wide. The flowers, rarely seen in cultivation, are borne in profusion along the end of the stem; they are 3mm/⅛in wide and light pink. The variegated form differs from the standard one, not only in its white leaf margins but also in a less upright growth form; it can be trained for a hanging basket. While this species bears a slight

resemblance to *Crassula portulacea*, the common "jade tree", it can tolerate brighter light and higher temperatures and this makes it a good beginner's plant for succulent bonsai; it must still be protected from frost, however. It is mostly grown from cuttings.

Natural habitat: Africa

PSEUDOLITHOS
(*Asclepiadaceae*)

While the genus has only a few members, its unusual, rock-like, succulent stems and comparative rarity have made plants of this group highly sought after. They have also earned the deserved reputation for being difficult to grow and short-lived in collections. They require bright light, moderate heat and a very well-drained compost (potting soil). The shape and colour of the flowers vary from species to species but all are quite small, no more than 1cm/½in wide. All species come from Africa.

△ *Pseudolithos migurtinus*

Although it is the most common and easiest to cultivate of the species in this genus, this species is still rare in collections and often short-lived. The tuberculate stem is initially spherical, becoming taller than it is wide in time and offsetting in age. The small, brown flowers are borne in the autumn (fall), in clusters from

the sides of the plant. It requires bright light and moderate, but not intense, heat. It is rot-prone and can be sunburned in intense light. Grafting increases the longevity of this plant. It is grown from seed.

Natural habitat: Somalia

RAPHIONACME (*Asclepiadaceae*)

This small African genus is grown for its large, underground caudices, which can be raised for effect. They produce annual vines with small flowers, some smaller than 5mm/¼in and ranging in colour from green to purple. Several species are commonly available, forming large roots fairly quickly but subject to rot in the winter.

▷ **Raphionacme flanaganii**

The most common and fastest-growing of the species, this can form a brown-skinned caudex more than 10cm/4in wide and long. During the summer, it grows more than 1m/1yd long vines, with dark green leaves, 1cm/½in wide and 4cm/1½in long. The vines tolerate a hot, bright exposure, but the roots should be shaded. It will not survive any exposure to frost and should be kept fairly dry during the winter. It is grown from seed.

Natural habitat: Africa

SANSEVIERIA (*Agavaceae*)

Some species of these African and Indian representatives of the Agavaceae are very common houseplants, such as S. *trifasciata* and S. *hahnii*. These less succulent species will tolerate low light and water. The more succulent species need more light but they will also survive a little neglect. The white flowers are borne on a short, unbranched spike and are often heavily scented at night. Many variegated cultivars are available. Propagation is by seed, from suckers, or from leaves.

▷ **Sansevieria pinguicula**

A fairly new species to cultivation, this forms rounded rosettes of thick, 10cm/4in long leaves, tipped with a stout spine. It is slow-growing but is not difficult. Its propagation is by seed or from leaf cuttings or offsets; the latter should develop roots before being removed from the parent plant. It will not withstand any frost.

Natural habitat: Africa

SANSEVIERIA

◁ *Sansevieria singularis*

This interesting species has juvenile and mature growth forms. The juvenile form produces clustering, fat, low-growing leaves, with a fattened upper surface. The mature form has 30cm/12in tall, round, upright leaves, which emerge from the soil a short distance away from the original. It will not withstand any frost. It is grown from offsets, leaf cuttings or seeds.

Natural habitat: Africa

SEDUM
(*Crassulacaeae*)

In northern rock gardens, these, along with *Semper-vivum*, are the most common succulent species grown. This genus occurs in the New and Old Worlds, with forms from low mats to thick, trunked, tree-like plants that are interesting to the caudiciform collector. The flowers are five-petalled and borne on much-branched, upright inflorescences. The flowers range from white to red and yellow. Many species are incredibly cold-hardy, but these tend to be able to tolerate little heat; conversely, the heat-tolerant species are frost-sensitive. Most are grown easily from cuttings and, occasionally, from seed.

△ *Sedum praealtum cristata*

This is one of the more common tree sedums. The normal plant forms a dense bush 1m/1yd tall, with a main trunk 2cm/¾in thick. The cristate (crested) form tends to be much shorter and to produce normal shoots, which should be removed to maintain the vigour of the crest. Both will tolerate fairly intense heat, bright, indirect light and light frost, and grow fast from cuttings.

Natural habitat: Mexico

SEMPERVIVUM (*Crassulaceae*)

This large genus extends east from Europe to eastern Asia and south into the mountains in northern Africa. There are many species in cultivation as well as hybrids, both natural and artificial. Called "houseleeks" or "hens and chicks", these are some of the most common garden succulents in Europe and the colder areas of the USA. They form low rosettes from 2cm/¾in to more than 20cm/8in wide, clustering more or less heavily into large mats. The rosettes are monocarpic (flowering once only, then dying), producing a single, many-branched flower spike and then dying. The many-petalled flowers range from green to white, through yellow and pink, to red. Most *Sempervivum* will tolerate extended periods down to −18°C/0°F, but require shade from hot sun; few will survive temperatures over 38°C/100°F.

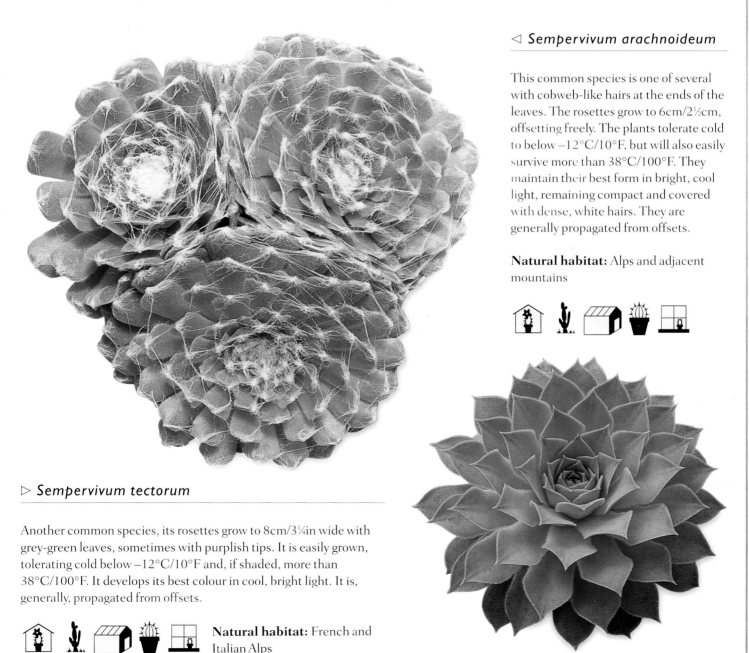

◁ *Sempervivum arachnoideum*

This common species is one of several with cobweb-like hairs at the ends of the leaves. The rosettes grow to 6cm/2½cm, offsetting freely. The plants tolerate cold to below −12°C/10°F, but will also easily survive more than 38°C/100°F. They maintain their best form in bright, cool light, remaining compact and covered with dense, white hairs. They are generally propagated from offsets.

Natural habitat: Alps and adjacent mountains

▷ *Sempervivum tectorum*

Another common species, its rosettes grow to 8cm/3¼in wide with grey-green leaves, sometimes with purplish tips. It is easily grown, tolerating cold below −12°C/10°F and, if shaded, more than 38°C/100°F. It develops its best colour in cool, bright light. It is, generally, propagated from offsets.

Natural habitat: French and Italian Alps

SENECIO (*Asteraceae*)

This genus is composed of over a thousand species of small perennial or annual shrubs and vines. The succulent species range from vines with succulent leaves to thick-leaved shrubs with or without thickened stems or tuberous roots. The five-petalled flowers are 2–4mm/about ⅛in wide, borne in a many-flowered head. They are white, yellow to orange and pink to purple. Many have been popular houseplants for decades. They tolerate bright light and moderate heat. Succulent species occur in Africa, Madagascar and Mexico, as well as the Canary Islands and the East Indies.

△ *Senecio articulatus*

The jointed, upright stems of this species grow to more than 40cm/16in tall, bearing small-lobed, arrow-shaped, light grey leaves. The flowers are yellow but are rarely seen. It will tolerate bright light as well as lower light levels, and moderate heat but no frost. It is grown mostly from stem cuttings, which readily break off at the joints, but can also be grown from seed.

Natural habitat: South Africa

◁ *Senecio ballyi*

This is one of several species of greater interest to the collector and has somewhat more difficult cultural requirements. It develops a thickened, tuberous root, which produces two separate forms of growth at two different times. When producing vegetative growth, it forms short stems, up to 8cm/3¼in long, with large leaves, 4cm/1½in wide by 8cm/3¼in long. During the flowering season, the growth is produced as a long, thick stem with small, scale-like leaves. This terminates in flowering heads with orange flowers. It requires bright, indirect light and moderately hot temperatures, with protection from frost. It is prone to root rot and should be protected from intense heat and sunlight. It is grown from cuttings or seed.

Natural habitat: Kenya

SESAMOTHAMNUS (*Pedaliaceae*)

This small genus contains caudiciform shrubs, occurring through-out Africa. The deciduous leaves are small. The flowers are borne while the plant is leafless. The colour ranges from white to yellow, sometimes with a blush of pink. Like the related caudiciform genus *Pterodiscus*, its seeds are, sometimes, winged.

▷ *Sesamothamnus lugardae*

This is the most common species generally available. The stems are fleshy, with small, tan spines. In its habitat, it forms a caudex 2m/6½ft or more thick. The leaves are grey-green, with a felted surface, and they drop in the autumn (fall). It requires high light and will tolerate intense heat. It is grown from seed and, occasionally, from cuttings.

Natural habitat: tropical to south-west Africa

203

SEYRIGIA (*Cucurbitaceae*)

This small genus of about four species comes from Mada-gascar. The plants consist of succulent, leafless, vining stems, with tuberous roots. The stems can be round or square, and smooth or covered with fine white fuzz. The dioecious flowers are borne singly from the nodes in female plants or in multiples from a short spur in males. The flowers are only 2–3mm/about ⅛in broad, and nondescript. This genus will toler-ate bright light and moderate heat, but no frost.

△ *Seyrigia humbertii*

The most attractive and robust of the genus, this will form masses of potato-like tubers, attached to the plant by thin, short roots. The square stems are covered with dense, white felt, up to 1cm/½in thick, producing 30cm/12in of growth in a season. It prefers bright, indirect light and can tolerate intense heat. The roots can be raised for effect, but should be protected from hot sun. It can be grown from seed, which is rarely available, but also grows well from cuttings, which are most successful if a section of the stem below the node is included.

Natural habitat: Madagascar

STAPELIA (*Asclepiadaceae*)

One of the four biggest genera in this family, along with *Caralluma*, *Hoya* and *Huernia*, this has been subjugated over the years but still contains many species. These generally have spineless, upright, green stems, which branch from the base to form large clusters. The flowers are among the largest in the family, some in excess of 20cm/8in wide in shades of tan, pink or yellow to dark purple, with darker bands running across the petals. Often, the flowers are quite hairy, with hair along the edges of the petals, sometimes densely clothing the entire flower. Like *Caralluma*, this genus is known for the foul odour of the flowers. They are some of the easiest stapeliads to grow but do require space for their large size. They occur over southern Africa.

◁ △ **Stapelia leendertziae** and **Stapelia leendertziae cristata**

The stems of this fast-growing species are four-angled, 1.5cm/⅝in wide and 10cm/4in tall. It branches from the base; a small piece can grow to 30cm/12in in a greenhouse bed in one season, but is much more easily contained in a shallow hanging basket. The flowers are borne in the autumn (fall), from the newest growth. The liver-coloured flowers are tubular, with petals united halfway, with the tube 4cm/1½in wide and petals more than 10cm/4in long. The cristate (crested) form has recently become available. It grows as easily as the normal plant but will not flower. It will tolerate intense heat, but requires some shade and protection from frost. It is grown from seed or cuttings.

Natural habitat: South Africa

STAPELIANTHUS (*Asclepiadaceae*)

From Madagascar, this small genus of creeping stapeliads is not the most easily grown, but produces unusual flowers, often urn-shaped, with a small opening. They are fairly slow-growing and rot-prone, requiring moderate light and temperature levels. They are grown from seed or cuttings.

◁ *Stapelianthus neronis*

Still uncommon, this species forms a low, compact clump of soft, purple stems 1.5cm/⅝in wide by 4cm/1½in long. The flowers are borne in the autumn (fall) along the outer edges of the cluster, and are urn-shaped, with a small pore at the tip. The inside of the petals is white; the outside of the flower is a velvety purple. It requires warmth, bright, indirect light, and grows well from seed or cuttings.

Natural habitat: Madagascar

TALINUM (*Portulacaceae*)

This genus occurs both in Africa and in North and South America. It contains herbaceous species with tuberous roots as well as thick-stemmed shrubs. The leaves are deciduous and often fleshy, with considerable variability in the genus. The flowers are five-petalled, opening late on hot afternoons, and range from white to yellow or orange and pink to red. Many of the species are self-fertile and several are so prolific as to be called weeds. Many species will tolerate fairly intense heat and those herbaceous perennials with subterranean tubers will tolerate heavy frost. They can be grown from cuttings but are generally grown from seed.

△ *Talinum aurantiacum*

This common species forms solitary or branched, underground tubers, up to 10cm/4in long. The annual stems are thick, sparingly branched and up to 15cm/6in tall. On hot afternoons from mid to late summer, the flowers open for several hours; they are yellow and 1.5cm/⅝in wide. It is self-fertile, but tends not to become a weeding problem. It can be grown from seed or cuttings.

Natural habitat: New Mexico and Texas, south into Mexico

TAVARESIA (*Asclepiadaceae*)

From south and south-west Africa, these stapeliads have upright stems, with many ribs covered with small, brittle spines. The flowers are funnel-shaped, opening widely at the end, and cream-coloured, with maroon markings. They grow well from seed or cuttings and tolerate fairly high temperatures, if shaded.

▷ *Tavaresia barklyi*

Recently united with *T. grandiflora*, both species are now known as *T. barklyi*. The stems are light green, growing to 2cm/¾in wide, and over 10cm/4in long. In cultivation, it can form a clump 15cm/6in broad in a couple of seasons. The flowers are borne in the autumn (fall), varying considerably in size, but they can grow up to 7cm/2¾in wide and 10cm/4in long. It will tolerate intense heat if grown in bright, indirect light and it must be protected from frost. It is grown from seed or cuttings.

Natural habitat: South Africa

TITANOPSIS (*Mesembryanthemaceae*)

This South African genus is made up of highly succulent dwarfs. The species have variously coloured leaves, with rough, pimply ends, and they form low, clustering rosettes. They grow quickly from seed, often flowering in the second season. They will tolerate intense heat and heavy frost.

▷ *Titanopsis calcareum*

This is the most common species in the genus. Its grey leaves are flattened and slightly pointed, 1.5cm/⅝in wide and 2cm/¾in long, on the ends of which are many tuberculate bumps of various sizes. In its habitat, it grows on limestone, its colour and texture mimicking its environment. In the autumn (fall), it bears yellow flowers 2cm/¾in wide. It will tolerate intense heat and bright light as well as −4°C/25°F, briefly.

Natural habitat: south-west Africa

TOMATRICHE (*Asclepiadaceae*)

The species in this small genus form long stems, which are sparsely branched and bear brown to purple flowers, with reflexed petals. They will tolerate intense heat and bright, indirect light but must be kept protected from frost. They are grown from seed or cuttings.

▷ *Tomatriche revoluta bicolor*

The plant pictured is an unusual form of a common species. The stems are grey-green, 1.5cm/⅝in thick and more than 25cm/10in long. The flowers are borne in late summer and autumn (fall), near the ends of the stems; they are 2.5cm/1in wide, with dark purple petals recurved behind the flower and an apple-green centre. This differs from the common form, which is entirely dark purple. The edges of the petal bear purple hairs, which stir in the slightest breeze. The flowers have a carrion scent, but it is only detectable at close range. It will tolerate intense heat and bright light but must be protected from frost.

Natural habitat: South Africa

207

TRICHOCAULON (*Asclepiadaceae*)

This South African genus is considered by some to be defunct. Of the species originally included in this small genus, there are two distinct forms of growth. The group of species with stems that have stiff, raised ribs or stiff tubercles tipped with short, stiff spines are now considered members of *Hoodia*. The group with soft, spineless, tuberculate stems have been considered for a couple of genera, including the novel genus *Lavrania*, but there does not seem to be a consensus at this time. These spineless species are still primarily associated with this genus by most collectors. They cluster sparingly, growing stems 5cm/2in wide by 15cm/6in long. The flowers are numerous, borne near the tip of the stem. They are yellow with maroon dots or stripes, and less than 1cm/½in wide. These species will not tolerate intense heat but need bright, indirect light, a very well-drained potting compost (potting soil), and protection from cold. They are grown from seed and often grafted.

▷ **Trichocaulon cactiforme**

Several species are commercially available, but this is the most common. The soft, tuberculate stems grow to 5cm/2in wide and 10cm/4in tall, clustering sparingly from the base. The flowers are yellow, with maroon dots or bands, and are 6m/20ft wide. If pollination takes place, two seed horns typical of the stapeliads grow to more than 10cm/4in long. It is quite rot-prone, requiring bright, indirect light and high temperatures – but not intensely so. In the winter, it should be protected from frost and kept fairly dry, requiring occasional high temperatures. It is propagated from seed and often grafted.

Natural habitat: South Africa

TRICHODIADEMA (*Mesembryanthemaceae*)

There are more than 25 species in this genus. The genus is made up of short shrubs with tuberous or woody roots. The stems are thin and have succulent leaves, tipped with a crown of spines, hence the generic name (which means "hairy-crowned"). During the summer, pink to purple flowers 2cm/¾in wide are borne sporadically. These species will tolerate intense heat and half a day of sun, as well as light frost. A few of the species lend themselves well to succulent bonsai. All are easily grown from cuttings or seed.

▷ *Trichodiadema bulbosum*

This is the best-known species in this genus. The leaves are light green and 5mm/¼in long, bearing the typical crown of soft white spines. The stems branch heavily, forming a low, rounded shrublet. After several years, seedlings or cuttings will develop several thickened roots, which can be raised for effect. This species is widely used for succulent bonsai. The flowers are purple, 2cm/¾in wide and produced more or less freely during the summer, even on small cuttings. It will tolerate morning sun and intense heat during the summer. It will also tolerate brief periods to −4°C/25°F.

Natural habitat: South Africa

TYLECODON (*Crassulaceae*)

This genus was formed from the members of *Cotyledon* with caudiciform or tuberous stems, succulent deciduous leaves and flowers that are borne upright, rather than being pendulous. Many of these species make attractive, succulent bonsai specimens. They are winter-growers, and must be provided with bright light and warmth at that time. They will tolerate brief periods near 0°C/32°F but require daytime temperatures of at least 27°C/80°F occasionally. They range from Namibia to South Africa.

▷ *Tylecodon paniculata*

The tallest and fastest-growing species of *Tylecodon*, this seems to be the easiest to keep alive. In its habitat, the trunk can grow to more than 50cm/20in thick and 2m/6½ft tall. In the autumn (fall), it produces lively, green, succulent leaves 3cm/1¼in wide by 6cm/2½in long. It will tolerate intense heat, bright, indirect light and light frost. It is grown from cuttings and, occasionally, from seed.

Natural habitat: South Africa

UNCARINA *(Pedaliaceae)*

Several species of this newly introduced genus are endemic to Madagascar. In their habitat, they form much-branched trees and shrubs more than 7m/23ft tall, with large, deciduous, fuzzy green leaves and a thickened base. The flowers are showy, yellow to orange, and borne during the summer. The fruit is unique: a flattened, pointed pod, armed with numerous barbed hooks, for dispersal by animals. These plants can grow quite quickly, if provided with adequate water, warmth and root run. They can easily become a problem if planted in a greenhouse ground bed, producing 2m/6½ft of stem growth in a season. They will tolerate intense heat and sun, when provided with adequate water, but must be protected from frost.

△ *Uncarina decaryi*

This species can form a sizeable shrub in a few seasons. The white-barked trunk is thickened at the base, tapering to 1.5cm/⅝in thick branches, topped with fuzzy, light green leaves. Keep the plants fairly dry in the winter, and do not let the temperature fall below 0°C/32°F for any length of time. It is grown from seed or cuttings.

Natural habitat: Madagascar

210

YUCCA *(Agavaceae)*

This large, North American genus is composed of xerophytic species, most of which are not truly succulent. Common to many gardens and landscapes in warmer areas, the body form can vary from more or less stemless rosettes of long, thin leaves to tree-like species with substantial trunks. While some species produce a solitary rosette, more commonly the plants make clusters, particularly upon reaching flowering size. After flowering, the rosette does not die, as is the case with agaves, but flowers year after year or, in the case of some larger species, every other year. The flowers are generally waxy and white and borne on an upright or, occasionally, pendulous stock. Most species can tolerate intense sun and heat and many will tolerate substantial cold. Propagation is generally from seed and, occasionally, by dividing clusters.

△ *Yucca rigida*

Attractive, 1m/1yd long, powder blue leaves form a rosette on top of a trunk up to 2m/6½ft tall. It is only now becoming available as a landscape plant, and does well as a container plant. It will tolerate −12°C/10°F for short periods. It is grown from seed.

Natural habitat: Texas (USA), Mexico

▷ *Yucca carnerosana*

Growing to 10m/30ft tall, this imposing species is now becoming available as a landscape plant. Although it will not flower until more than a 1m/1yd tall, the flower spike is 1.5m/1½yds tall and is produced every other year. Cold-hardy to −12°C/10°F, for short periods, it is best grown as a landscape plant. It is propagated from seed.

Natural habitat: Texas (USA), Mexico

ZAMIACAULCAS (*Araceae*)

These odd African succulents may be considered to make ideal house-plants. They thrive in low light and bright light and tolerate both considerable moisture and drought. They form a large underground tuber, which sprouts both roots and long, green leaves from the apex. Although the family is known for its foul-smelling flowers, this genus does not share this reputation. They are propagated from leaves, which, when cut into sections with one leaflet, produce plantlets readily.

▷ *Zamiacaulcas zamiafolia*

Although there are a couple of species in cultivation, this is by far the most common. The leaves grow to 10cm/4in wide and 40cm/16in long. While the tuber will grow larger than 15cm/6in across, it cannot be displayed as the roots emerge from the top. Specimens are known to break their pots as the tuber grows. It will tolerate intense heat and bright, indirect light, but survives in low light and cooler temperatures. It is grown from leaves.

Natural habitat: Africa

care and cultivation

After purchasing new species of cacti and succulents, you will be faced with the task of successfully growing them. Clearly, the proper maintenance of these plants is every bit as important as acquiring them in the first place. After talking to other enthusiasts, you will soon realize that each grower has a different approach to succulent cultivation. The wide variety of composts (potting soils) and care strategies are linked to both the local climate and the availability of horticultural supplies. A grower's success comes from the ability to modify the care of succulents, using the materials available, to take the best advantage of local conditions.

◁ *Reputable nurseries will sell healthy plants free of pests and diseases.*
Most will be able to advise on caring for your plants.

TOOLS AND EQUIPMENT

Although no gardening tools or equipment are manufactured specifically for succulents, many of those used for general gardening are applicable. There are a few items, shown here, which are particularly useful.

CULTIVATION TOOLS

Good-quality tools are always worth the extra expense because they are easy to work with and durable. A few items are invaluable for proctection such as thick gloves, a paper sleeve, or a cloth wad.

A pocket knife or a retractable-blade knife is good for tender cuttings, delicate work and most grafting. While thinner and less durable than typical pocket knives, retractable-blade knives have replaceable blades, ensuring a clean, razor-sharp edge. Whatever the cutting tool, keep its edges sharp, clean and sterile. Rubbing alcohol or bleach are readily available and fairly effective for sterilization. While alcohol is not so effective as bleach, it does not damage the tissue of delicate cuttings or etch cutting tools, as bleach can. Flame sterilization is also quite effective, but works best with small, disposable blades, since larger blades take too much time and flame sterilization ruins their temper. Fleshy stems with a slightly woody core are best cut with serrated knives; very woody cuttings may require a pruning saw. Secateurs (pruning shears) can be used on smaller woody cuttings. After use, these tools should be cleaned, dried and, in areas of high humidity, oiled as well.

Small hoes are a necessity for weeding and cultivating around specimens in plantings. For smaller weeding jobs, long tweezers are quite handy.

◁ **Dibber (Dibbler)**

Dibbers, or dibblers, are made from a variety of materials, even an old pencil or piece of dowel, and are used to make holes in compost (potting soil) for planting seedlings or cuttings.

▷ **Widger**

Widgers are useful for removing seedlings from seed pots without damaging the tender young roots. They can also be used in the place of a dibber to plant seedlings without compacting the soil mix.

△ **Gloves**

Heavy leather gloves offer protection from most spines. If only lightweight gloves are available or you need more protection, wrap the fingers of the gloves with several layers of masking tape or duct tape. When the tape becomes full of spines, cut it off and re-tape the gloves.

◁ **Knife**

Knives are essential for any small cutting operations. These include making cuttings, dividing clusters, pruning tender shoots and removing rot. Locking knives are excellent since they provide greater safety with a mechanism that prevents the blade from folding back on your fingers. Large straight knives, particularly those with serrated edges, are excellent for making cuttings from all but very woody plants.

214

◁ Minimum-maximum Thermometer

As the name suggests, this kind of thermometer records the highest and lowest temperatures in a given spot. It can be used to determine the upper and lower temperature thresholds of plants, as well as to help choose a location for particular species. Using several of these at different locations in a greenhouse, house, or outdoors can provide valuable information about localized temperature variation.

▽ Trowels

Having several sizes of trowel is particularly handy when working in ground beds and rock gardens: use a larger one for mixing soil and a smaller one for working in tight spaces.

▽ Spoon

A spoon can be used to remove larger seedlings and rooted cuttings, and is handy for scooping out soil from spaces too small for a trowel.

◁ Folding Pruning Saw

Pruning saws are a necessity when plants become too large and woody for pruning shears. Because the toothed blade leaves a ragged edge, however, it is not ideal for taking cuttings.

◁ Secateurs (Pruning Shears)

Secateurs (pruning shears) are most useful for shaping plants, removing hard, dead material, and making cuttings of plants with a woody core. The anvil type, which is generally less expensive, cuts less cleanly than the scissors type. There are also pruners made specifically for bonsai which are useful for shaping caudiciforms.

CONTAINERS

Porous clay pots, while heavier and more expensive than plastic pots, have long been used by hobbyists for their ability to "breathe" and dry out faster. Commercial growers use mostly plastic pots, which require more porous composts (potting soils). "Pans" (pots that are more wide than tall) are perfectly designed for a succulent's shallow roots and are available in clay and plastic. Glazed pots and most stoneware containers, while clay in origin, are not porous and should be watered like plastic pots. Bonsai-style pots also work well for succulents, since they are shallow and dry out quickly. Saucers are generally used to protect interior surfaces from water damage, but can also be useful if watering seeds and young seedlings from underneath to avoid washing them out with overhead watering. In most cases, the saucer should be emptied of standing water, as this may promote rot once the compost (potting soil) is moist.

TOP DRESSINGS

Top dressings, usually different sizes and colours of gravel, serve several functions and can be critical to the health of the plant. Superficially, they enhance the appearance of the plant in the pot: many growers prefer to have several colours and grades of material so they can choose which best accents a particular plant. More important, top dressings slow moisture loss and moderate soil temperature, which is particularly important for tender young plants and in arid regions. A top dressing can also inhibit algal growth.

△ Labels

Whether plastic, wood or metal, labels are a necessity. In addition to the Latin plant name, collectors often include the origin of the plant, the date it was acquired and the time of the last transplanting. All but the sturdiest labels will rot, break or fade in time, and will need to be replaced periodically to ensure the information is not lost.

Moisture Meter

These useful devices are indispensable to the novice grower for determining when to water. In larger pots, the top layer of compost (potting soil) can be dry while the compost in the centre and bottom is still quite wet. Moisture meters can detect the presence of moisture, although their accuracy varies according to the saltiness of the water.

▽ Seed Trays

Seed trays are used not only for starting seeds and nurturing seedlings but also for rooting cuttings. Since they dry out more quickly than deep pots, the moisture level in the compost is easier to control.

◁ Brushes

Small paintbrushes have several uses. They are used primarily to pollinate plants and it is wise to have several sizes as flower sizes vary widely. Brushes made from animal hair seem to work best, since the pollen adheres well to the rougher material. Brushes can be used to gently clean dirt and spider webs from plants. They are also perfect for spot applications of dusting sulphur and rooting hormone.

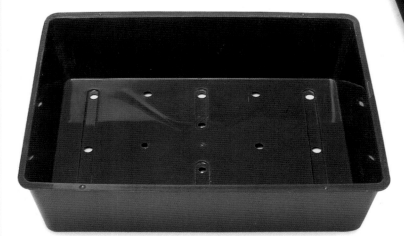

SOIL MIXES

If asked about the perfect growing medium for succulents, ten growers would give 20 different answers! In fact, hobbyists may spend as much time debating composts (potting soils) as they do talking about their plants. General-purpose, commercial composts are widely available, making it easier to consistently produce a good-quality succulent mix. Unfortunately for hobbyists, certain components used to produce potting composts, such as pumice, are often only regionally available. Most basic cactus and succulent composts have 25–50 per cent organic matter, combined with an inorganic ingredient. They should be loose and well aerated, even when wet, to prevent waterlogging and root rot. A good succulent compost allows for easy root growth, while holding less water than a typical houseplant compost. Composts used by commercial growers are entirely soilless, which often makes them physically lighter and free from pests and diseases.

INORGANIC BASES FOR COMPOSTS (POTTING SOILS)

Pumice and perlite are the most common porous, inorganic bases for succulent composts (potting mixes). While often considered interchangeable, they do have slightly different characteristics. Pumice is preferred by many growers, since it makes a superior, long-lasting compost. Perlite is more widely available and less expensive. Perlite's drawbacks are twofold, however: first, unless a top dressing is used, the perlite tends to float out of the compost during watering; secondly, perlite breaks down over time, compacting in the pot and making more frequent repotting necessary. Another porous material occasionally used is scoria, or crushed lava rock. It has about similar qualities to pumice, but ranges from red to black in colour, and the particles are generally larger in size than pumice or perlite. When porous materials are not available to form the basic compost, stones from fine grit up to gravel are used. These do not provide high porosity, but they do limit the amount of water the compost can hold. While they add considerable weight to a compost, grit and gravel make adequate, long-lasting substitutes for pumice or perlite.

ORGANIC ADDITIONS TO COMPOSTS (POTTING SOILS)

Although some succulents prefer little or no organic matter, most benefit from its presence. It increases both the volume of water a compost can hold and its ability to absorb nutrients. Peat, coir and mulch are the most common organic additions. Peat is the most stable and long lasting but, when dry, becomes hydrophobic, making it hard to re-wet. Coir is produced from ground coconut husk, and is becoming popular since it is light and inexpensive and takes up water readily, even when completely dry. Bagged "mulch" is quite variable, since it is produced regionally from timber or other agricultural by-products. Well-composted mulch is an excellent substitute for peat or coir. However, low-quality material can contain fungal pathogens and weed seeds; and, if it is only partially composted, it will draw nitrogen from the compost as it decomposes, slowing the plant's growth.

NUTRIENTS AND OTHER ADDITIONS

A number of other additions are used to further modify composts and provide the nutrients necessary for normal growth. Limestone, either crushed, powdered or pelletized, is often added to neutralize the acidity from organic matter, and to provide calcium. Gypsum is also occasionally used to add calcium, but it can acidify the mix. Phosphorus and potassium can be added in powdered or pelletized forms but, if the grower plans to use a soluble, balanced fertilizer, these may not be necessary. Several powdered, pelletized or encapsulated slow-release fertilizers are readily available and provide a constant low level of nutrients for the plants. Since these are eventually used up by the plant or leached through repeated watering, they should not be the only source of fertilizer.

217

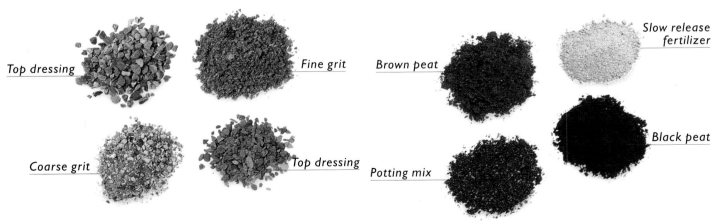

Top dressing   Fine grit
Coarse grit   Top dressing
Brown peat   Slow release fertilizer
Potting mix   Black peat

△ *Most growers formulate their own composts (potting soils) and top-dressings from materials locally available. Commercial houseplant composts (potting soils) can be modified with pumice, perlite or various sizes of grit. A compost (potting soil) can also be made from raw materials such as peat or mulch, and grit or porous inorganic materials. Nutrients and slow-release fertilizers are added.*

BUYING CACTI AND SUCCULENTS

Acquiring new plants certainly provides a great amount of joy to growers, but also no small amount of anxiety. Because of the enormous numbers of succulent species, finding one in particular is often difficult. Once-common plants become hard to find as interest in them wanes, often to be renewed a few years later. Most collectors purchase their first plants at local nurseries, markets or department stores. As the cactus and succulent industry grows, the diversity and quality of the plants commonly available also increases. Rare, slow-growing and less popular species, however, are rarely mass produced and are often only available from smaller speciality nurseries and mail-order companies.

MAIL-ORDER PLANTS

Because local demand for succulent plants is generally limited, many nurseries specializing in cacti and succulents also offer plants by post (mail). Mail-order companies also offer the greatest numbers of species, common and rare. While the size and cost of plants available via mail order varies considerably, the plants are, generally, healthy and of good quality.

▷ *The scarring on the sides of this plant not only mars its appearance, but may have been caused by a fungus or other pathogen that could infect neighbouring plants.*

▷ *These cacti are healthy and actively growing. They have good colour and are apparently free from pests and diseases. The only other inspection required would be to remove the pot and inspect the roots for mealy bugs.*

△ *Although otherwise healthy, this* Trichocereus *has been grown with too little light, causing it to produce thin, pale green growth. It could still form an attractive plant if the tip were removed and rooted and then left to form a cluster at the base, but this would take one or two seasons.*

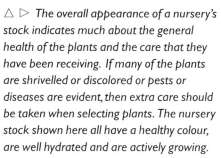

△ ▷ *The overall appearance of a nursery's stock indicates much about the general health of the plants and the care that they have been receiving. If many of the plants are shrivelled or discolored or pests or diseases are evident, then extra care should be taken when selecting plants. The nursery stock shown here all have a healthy colour, are well hydrated and are actively growing.*

△ *Although this* Orbea variegata *may appear limp and in questionable health to the novice, it is perfectly healthy. Becoming familiar with the normal appearance of species will help you when buying succulents.*

BUYING PLANTS

The novice should always select plants which are healthy and free from pests and diseases, if at all possible. That a plant be plump and actively growing is not necessarily important, since it may normally be dormant at that particular time of year. At the very least, a specimen should be visually free from insects or their eggs, mites and spots of rot. Superficial imperfections, such as blemishes, old insect injuries or pruning scars, are inevitable in larger specimens and should not be a basis for rejection. As the collector learns to recognize pests and diseases, he or she can distinguish which plants can be nursed back to health and which are beyond help. Although the overall appearance of a nursery's stock indicates much about the general health and the care that the plants have been receiving, some species have an unusual appearance which can make them look sick. By becoming acquainted with the normal appearance of such species and by asking the nursery staff and other collectors the novice will learn to make a more informed choice.

FIELD-COLLECTED PLANTS

Plants of wild origin should be avoided. Aside from ethical or legal questions, they are hard to re-establish and are often short-lived in cultivation, requiring re-collection to supply the demand. Occasionally, plants are available that have been salvaged from areas cleared for development. These pose less of an ethical dilemma, provided there is proof of their legal collection, but the problem of re-establishing and maintaining them still remains. The conscientious collector should make a point of buying only artificially propagated specimens.

PROVIDING THE RIGHT CONDITIONS

Many species have their own specific care requirements. Apart from the initial health of the plant and the medium in which it is grown, the things important to proper plant growth are light, temperature, water, and fertilizer. By adjusting these, you can grow attractive and healthy plants.

LIGHT

Providing proper light, particularly indoors, can cause more anxiety than anything else. Fluorescent lighting offers a remedy to low light, but does not provide much heat, and the bulbs have to be mounted no more than 10–30cm (4–12in) above the plants to get results. High-pressure halide lights have remedied these problems, providing both light and heat, but at an increased energy usage. Many species of succulents grown in lower light will merely survive but not flourish or flower. Other species will grow well in lower light, provided water and fertilizer are monitored closely.

Too much sunlight is as bad as not enough for certain species and its effects are often rapid and spectacular. Sunburn damage appears first as a bleaching of the sunny side of the plant; this can develop into a permanent scar. This can affect both shade-loving species and sun-hardy species that have been initially grown in

△ *If bright, diffuse, even lighting can be provided, it will produce the best quality and quantity of growth, even when plants are densely packed together.*

shade and then moved too quickly into a sunny situation. Tender plants moved to the wrong exposure can be damaged in less than a hour. Damage from excessive sun can also occur gradually in plants that are already acclimatized to the sun. During exceptionally hot periods or a dry spell following a period of high humidity a plant can begin to yellow. When recognized in its early stages, sun stress of this kind can be remedied, either by moving the plant to a less sunny position or temporarily covering it with shade cloth or muslin (cheesecloth).

TEMPERATURE

Providing adequate warmth is certainly the greatest expense and ordeal faced by growers of succulents. This is particularly true in areas that have long, cool winters, with a minimum of sunlight. Temperatures in the desert often fluctuate by as much as 5–10°C (40–50°F) each day. Having adapted to these extremes, even tropical succulents will tolerate low nightly temperatures, so long as they receive sunlight and warmth during the day. When subjected to long periods of low light and consistently low temperatures, however, these same species cease to thrive and may well die. The minimum temperature that has been provided with each species in the plant directories is derived from plants grown with these oscillating temperatures, rather than static ones. In order to maintain many of the tropical species in climates with long winters and short, cloudy days, the minimum temperature must be increased considerably. The genus *Adenium*, for example, provided with a daily high of 15–21°C (60–70°F) and bright sunlight, will easily tolerate a nightly low of 3–5°C (38–40°F). However, when consistently kept at 5–10°C (40–50°F) in low light, they inevitably rot and die. For *Adenium* to survive static winter conditions, the minimum temperature must be raised to at least 15°C (60°F). Another phenomenon can occur during the summer if there is no nightly cooling. When the lowest temperature still exceeds 27–32°C (80–90°F), many succulents will go dormant. Their stomates remain shut, they will not take up water and they will rot if normal watering is continued. In tropical climates, the grower can only wait until conditions become favourable for growth. In greenhouses and drier climates, however, nightly misting, extractor (exhaust) fans and circulating fans can be used to lower the temperature.

WATERING

More succulents die from overwatering than from anything else. It is best to allow the soil to become almost dry between waterings. It is also dangerous to allow the plant to remain completely dry for a long time, as the roots will start to die back. The best way to determine when to water is to examine the soil for moisture. Moisture meters are helpful to check for this, particularly in larger potted specimens. The amount of water should vary according to the season; postpone watering if cold or wet weather is expected. During the growing season, water the

◁ △ As well as promoting growth and flowering, fertilization aids in disease resistance. Growers can introduce the fertilizer with hose attachments or simply apply the fertilizer with a watering can. The plant should be watered with the same amount of fertilizer solution as would be given in a normal watering. Liquid (pictured above) or soluble formulations of fertilizer generally produce more consistent growth when applied twice as often as the recommended frequency but at a half to one-quarter the recommended rate.

plants more thoroughly, so that some water runs out of the bottom of the pot. This keeps dissolved salts from accumulating in the compost (potting soil). While the plant is dormant, water it less frequently and more lightly, in order to moisten, but not soak, the compost. Early morning is generally the best time to water, since this allows the plant to dry out during the heat of the day. Plants with dense spines or many crevices require extra care, so that water does not remain trapped and promote rot.

FERTILIZATION

While a soilless compost (potting soil) is the most reliably consistent growing medium, it usually has no innate fertility. Any nutrients necessary for plant growth must be added. Even amended mixes eventually require supplementary fertilization. Some fertilizers, like fish emulsion, provide only nitrogen. The best growth is provided by a balanced fertilizer with micronutrients. While there is much debate over the exact ratio of nitrogen (N) to phosphorus (P) to potassium (K), or N:P:K, to promote the best growth, there are some things the grower should bear in mind. A higher ratio of nitrogen, 30:10:10, will promote more growth; higher potassium, 10:30:10, better flowering; and higher phosphorus, 10:10:30, better disease resistance. Succulents are not heavy feeders so, rather than applying the fertilizer at full strength, it is better applied at a quarter or half strength at every or every other watering during the growing season. Plants grown in low light conditions should be fertilized sparingly, to prevent thin, weak growth. As the end of the growing season approaches, gradually decrease fertilization so that the plants will not make soft, tender growth.

△ Plants that are exposed to too-low temperatures can suffer stem tip damage or even stem collapse. Rot often attacks the affected areas. Increase the temperature so that the dead tissue can dry out or cut out all the damaged tissue.

GROWING INDOORS

Virtually any succulent species can be kept alive indoors, but this environment limits the species that will really flourish, produce typical growth and flower. Fertilization and watering must be limited to prevent thin, weak growth or root rot. Because of the reduced heat, light, water and fertility, plants mature much more slowly indoors. Plants can also suffer from sunburn when placed too near a bright, hot window. Watering may also need to be adjusted because of low humidity caused by the use of heaters during the winter or air conditioning during the summer.

GROWING OUTDOORS

The quality and quantity of growth produced by plants outside far exceeds what is possible indoors. The range of species possible is far wider, as well. There is, however, less control over the plant's environment. Weather conditions can affect plants adversely. Insects and animals can become problems. Increased care is also required. Many tropical and tender species can be grown outside when danger of frost is past, and then moved back indoors in the autumn (fall). Take care not to move plants too quickly into hot sunlight, as sunburn can result.

Benefits from Growing Outdoors

There are additional benefits gained from growing in the ground. Some species can be bedded out for the summer, and then be dug up and stored, bare-rooted, for the winter. This works particularly well with some caudiciforms, like *Cyphostemma juttae*. Potted plants can also be bedded out in their pots. At the end of the season, exhume the pot, trim the roots growing through the drainage holes and move the plant indoors. It is the moderating influence of the soil or growing medium which promotes better root growth. Ground beds have less severe fluctuations in moisture and temperature, and often maintain greater fertility. Patio plants must be watered more often than indoor plants, unless they receive rainfall. Ground beds, once established, need

△ *Greenhouses allow the grower to cultivate the greatest variety of plant species. Here, species of* Gasteria, Haworthia *and* Aloe *grow equally well together. Instead of benches, these plants are maintained on a bed of gravel, which prevents the growth of weeds, provides no hiding place for slugs or snails and allows excess water to run off.*

thorough irrigation for good root development and time to dry between watering. However, well-drained beds exposed to frequent rains will not necessarily cause rot. Rain water, partly due to its acidity, does not promote rot as easily as tap water.

GROWING IN THE GREENHOUSE

Greenhouses offer the potential to grow virtually any species of succulent well. With the right equipment, light, temperature, air circulation and even humidity can be controlled. Unfortunately, this closed system which allow plants to thrive is also perfect for the rapid spread of pests and diseases.

Hobbyists new to greenhouse growing often find that they have too much light, resulting in sunburn and excessive heating. This is easily remedied by applying a coat of white paint to the outside of the greenhouse or a layer of shade cloth. Winter heating is the most common and costly means of moderating temperature. Generally, the cheapest sources of energy are used; heaters are available which use electricity, methane, propane or heating oil. Be careful with any heating device, since many greenhouse materials are very combustible and carbon monoxide can accumulate in closed structures. High temperatures can also be a problem, and many greenhouses are designed to be opened during the summer. Some have extractor (exhaust) fans to bring in outside air. Stagnant air and high humidity can promote fungal diseases. To avoid the need for chemical control, use circulating fans to remove condensation from plants. While humidity can easily be increased by spraying a mist of water, removing excess moisture is more difficult. This can be accomplished by using a dehumidifier or, less expensively, by using extractor (exhaust) fans.

△ *The quality and quantity of growth, as well as flowers, produced by plants outside far exceeds what is possible indoors. The range of possible species is far wider, as well.*

GROUP PLANTINGS

For group plantings, choose species that vary in colour and texture and make stunning arrangements. It is important to select those which have similar light and water requirements since individual care is difficult to provide in group plantings. If the planting is to be for the long term, choose and position species with their eventual sizes in mind, as well. The plants intended for seasonal and short-term plantings, however, need only have the same cultural requirements. When succulents are to be transplanted into a very different compost (potting soil), knead the rootball to remove most of the original compost. If this is not done, moisture will not travel from one compost to another.

PLANTING IN CONTAINERS

Container plantings, by their nature, have a limited duration before they need to be thinned or replanted. If the species are carefully selected, with similar growth rates and a relatively small mature size, a planting can last from two to four years before it needs replanting. When planted with miniature species, it will last even longer. The down side to selecting plants for a long-term container planting is that the grower is limited to a much narrower range of species. Most commercially produced

"dish gardens" include plants with vastly different growth rates, and species from miniatures to giants planted side by side, since they are planted for short-term effect. These plantings have a life span of one or two years before they must be thinned or replanted. While this requires extra maintenance, it provides more aesthetic appeal than a container filled with plants of similar shapes and sizes. Shallow containers are generally best for group plantings, since they weigh less and dry out more quickly.

PLANTING IN A BED

Cacti and succulents appear most natural when planted out in beds. This can be emphasized by the use of various top dressings and larger stones. Since succulent plants will tolerate transplanting more often than other plants, they can easily be added to or removed from plantings. The more stable moisture and temperature of the larger volume of compost (potting soil) promotes better growth. Beds do not work well indoors, and are best either outdoors or in a greenhouse, where they will receive adequate heat, light and air movement.

While well-drained soil and low rainfall allow some growers to do plantings in beds at ground level, most must be raised beds, which require more preparation. Depending on the desired look and the life expectancy of the bed, the sides can be made from any number of materials. Brick, concrete blocks, treated wood or mortared stones are the most common. Fill raised beds that sit directly on the ground entirely with the growing medium or, if increased drainage is needed, have a layer of gravel at the bottom.

223

◁ *Air movement in a greenhouse is critical for disease prevention. Some growers find it necessary to use circulating fans throughout the year.*

△ *A bed of succulents can provide a jungle-like appearance, combining many colours and textures.*

PLANTING BOWLS, BASKETS AND BEDS

PLANTING A BOWL GARDEN

1 A good selection of plants, with a variety of forms, colours and sizes, is important. It is also very important to choose plants with similar watering requirements; generally, cacti are not combined with other succulents. It is helpful to arrange the plants before planting them, as they will be harder to handle when unpotted, particularly spiny plants. If the finished bowl is to be displayed in a central location, it will look best with the tallest plants in the centre. For display against a wall, they should be arranged from short to tall, front to back.

2 There are two ways of adding the compost (potting soil). Either fill the container with compost and then scoop it out to make room for each rootball; or partially fill it, arrange the plants in place and add compost to fill the spaces between the rootballs. If very shallow pots, particularly bonsai pots, are used, flatten out or trim the rootballs to set the plant at the proper level.

3 After the plants have been placed and the compost (potting soil) tamped down and levelled, there should be enough room left at the top of the pot to finish the planting with top dressing, stones or other accents.

4 Water succulents immediately; cactus plantings should not be watered for several days and then only lightly for the first couple of times.

5 Once the top dressing and stones or other materials have been added, a soft brush can be used to remove bits of compost (potting soil) from the plants.

PLANTING A HANGING BASKET

1 Before starting, have all materials at hand: plants, slightly moist succulent compost (potting soil), hanging pot with hanger. It is generally easier to remove the chain or other hanger before planting, and then re-attach it afterwards.

2 Fill the planter with compost (potting soil). Scoop out an amount of compost the same volume as the rootball of each plant and set the plant in the hole. If the compost falls back in the holes, it is too dry and must be moistened.

3 Fill any low areas level to the tops of the rootballs with compost (potting soil) and gently tap the container. The level of the soil should be at least 1–2cm/½–¾in lower than the edge of the container to allow for water. Arrange the hanging portions of the cuttings and attach the hanger.

4 If the conditions are fairly warm and dry, the basket can be watered lightly immediately after planting, otherwise watering should be delayed for several days.

PLANTING A BED

1 Once the sides are erected, the bed can be filled with compost (potting soil). If greater drainage is required, add a layer of gravel first, then top with a sheet of water-permeable material.

2 Fill the bed with compost (potting soil). If mounds or large stones are to be included, they need to be added before planting. As you select each spot for planting, scoop out the soil and insert the plant.

3 When the plants and compost are in place, top with a dressing of small stones. Water a succulent bed lightly immediately after planting, but withhold watering from a cactus planting for several days. This will allow damaged roots to heal.

4 Once the planting becomes established, water and fertilize as often as it dries out. In future, individual plants can be added or removed without disturbing the entire planting.

ROUTINE MAINTENANCE

In addition to periodic watering and occasional fertilization, cacti and succulents benefit from regular attention to maintain their appearance and health. By routinely examining their plants, growers can prevent potential problems, such as the spread of pests and diseases, and check the quality of a plant's growth and adjust its care accordingly. The amount of care will vary seasonally, with its highest level during the plant's growing season.

HANDLING

Some succulents, like *Adromischus* and *Pachyphytum* species, and some cacti, particularly many *Opuntia* species, have leaves or segments which easily break off if they are roughly handled. Handling these as little as possible is generally the only solution. Many cacti and succulents have a waxy coating on the leaves or stems which brushes off when touched, leaving permanent fingerprints. Gripping these plants by their base will limit this. Aside from injuring their plants, growers need to avoid injury to themselves. Many succulents, *Euphorbia* species, especially, have poisonous or caustic sap. The hobbyist should wear gloves and eye protection when pruning these plants. Wash off sap that does come in contact with the skin with alcohol, followed by washing with soap and water. The same attractive spination which appeals to hobbyists also makes heavily spined plants difficult to handle. Tongs, heavy gloves, or a sleeve of paper or thick fabric can be used to manipulate these species.

PRUNING

Many succulents become rank and weedy without occasional shaping and pruning. Even small species may need to be trimmed back, lest they outgrow their allotted space. Pruning tools vary from knives to scissors, secateurs (pruning shears) or, for the largest jobs, a pruning saw. These should be very sharp, so they will cut rather than crush the tissue, and should also be kept clean and sterilized, to avoid spreading bacteria, fungi or viruses.

Pruning can serve several purposes; to thin or shorten stems on overgrown plants; to remove damaged portions of the plant; or to shape a plant for a more desirable appearance. Shrubby caudiciforms often need intensive pruning and shaping to acquire the gnarled shape typical of their growth in the wild. Many caudiciforms and other succulents lend themselves so well to shaping that they are becoming popular subjects for bonsai, tolerating the harsh training more easily than non-succulent trees and shrubs. Additionally, since many succulents grow well from cuttings, the hobbyist may prune an overgrown specimen and propagate it simultaneously.

DUSTING
Where overhead watering is not practised, dust and cobwebs can accumulate. Use a soft brush, gently, to remove this debris without damaging the plant or breaking its spines.

REMOVING DIRT
Accumulations of dirt and other material can often be removed with a stiff spray of water. Where this is not possible or more delicacy is required, an atomizer and soft brush will suffice.

HANDLING

HANDLING *EUPHORBIA* SPECIES

Care should be taken when handling Euphorbia species to avoid coming in contact with the often caustic and poisonous sap. While heavy rubber gloves offer the best protection, a sleeve of paper works quite well and can be discarded afterwards.

HANDLING *OPUNTIA* SPECIES

In addition to the spines normally present in cacti, species of Opuntia also bear glochids. These tiny, barbed spines are extremely numerous and very irritating. They can also become airborne when the plant is disturbed; misting the plant with water immediately before handling will help. Use tongs or, as in this case, a piece of foam, to hold the plant. Avoid wearing gloves, since they would become impregnated with glochids and have to be thrown out.

TAKING LARGE CUTTINGS

Several layers of cloth provide adequate protection when taking large cuttings. For exceptionally long-spined species, old carpeting with an outer layer of cardboard may be necessary.

PRUNING

1 *Pruning begins with the removal of all unhealthy growth.*

2 *Next, trim any stems which will detract from the appearance of the plant. At this point, the plant's future appearance and size needs to be considered. For example, if the plant is to look best when it is 1 m/1 yd tall, it should be trimmed to well below that height. This will allow the new growth to cover the pruning scars and produce an attractive plant with the desired height.*

3 *After a period of time, the pruned plant will have produced clean, healthy new growth.*

227

ECHEVERIA MAINTENANCE

1 *Many rosette succulents, Echeveria in particular, become leggy with age, forming long stems and successively smaller rosettes. These need special maintenance every couple of years. First, cut or gently pull off the old flower stalks.*

2 *Next, remove the withered leaves below the rosette. They can often be easily removed by hand, but other succulents may require scissors or secateurs (pruning shears).*

3 *Then cut the stem below the rosette. You can treat it with sulphur or rooting hormone, but allow it to heal for one or two weeks before replanting it. If the rooted portion of the stem appears vigorous, save it, since it may produce more rosettes.*

DAMAGED PLANTS

REMOVING STEM DAMAGED BY ROT
Rotted stems and portions of plants should be removed as completely as possible. If rotted sections are being removed from living stems, sterilize the pruning tool prior to making the last cut into healthy tissue, and sterilize it afterwards, as well.

REMOVING STEM DAMAGED BY OTHER CAUSES
It is good practice to remove tips damaged by frost or other causes, or dead stubs of leaves from previous pruning. In some species, additional dieback will result by cutting into the living tissue; in these, take care to remove only the dead tissue.

REMOVING OLD LEAF (ON LITHOPS)
In the wild, the withered leaves which accumulate around plants are beneficial, providing additional fertility as they decompose. In cultivation, these are generally removed, since they hold excess moisture and promote rot, and can harbour pests and diseases. Gently remove them with fingers or tweezers.

REPOTTING

While novice growers usually associate repotting with moving a plant into a larger container to promote growth, it is also performed to remove old, spent compost (potting soil) or to replace an unfamiliar compost. The last thing that occurs to most beginners to do after buying a new plant is repotting it. Many advanced growers, however, consider this a first priority. There are so many different composts being used that, unless the grower is familiar with the properties of the particular one used for the new plant, they will repot the new plant immediately. This not only places the plant in a familiar growing medium, it allows the grower to examine closely the health of the root system and check for pests, particularly mealy bugs.

Changing the Soil

Akin to this procedure is changing the soil on specimen plants. Since many succulents have a modest size when mature, a grower may wish to keep a particular plant in a pot selected for it. Most composts (potting soils) have a certain life span and, over a period of years, dead roots accumulate and the cramped root system loses vigour. The fine hair roots, which are an extension from one cell (and each cell only produces one) and which take up the water and nutrients for the plant, are fairly short lived, particularly when the compost (potting soil) is allowed to dry completely between waterings. After a long time root-bound in a pot, plants sometimes have no room left to make new roots and few cells left to produce hair roots. By trimming old, matted roots, you can re-establish the plant in the same pot, with room to grow more roots.

Repotting a Root-bound Succulent

To do this, unpot the plant and remove much of the compost. Also remove any rotted or dead roots and, if necessary, trim the roots as well. Dust the roots with sulphur and/or a rooting hormone and allow them to heal for one to three weeks before replanting. The rootball should be lightly shaded and protected from intensely hot, dry winds (if the plant is stored in a humid environment with poor air movement, however, the newly trimmed roots can develop rot). If possible, repot in good weather and it can restore vigour to specimens while maintaining them in a favourite pot.

It is generally best to choose a container that is only slightly larger than the original. Occasionally, a wider but more shallow pot may be chosen, but many cacti and succulents have stout or tuberous roots which make this impractical.

Raising Caudiciforms

The tuberous nature of many succulents has led to the practice of raising their underground storage structures. Many have thick, gnarled roots, giving the illusion of extreme age. Others have large, round trunks, which resemble rocks. Whatever their appearance, a large, well-displayed caudex inevitably generates interest when shown in public. Since this is usually not normal for the plant, growers need to be aware of particular guidelines. A submerged caudex generally grows faster than one that has been raised. Many growers have selected a beautiful pot and proudly displayed the caudex of some seedling caudiciform, only to see it remain essentially the same size year after year. Patience and occasional repotting will yield a large caudex for future display. Newly raised roots also need protection from sunburn while their skin thickens. Certain species, particularly tuberous *Ceropegia* and their kin, will never tolerate intense heat and sunlight.

Repotting Caudiciforms

Raising the plant can be performed in a new container or the original. To replant in the same container, lift the plant, roots and all, out of the pot and add a layer of new compost (potting soil). Replant at this new, higher level. Before adding the top dressing, to finish the process, use a soft brush to remove the compost from the newly raised portion.

▷ *Many tropical caudiciforms respond well to deep, fertile, well-drained soil and plenty of water, and can produce massive caudices in one or two seasons. Most outdoor plantings are seasonal, since few climates are suitable for growing tropical species outside all year. This bed was planted in the spring with* Adenium, Bursera, Cyphostemma, Momordica *and other caudiciform species. While growers with outdoor beds might be tempted to leave the plants in the ground for as long as possible, the plants must be dug up and re-established indoors before winter.*

REPOTTING A SUCCULENT

1 *All of the materials should be at hand: pots, compost (potting soil), top dressing, and some paper to handle the plant.*

2 *Gently remove the plant from the pot. Sometimes it is necessary to run a knife around the inside of the pot.*

3 *To protect the plant and/or planter, a paper sleeve can be used to hold the succulent.*

4 *Loosen the rootball and shake off some of the old compost.*

5 *Add a layer of compost (potting soil) to the new pot, to raise the plant to its previous level. Succulents can rot if planted below grade and are not generally raised high.*

6 *Pour compost (potting soil) around the roots, gently tapping and tamping down to fill all the spaces.*

7 *Add the top dressing around the plant. It will prevent lighter portions of the compost from floating if it is 5mm/¼in or more thick. Water in most succulents lightly, immediately after repotting.*

◁ *This dwarf hybrid has been planted in a shallow pot that is well suited for its fibrous roots. It should be comfortable in this for several seasons.*

230

REPOTTING A CACTUS

1 *Repot a cactus in essentially the same way as any other succulent, taking even greater care not to injure it. Carefully remove the cactus from its pot.*

2 *Before replanting, slightly loosen the rootball, to separate, but not damage, the roots. If the rootball is too dense it will prevent water from entering and starve the inner roots of water. When examined later, the original rootball will be intact, with only a few new roots growing out. As the plant is positioned and planted, take care to place the plant at its original level in the compost (potting soil).*

3 *The compost (potting soil) and top dressing should be added carefully; it can get caught in the spines, is difficult to remove and detracts from the appearance. After repotting, cacti should not be watered for a week or more and then, initially, more lightly than normal.*

△ *Cacti should be in proportion to their pots. Smaller pots need approximately 1–2cm/ ½–¾in of space between the plant and the side of the pot, larger plants require more space, up to 2.5–5cm/1–2in.*

REPOTTING DELICATE CACTI

1 *Plants with delicate root systems, which will not tolerate much handling, can be repotted by nesting a pot the same size as the rootball into the larger one and filling in around it with compost (potting soil).*

2 *Carefully remove the inner pot and replace it with the cactus. If the cactus is too deep, gently raise it to the right level and tap the pot, the compost (potting soil) should fill the space under the rootball.*

3 *Add additional compost (potting soil), as needed, followed by top dressing. Many delicate species are prone to rot if compost gets on top of them, so any stray compost should be carefully brushed or blown away.*

PROPAGATION

As the habitats of these marvellous and unusual plants declines each year, through agriculture and urbanization, the need to propagate and maintain these species becomes imperative. Already, many species are extinct in the wild, existing now only in cultivation. Apart from species preservation, starting new plants and watching them develop and mature fills many growers with a sense of awe and fulfilment unequalled in this hobby.

IN THE WILD

Reproduction from seed is the most common method of propagation. Since few seedlings survive to maturity, great numbers of seeds must be produced to guarantee a plant's successor. A giant Saguaro cactus, *Carnegiea gigantea*, may produce one million seeds over its life span, with a couple of these, or only one, surviving to maturity. In addition to reproducing sexually, plants have several forms of asexual propagation. Rhizomes or other underground shoots are common in *Agave* and *Sansevieria*, and often emerge as small plants some distance from the parent. Several species of *Kalanchoe* produce plantlets from the leaf margins. These eventually fall to the ground and root, forming dense stands. Sometimes plantlets are formed on flower stalks, as a response to poor pollination. In *Agave*, several thousand of these small plants, called bulbils, may develop as the plant's last effort to reproduce before it dies. In *Haworthia* and *Gasteria*, one or two plantlets often sprout from an unpollinated flower spike. In the Crassulaceae, many species produce propagules from leaves that have been accidentally broken off. Some vining succulents will root as they grow, forming independent plants. It is not unusual in the cactus family for joints and sections of stems to root and form new plants. This is quite common in the genus *Opuntia*, and some species, such as *Opuntia fulgida*, grow so successfully from cuttings that they have lost the ability to reproduce from seed.

IN CULTIVATION

As the hobbyist can provide more uniform conditions, seedlings and other propagules have the potential for greater survival than in nature. By the same token, however, 100 per cent mortality can occur if simple mistakes are made. The same conditions which promote the best germination and growth for seedlings are also perfect for bacterial and fungal growth. To achieve maximum survival and growth, the grower may need to control temperature, light and humidity, and use fertilizers, fungicides and rooting hormones.

RAISING SUCCULENTS FROM SEED

Seeds are relatively inexpensive, easy to ship and, if stored correctly, long-lived. The majority of cacti and succulents require only general care. Seedlings are often started in aquariums or with plastic bags over the pots to hold the moisture. When provided with a constant supply of moisture, high humidity and the right temperature, 21–27°C/70–80°F, seeds will take up water and germinate. Newly germinated seedlings are often very tender and quite susceptible to drought and extremes of light and temperature.

Unfortunately, the conditions which provide for optimum germination are also perfect for fungal and bacterial pathogens. The effects of these can be minimized by sterilizing the materials before planting, and by the use of chemicals. Local nurseries are usually the best source of information about the most effective chemicals. These should be applied following the recommendations on the label. By "hardening off" seedlings, or acclimatizing them to conditions with lower humidity, as quickly as possible, the grower will reduce the chances of rot. This may take weeks or months for small-seeded species, but species from very large seeds should be hardened off immediately, lest they become tender and leggy in a highly humid environment.

△ *Visible in this cross-section of a* Schlumbergera *flower are the many long, white stamens and long red pistil, which are surrounded by the brightly coloured petals.*

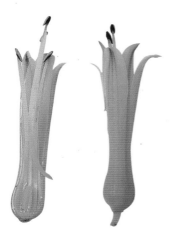

△ *Flowers of* Aloe *have essentially the same parts as a cactus flower, but they vary in number and shape.*

PLANTING AND SOWING SEEDS

1 *Fill and level the pot with a general-purpose cactus and succulent compost (potting soil). If the compost is very coarse or the seeds very tiny, top with a thin layer of finer compost.*

2 *Carefully sprinkle the seeds evenly over the compost. If the seeds are planted too thickly or in clumps, the seedlings will push out of the growing medium and will eventually dehydrate and die.*

3 *The amount and size of grit used to cover the seeds will vary depending on their size. Dust-fine seeds may need little, if any, covering as they will filter down among the grains of compost. Medium-sized seeds should be barely covered with a single layer of grit. Large seeds will need to be completely covered by a deeper layer of grit and the largest should be pressed into the mix before adding the grit. Moisten the pot carefully and place it where it will have high humidity and warmth.*

4 *Although the above-ground portion of this seedling is fairly robust, it has a shallow, delicate root system, which can be harmed by underwatering.*

5 *Upon germination, cacti and succulents form one or two cotyledons, or seed leaves. In some species these can be large, but in most cacti they are obscured by areoles and spines.*

233

TRANSPLANTING SEEDLINGS

1 *In time, healthy seedlings will be large enough to transplant. Allowing the tray to become overgrown and crowded can promote rot, so prompt repotting is necessary.*

2 *The seedlings must be gently separated to avoid damaging the roots. This is easier to do if the soil is slightly moist.*

3 *Seedlings can be potted up singly or several to a pot. When planted several to a pot, small seedlings seem to re-establish and grow more quickly than lone seedlings do.*

△ *Originally, this was an unbranched tip cutting. Once established the tip of this plant was removed to make another cutting, which forced it to branch, making a fine specimen.*

GROWING FROM CUTTINGS

While some species of succulents have proved extremely difficult or impossible to propagate from cuttings, many are quite simple. Cuttings and unrooted offsets are generally best taken during the growing season. Tools should be sterilized, to keep them from infecting the cuttings as well as the parent plant with harmful fungi or bacteria. Although many species will produce roots without synthetic rooting hormones, most benefit from them. Rooting hormones are available in powdered and, occasionally, in liquid forms. Some may also contain fungicides, making them doubly useful. These are applied by dipping the cut end of the plant into the compound, shortly after the cuttings are taken (if the cut end is allowed to dry, a powdered hormone mixture will not adhere to or be absorbed by the plant tissue). The white latex common to *Euphorbia* and their relatives should be rinsed from the cut end before the hormone is applied.

All but the most tender or non-succulent woody cuttings need to heal before planting. Cacti and thick-stemmed succulents, like *Euphorbia*, may require days or weeks to heal, since the cut end must form a hard calloused layer, which excludes pathogens. New roots will sometimes burst through this layer, even before the cutting is planted. The grower should not wait for the roots to emerge from unpotted cuttings, however, since some species will not produce roots until the cutting is planted. Cuttings are ready for planting when the callous does not crack when gently pushed with the tip of a fingernail.

GROWING FROM CUTTINGS

1 *Larger cuttings, like those of* Cereus hildmannianus, *require extra-careful handling to prevent injury either to the grower or to the plant. Larger cuttings also develop a woody centre but are cut easily with a serrated blade, which should be sterile. After cutting, dip them in sulphur or a rooting hormone and allow the cut to heal for several weeks.*

2 *To establish numerous unrooted offsets or small cuttings, partly fill a shallow pan with compost (potting soil) and then top it with a thick layer of coarse grit.*

3 *Once the offsets or cuttings have healed sufficiently, plant them in the coarse grit on top. This will keep the cut end from remaining too wet and allow the roots to grow into the richer compost below.*

TAKING STEM CUTTINGS FROM SUCCULENTS

1 *Use sharp, sterile secateurs (pruning shears) to remove the cutting from the parent plant. When taking cuttings from plants with irritating sap, like this specimen of* Euphorbia ferox, *wear hand and eye protection. Spray the white sap off the stock plant and cuttings with clean water. Dip the cuttings in rooting hormone.*

2 *Allow the cutting to heal for several days at least before planting it. Cuttings are often planted in a coarse grit, which will promote rooting without keeping them too wet.*

3 *After the cutting has developed a good root system, transplant it into a general-purpose succulent compost (potting soil).*

4 *When preparing a leafy succulent stem cutting, remove the bottom leaves from the portion of the stem that will be buried.*

5 *Allow the cutting to heal for a couple of days before planting it in coarse grit to begin rooting.*

DIVIDING

Clustering species, such as Agave, once unpotted, are easily divided with secateurs (pruning shears).

TAKING LEAF CUTTINGS

1 Echeveria nodulosa, *like many members of the Crassulaceae family, can be propagated from leaves. Strip only the healthy leaves from the stem. The entire leaf is needed, since the plantlets will emerge from the base of the leaf.*

2 *Allow the leaves to heal for one to three weeks, in a slightly shaded location.*

3 *Plant them in a shallow pan filled with coarse compost (potting soil). Place in a shaded location, protected from extreme heat or cold.*

4 *After the plantlets form, remove them from the pan and replant them. It generally takes at least a season to produce a batch of plantlets from leaf cuttings.*

235

DIVISION

Taking rooted offsets and separating clusters is the fastest and most trouble-free method of propagation. Although the secondary stems or rosettes are often still attached to the main stem, they generally have some roots of their own. Rooted offsets can often be removed without disturbing the parent plant. However, if they are firmly attached or a quantity is desired, the plant should be unpotted and carefully separated. This may require a knife or pair of secateurs (pruning shears). Any wounds should be treated with dusting sulphur or rooting hormone. If larger wounds are made while separating a cluster, allow the plants to heal for a few days before they are planted.

CROSS-POLLINATION

Many species of succulents are quite easily pollinated, requiring only a small paintbrush to move pollen from the anthers of a flower on one plant to the stigma of a flower on another. A fair number of succulents are self-fertile, requiring only one plant to produce seed, although pollination is often still necessary. Many caudiciform species and many *Euphorbia* are dioecious, so the growers must have both a female and a male of the species. Putting aside complicated procedures, the grower then has the choice of producing pure seed or hybrid seed. Because many succulents hybridize easily, commercial seed producers prefer to have buildings which exclude bees and other pollinators, and thus hand-pollinate all of their stock.

GRAFTING

The first grafted cacti most people encounter are the bright red *Gymnocalycium* sold as "ruby balls" or "red caps". Almost always grafted on tender, tropical *Hylocereus* stocks, these generally live little more than a year or two. Generally, grafting is used to mass produce new species and cultivars as well as to speed rare species to flowering size. It also allows exotic species to be grown under far harsher conditions than they might otherwise survive. Grafting is made possible by the vascular cambium, a special ring of tissue only one cell thick, which occurs in the stems of all

△ *In the cross-section of this* Opuntia *flower, the ovary is clearly visible at its base. The hollow in the centre contains many ovules, the small yellow projections inside. Once pollinated, these will produce the seed.*

flowering plants. When the vascular cambium from the scion (the top part of the graft) is placed in contact with that of the stock (the bottom), it grows together, allowing for the exchange of water and nutrients. More amazingly, the rings need only touch at one point for a graft to be successful.

The most basic rules of grafting are as follows: the scion and stock of a graft almost always need to be in the same plant family; the portion of the stock to be used should be plump, young, actively growing tissue; and the cutting implement must be sterile and razor-sharp. Without these essentials, most grafts will fail. The two most common styles of grafting are the flat graft and the split or wedge graft. While the scion can be virtually any species that the grower wishes to propagate, the stock must fulfill the requirements of the grower. Some of the traits to look for in potential stock are longevity, cold or heat tolerance, speed of growth, and reluctance to offset. Above all, the stock should grow well under the conditions available to the grower.

CROSS POLLINATION

1 *A small paintbrush is commonly used to transfer pollen from flower to flower. The natural roughness of hair bristles works better than plastic bristles.*

2 *After pollination, the ovary of a typical cactus swells, and once ripe it often changes colour to attract animals which disperse the seed.*

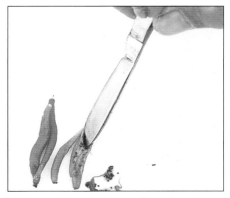

3 *The ripe fruit of a* Mammillaria *have been cut open to reveal the seeds. Depending on the species, a cactus fruit can contain from fewer than ten to several hundred seeds.*

FLAT-GRAFTING CACTI

1 *Choose an actively growing stock that is well hydrated. While some species make better grafting stocks than others, virtually any species can be used for a root stock. The hardier the stock, the longer the graft will last.*

2 *Using a razor-sharp, sterile blade, make the initial cut at just above the level planned for the finished graft. If the tip is large enough, it can be saved, rooted and used again.*

3 *Making several cuts to bevel the top of the stock will make it slightly domed when the graft has healed, allowing it to shed water. Without bevelling, stocks will have a concave top, where water can accumulate and cause the scion to rot.*

4 *Before making the final cut on the stock, prepare the scion with a single cut, since scions generally do not need to be bevelled.*

5 *As soon as the scion is cut, make the final cut on the stock. Neither cut end should touch any surface, since this can contaminate the graft and promote rot.*

▽ *While Astrophytum myriostigma is propagated mainly from seed, some of the cultivars are grafted to speed their growth. Even with species that are easy to grow, grafting enables them to be grown faster and under a broader range of conditions*

6 *Align the scion and stock so that the vascular cambium of each is touching in at least one spot. This layer of cells is located at the outer edge of the white ring of tissue near the centre of the stem. The stock and scion must be united soon after making the final cuts. If the tissue dries or touches an unsterile surface, the ends must be recut.*

7 *Use rubber bands to secure new grafts. Loop the bands under the pot, then gently position them over the scion. Hold the scion firmly enough to exclude air, but not hard enough to crush the tissue. Protect the graft from extreme temperatures, hot dry draughts or stagnant humidity for a week or more. Remove the rubber bands after 3–5 days.*

237

FLAT-GRAFTING EUPHORBIA

1 *Besides cacti,* Euphorbia *are the most commonly grafted succulents. The technique is essentially the same but there are some notable differences. First, many people wear hand and eye protection when cutting* Euphorbia *as the sap is caustic. The stock must be cut near the tip, since older tissue lower on the stem will not accept the scion.*

2 *Bevel the stock. If the knife becomes too sticky with sap, a spray of alcohol from an atomizer will clean the blade.*

3 *After bevelling the stock but before making the final cut, rinse the sap from the stock with cold, clean water, not alcohol.*

4 *Prepare the scion before cutting the stock for the final time.*

5 *Place the scion and stock together, making sure the vascular systems touch. Do not spray any water on these final cut surfaces.*

6 *Attach rubber bands as for cacti and protect the plants from extreme conditions for a week or so, before removing the rubber bands.*

▷ *Many* Euphorbia *crests are grafted, both to ensure survival and to facilitate faster growth. After several seasons, the grafting stock is often hardly noticeable.*

SPLIT OR WEDGE GRAFTING

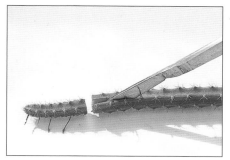

1 *This technique is most useful with thin cacti, such as* Epiphyllum *and* Schlumbergera. *Make shallow cuts on one or both sides of the end of the scion, producing a sharp wedge of tissue.*

2 *Cut the tip of the stock and then split this cut end down the middle.*

3 *Insert the scion in the bottom of the incision. Push a clean cactus spine through the stock and scion, to hold the scion in place. Use gentle pressure to hold the incision tightly shut. Protect the graft from extreme conditions for a week.*

GRAFTING SEEDLINGS

1 *Small seedlings are often grafted. Some growers are loath to waste any portion of rare or new plants. This seedling of* Astrophytum myriostigma *'Onzuka' has been split in half diagonally, then both its top and bottom were grafted.*

2 *While the top of the seedling continues to grow normally, the bottom must form a new growing point or, in this case, several. This graft is a month older than in the previous picture.*

PESTS AND DISEASES

Hobbyists new to cacti and succulents are often surprised to find that many of the same pests and diseases that plague leafy house and garden plants are also injurious to their succulents.

Prevention is always the best initial step in controlling diseases and pests. Providing conditions that are beneficial for the growth of the plant but unfavourable for the pest or disease will ensure that the grower will have fewer problems to begin with. A good first step in prevention is to place new plants in a quarantine area for several weeks. This allows the grower to discover and treat any pest or disease before it is introduced into the collection.

Proper identification of the causal agent of pest or disease damage is the most important step in dealing with it, since many of the treatments are very specific and incorrect diagnosis and treatment can worsen the problem. Local nurseries, agricultural services and long-time hobbyists are generally most useful in identifying problems.

Using Chemicals

Applying fungicides and pesticides should not be undertaken lightly by the hobbyist. These chemicals, if used improperly, can do as much harm as good, so the manufacturer's instructions should be followed closely. Often, repeat applications are required: in this case, applying twice as much at one time is not an adequate substitute for two separate applications; it may damage the plant and will not necessarily control the organism. Many chemicals use a petroleum base, which can burn the plant if it is applied during the heat of the day. For this reason, chemicals should be applied in the cool of the morning or late in the day.

PESTS

Aphids (Greenfly)

Identification Anyone who has cultivated a garden will recognize these small insects by their fat, teardrop-shaped bodies. They come in a variety of colours, green being the most common, and are found, often in great numbers, sucking on tender young leaves and flowers at the ends of the stems. They also expel great quantities of sugar water, or honeydew, as they feed. This often promotes the growth of black sooty mould, and can ruin the appearance of the plant. This sugary substance can be removed with a spray of water.

Cause Aphids have a winged stage and, since females do not require sex for reproduction, it only takes one to start an infestation. They reproduce very quickly and can give birth to live young as well as eggs.

Control These are among the easiest of the pests to kill and most general insecticides are effective. The least toxic chemical controls are insecticidal soap and diatomaceous earth. Lacewings and ladybird beetles (ladybugs) are excellent biological methods of control.

Prevention Since a lone female or her eggs are hard to spot, new, quarantined plants should be frequently inspected for the beginnings of an infestation.

◁ *Large healthy mealy bugs are visible at the tip of the succulent's stem. The new leaves are deformed as a result of their feeding.*

△ *The dense infestation of mealy bugs on the crown of this Ferocactus should first be dislodged with a stiff spray of water. Then the whole plant can be treated with an appropriate insecticide.*

△ *The damage from spider mites and thrips is quite similar. In either case, the skin of the plant is extensively scarred. While this plant will not die, it will take years to outgrow this damage.*

△ *The fine, dense webbing is evidence of an extreme infestation of spider mites. Their feeding has killed the youngest leaves and given the mature leaves a yellow, unhealthy colour.*

241

Mealy Bugs

Identification These small, elliptical insects are generally white and are the most common pest in succulents and cacti. They get their name from a waxy (or mealy) white material they produce. A common misconception is that there is only one kind of mealy bug. There are least half-a-dozen different species, which can make their homes on the roots, stems, leaves and tender tips of the plants.

Spine mealies are an unusual species, which have caused much confusion. They get their name from the white egg cases, which are often deposited on the ends of spines. The insect, however, is a metallic grey colour, does not produce the typical white, waxy waste material and is found scattered over the body of the plant. Like aphids and whiteflies, these insects exude honeydew, which can promote the growth of sooty mould.

Cause Since these insects, depending on the species, can be found on virtually any portion of a plant, they can easily escape visual detection. The eggs can lie dormant for a long time in used compost (potting soil), pots and on and under benches, later reinfesting treated plants. Although they move very slowly, they will spread outward from an infested pot via the bench, or from plant to plant, when they are touching.

Control Insecticidal soap is a moderate means of control and commercial insecticides are available that are recommended for these pests. The biggest problem with controlling mealy bugs is applying the pesticide effectively. Their waxy waste material is very difficult for insecticides to penetrate. Adding a surfactant, or wetting agent, may remedy this. Root mealy bugs may require a soil drench for control, but this requires considerably more of the chemical and is not 100 per cent effective. The best remedy for these is to bare the roots of the plant, remove any visible sign of infestation by hand and then dip the plant in the dilute pesticide.

Prevention Quarantining new plants and inspecting them (and their roots) is the best way to prevent the introduction of new insects. When an infestation is located, sterilize the area to prevent a further infestation.

Scale

Identification There are several species of scale, which vary in shape from round to elliptical, in size from barely a millimetre to a centimetre (½in) across and from white to brown in colour; however, their life cycle is the same. Eggs hatch after they are laid by the large, hard-shelled female. This juvenile stage, known as a "crawler", will move a short distance and then produce a hard shell, then becoming permanently immobile.

Cause These are generally introduced to collections on infested plants.

Control A mature scale insect cannot re-attach itself and will die once it is brushed off a plant. If left in place they are almost impervious to most pesticides, and only systemic insecticides will offer much control. The juvenile crawling stage, however, is easily controllable with chemicals.

Prevention As scale insects do not move much in their lifetime, attentive growers can spot infestations early, before they have spread.

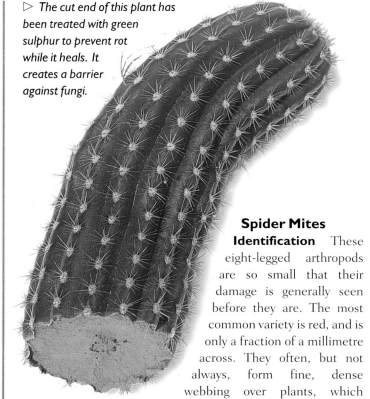

▷ *The cut end of this plant has been treated with green sulphur to prevent rot while it heals. It creates a barrier against fungi.*

242

Spider Mites

Identification These eight-legged arthropods are so small that their damage is generally seen before they are. The most common variety is red, and is only a fraction of a millimetre across. They often, but not always, form fine, dense webbing over plants, which should not be confused with the coarse, stranded webs made by ordinary spiders. An infested plant at first becomes lighter in colour and can eventually turn almost white or silvery, as the mites destroy the epidermis.

Cause Because of their minute size, it is often difficult to detect spider mites until there is a large infestation. They disperse by ballooning, in the same way as spiders, drifting on a breeze from a line of silk, and can be blown into a collection on the wind.

Control If mites are a problem, pay close attention to neighbouring plants to catch any new infestations early. Dusting sulphur is one of the oldest remedies, but it can burn the plants and is unattractive when applied. There are many miticides on the market; whichever you choose, you must follow the directions closely. Most require multiple treatments for control, since one application is virtually never 100 per cent effective. Using predatory mites, which hunt and eat spider mites, is one method of biological control.

Prevention Since mites are spread on the breeze, checking the plants which are upwind and downwind from an infestation may reveal the source of the infestation and new colonies of mites. Only perseverance and treatment will control mites.

Thrips

Identification These fast-moving, winged insects are a fraction of a millimetre long, tan in colour, and the shape of a grain of rice. They are the same as the flower thrips which cause damage in roses and other ornamental flowers. If you observe an infested plant, you will see them rapidly moving about the tender growing tips and flowers. Their damage appears as a bronze or silver cast from feeding on these tender tissues. Often, by the time the damage is noted, they have moved on to other plants.

Cause Thrips migrate locally and regionally throughout the growing season, so they often appear seemingly out of nowhere and can vanish as quickly.

Control The biggest problem in controlling these insects is noticing them in the first place. They are easily controlled by a wide variety of chemical controls, but repeated applications are necessary as more move into an area.

Prevention There is no convenient way to exclude these insects from a collection and only a watchful eye and early detection will prevent the damage they can cause.

Whiteflies

Identification These small, white, waxy, flying insects are a problem with leafy succulents, particularly *Euphorbia*. When an infested plant is shaken, they fly up from where they are feeding on the underside of the leaves. Their life cycle takes 14 days. Hatching from eggs as flightless nymphs, they feed for several days and then pupate for a short time and emerge as flying adults. This allows them to reproduce quickly and makes them difficult to control. The best indication of the size of the infestation is the presence of small, white, elliptical eggs and pupal cases on the underside of the leaves. Just like aphids, whiteflies produce copious quantities of honeydew and promote the growth of sooty mould.

Cause Although they are not strong fliers, whiteflies can be borne for, literally, hundreds of kilometres by strong winds. Most often, they are introduced to a collection as eggs on leafy succulents. They are encouraged when a plant is stressed.

Control Whiteflies can be controlled with chemicals but require repeated applications, since the eggs and pupae are highly resistant to insecticides. The larvae and adults, however, are easily killed by insecticidal soap.

Prevention New plants should always be checked for the presence of eggs and pupae on the underside of the leaves.

△ *The root rot is now slowly moving up this* Cleistocactus. *If a clean, rot-free cutting can be taken from the tip, it can be dipped, allowed to heal and rerooted.*

Other Insects and Animals

Occasionally, a grower will find one or several of their plants with large portions eaten away. Many larger insects, like crickets and grasshoppers, snails and slugs and virtually all rodents, from mice to squirrels, find cacti and succulents quite tasty. Before spraying toxic chemicals or putting down poisons which may kill harmless animals and insects, identify the exact cause of the damage. Sometimes, the culprit is a single grasshopper that has strayed into a greenhouse and which can do considerable damage. Once located, traditional control methods can be used: "place pest on block A, cover with block B, apply pressure!" Proper identification will allow the grower to use the most benign and effective form of control.

DISEASES

Basal and Root Rot

Identification Several fungi (and some bacteria) can attack the roots and lower stems of cacti and succulents. The most common symptom is a darkening of the tissue, which eventually turns soft and liquid as the pathogenic organism breaks down the tissue. This can spread upward and, eventually, kill the entire plant.

Cause These fungi are very common. Their spores can be present in the soil or on used pots. In addition, they can be spread by water splashing from one plant to another or, in a group planting, from one plant's roots to another's.

Control Portions of the plant can be saved if you can make healthy cuttings that are free from discoloration and rot. The remains of the plant and the infected compost (potting soil) should be disposed of and, if the pot is to be reused, it must be sterilized. Few fungicides are totally effective against root rot and, because they have to be applied as a drench, in some cases this extra water will aid the fungus and hasten the plant's decline.

Prevention Using a good, porous compost and careful watering will keep this at a minimum. The timely removal of any infected plants from a collection will also limit the problem.

Cold Damage

Identification Damage from cold can appear in two different ways. Following a brief cold snap, the plant may seem fine at first but, after several days, portions of the stems will turn colour, often black, and wither. Tissues of very tender plants or those which have been frozen solid will at first appear glassy and transparent, and will tend to liquefy soon after they thaw.

Cause Normally cold-hardy plants can be damaged by an early frost or if they are still actively growing too late in the season. Extremely tender species can be damaged even inside a heated structure, if placed too near the window or exposed to a cold draught for too long.

Control Withholding fertilizer and cutting back on water in the autumn (fall) will prepare hardy plants for winter. In a house or greenhouse, circulating fans will even out the temperature and prevent cold spots.

Prevention Plants should be carefully selected for their hardiness for specific locations. If the conditions become unexpectedly cold, taking extra precautions, such as covering the plants with a sheet, can prevent some damage.

◁ *This* Cleistocactus *has etiolated due to the lack of adequate sunlight. Note the thin new growth as the plant has leaned towards the light.*

△ *The damping-off fungus that is attacking these seedlings will quickly kill the remainder. While fungicides might halt the spread of the disease in this container, it is probably better to transplant the remaining healthy seedlings into clean fresh compost (potting soil) and then treat them.*

GLOSSARY

AREOLE The spine-bearing structure found in all of the members of the Cactaceae. It is a modified stem with virtually no elongation, with spines taking the place of the leaves.

BLOOM 1 A flower. 2 The white- to blue-coloured layer of waxy material coating the epidermis of a leaf or stem, primarily to prevent moisture loss.

BONSAI A plant that has been trained, through pruning and other cultivation techniques, to resemble a mature plant in miniature.

BRACT A modified leaf borne at the base of a flower or flowering head. Bracts are occasionally highly coloured, resembling petals.

CALLOUS A layer of protective tissue which forms at the cut end of a section of stem or leaf removed for propagation.

CAUDEX (pl. caudexes or caudices) Any swollen storage structure on a perennial plant. In succulents, the above-ground and/or buried, thickened portion of the plant. This commonly increases in size each season.

CREST Also called fasciation; a mutation that results when the growing point of a plant forms a long line, rather than a single point. In botanical terms, it is usually signified by *cristate*.

CRISTATE see Crest

CULTIVAR Short for *cultivated variety*, this is a form or hybrid of a species that is grown in cultivation and which is, generally, not of wild origin. Cultivar names are indicated by single inverted commas, for example, *Epiphyllum* x 'Reward'.

DORMANCY A break in a plant's growth brought on by the change in seasons, or by other factors unfavourable to growth, such as excess temperature or limited water or nutrients.

EPIDERMIS The outer, protective tissue of a plant. In succulents, this may bear other additional protective features, such as bloom or dense, fine hairs.

EPIPHYTE A plant that uses other plants, mostly trees and shrubs, for support, but does not derive any of its sustenance from the support plant.

FAMILY A group of closely related genera.

GENUS (pl. genera) A group of closely related species.

HYBRID A plant produced by cross-breeding two different species or varieties of plants. In botanical names, hybrid status is often indicated by an "x", as in *Epiphyllum* x 'Reward'.

NUTRIENTS The chemical elements necessary for proper plant growth, specifically those which must be provided by fertilization or additions to composts (potting soils). These are generally divided into two groups based on the relative quantities

necessary. The macronutrients are nitrogen (N), phosphorus (P), and potassium (K); the micronutrients are boron (B), copper (Cu), iron (Fe), magnesium (Mg), manganese (Mn), and zinc (Zn). Other nutrients are also necessary, such as calcium (Ca), but are often naturally present in the water or compost (potting soil).

MICRONUTRIENTS see Nutrients

MONSTROSE This mutation appears as randomly occurring growth from multiple growing points and, generally, results in a misshapen, club-like plant.

PATHOGEN Any micro-organism which causes disease, especially bacteria, fungi and viruses.

OFFSET A secondary branch produced from the side or base of a succulent, especially from a cactus.

SPECIES The taxonomic distinction representing a unique, interbreeding population of closely related plants. More specific than this are varieties (var.) and subspecies (ssp.), which represent highly localized variations of particular species.

SPP. This refers to all of the species in a genus.

STOMATA A pore on a plant's stem or leaf which, through opening and closing, governs the exchange of gases with the outside.

VARIEGATION A naturally occurring or virally induced mutation, which appears as stripes or whole sections of tissue that are without chlorophyll. Variegated varieties are often prized for the attractiveness of the markings caused by this mutation.

244

PLANT LISTS

PLANTS FOR BEGINNERS

These species are fairly common and easily grown.

SUCCULENTS FOR BEGINNERS

Abromeitiella brevifolia
Adromischus (most species)
Agave (most species), along with
Agave americana
Agave angustifolia var. *marginata*
Agave colorata
Agave ferox
Agave x 'Leopoldii'
Agave parryi var. *hauchucensis*
Agave parryi var. *truncata*
Agave victoria-reginae and varieties
Aloe (most species), along with
Aloe barbadensis
Aloe harlanii
Aloe humilis
Aloe x 'Doran Black'
Anacampseros rufescens 'Sunrise'
Cotyledon (most species), along with
Cotyledon undulata
Crassula (most species), along with
Crassula muscosa
Crassula x 'Morgan's Pink'
Echeveria (most species), along with
Echeveria agavoides
Echeveria lilacina
Echeveria purpusorum
Echeveria x 'Topsy Turvy'
Euphorbia (many species), along with
Euphorbia fruticosa
Euphorbia horrida var. *striata*
Euphorbia milii var. *bojeri*
Euphorbia royleana
Ficus palmeri
Gasteria (most species)
Graptopetalum (most species)
x *Graptoveria amethorum*
x *Graptoveria* 'Silver Star'
Haworthia (thin-leaved species), together with
Haworthia cuspidata variegata
Haworthia limifolia
Haworthia reinwardtii var. *chalumnensis*
Haworthia viscosa var. *caespitosa*
Hoya (most species)

Hoya carnosa
Kalanchoe (most species)
Lampranthus haworthii
Monadenium coccineum
x *Pachyveria hybrid*
Portulacaria afra
Sansevieria (most species), together with
Sansevieria pinguicula
Sansevieria singularis
Sempervivum (most species), together with
Sempervivum arachnoideum
Sempervivum tectorum
Senecio articulatus
Trichodiadema bulbosum
Zamiacaulcas zamiafolia

CACTI FOR BEGINNERS

Acanthocalycium violaceum
Aporocactus spp.
Arrojadoa dinae
Arrojadoa penicillata
Astrophytum ornatum
Borzicactus samaipatanus
Cereus (most species, especially, *Cereus hildmannianus*)
Cereus hildmannianus var. *monstrose*
Cleistocactus spp.
Coryphantha elephantidens
Echinocactus grusonii
Echinocereus luteus
Echinocereus pentalophus
Echinocereus reichenbachii
Echinopsis (many species), along with
Echinopsis aurea (yellow-flowered) and
Echinopsis aurea (red-flowered)
Echinopsis chamaecereus
Chamaecereus hybrids and
Chamaecereus x 'Fire Chief'
Echinopsis huascha
Echinopsis peruvianus
Echinopsis smurzianus
Echinopsis x 'Glorious'
Echinopsis x 'Green Gold'
Echinopsis x 'Los Angeles'
Eriosyce subgibbosa var. *nigrihorrida*
Eriosyce subgibbosa var. *wagenknechtii*
Espostoa lanata
Ferocactus glaucescens
Ferocactus herrerae
Ferocactus macrodiscus

Ferocactus pilosus
Ferocactus rectispinus
Gymnocalycium spp.
Hatiora salicornioides
Mammillaria (many species), together with
Mammillaria bocasana
Mammillaria bombycina
Mammillaria candida
Mammillaria compressa
Mammillaria geminispina
Mammillaria hahniana
Mammillaria lauii fma. *subducta*
Mammillaria nivosa
Mammillaria perbella fma. *pseudoperbella*
Mammillaria pringlei
Mammillaria prolifera
Mammillaria supertexta
Mammillaria zeilmanniana
Matucana aureiflora
Matucana formosa
Matucana intertexta
Matucana madisoniorum
Myrtillocactus geometrizans cristata
Opuntia (most species)
Oreocereus henricksenianus var. *densilanatus*
Oreocereus celsianus
Pachycereus pringlei
Parodia (most species)
Pereskia weberiana
Pilosocereus alensis
Rebutia (many species), together with

245

Rebutia albissima
Rebutia graciliflora var. *borealis*
Rebutia marsoneri
Rebutia mentosa
Rebutia miniscula fma. *senilis*
Rebutia muscula
Rebutia narvaecensis
Rebutia steinbachii fma. *bicolor*
Rebutia wessneriana var. *krainziana*
Stenocactus coptonogonus
Stenocereus thurberi
Stetsonia coryne
Tephrocactus articulatus
Thelocactus bicolor var. *bolansis*
Thelocactus bicolor var. *bicolor*
Thelocactus setispinus

PLANTS FOR THE ADVANCED COLLECTOR

These species require more specialized care. Many are slow-growing; they are often uncommon in cultivation and may perish if exposed to consistently low winter temperatures.

SUCCULENTS

Adenia spp.
Adenium spp.
Avonia spp.
Bombax ellypticum
Caralluma spp.
Cephalopentandra ecirrhosa
Ceraria pygmeae
Ceraria namaquensis
Ceropegia spp. (especially highly succulent and tuberous species)
Cheiridopsis peculiaris
Cissus saundersii
Cyphostemma spp.
Dioscorea elephantipes
Edithcolea grandis
Eulophia pettersii
Euphorbia (while many species are simple to grow, just as many are difficult)
Euphorbia abdelkuri
Euphorbia ambovombensis
Euphorbia balsamifera
Euphorbia bupleurifolia
Euphorbia cap-saintmariensis
Euphorbia clavarioides var. *truncata*
Euphorbia columnaris
Euphorbia cylindrifolia var. *tuberifera*
Euphorbia francoisii

Euphorbia piscidermis
Fockea spp.
Huernia kennedyana
Ibervillea spp.
Idria columnaris
Jacaratia hasseleriana
Jatropha (particularly tuberous species), together with
Jatropha cordata
Jatropha cuneata
Jatropha podagrica
x *Luckhoffia beukmannii*
Matelea (*Gonolobus*) *cyclophylla*
Momordica rostrata
Monadenium (particularly thick-stemmed and tuberous species), together with
Monadenium reflexum
Monadenium ritchiei
Monadenium rubellum
Monsonia (most species), together with
Monsonia penniculinum
Moringa droughardtii
Operculicarya decaryi
Othonna (most species), together with
Othonna clavifolia
Othonna herrei
Orbeopsis melanantha
Pachycormis discolor
Pachypodium (most species),

together with
Pachypodium x 'Arid Lands'
   (*P. namaquanum* x *P. succulentum*)
Pachypodium namaquanum
Pachypodium saundersii
Pachypodium succulentum
Pedilanthus macrocarpus
Pelargonium (the highly succulent and tuberous species), together with
Pelargonium klinghardtense
Pelargonium succulentum
Piaranthus foetidus
Pseudolithos migurtinus
Raphionacme flanaganii
Senecio ballyi
Sesamothamnus lugardae
Seyrigia humbertii
Stapelianthus neronis
Trichocaulon cactiforme
Tylecodon (most species), together with
Tylecodon paniculata
Uncarina decaryi

CACTI

These species are particularly difficult and require very well-drained compost (potting soil) and high temperatures to survive long winters with low light.

Ancistrocactus uncinatus var. *wrightii*
Ariocarpus spp.
Astrophytum asterias
Astrophytum asterias 'Super Kabuto'
Astrophytum myriostigma monstrose 'Lotusland'
Austrocephalocereus dybowskii
Austrocephalocereus lehmannianus
Aztekium ritteri
Copiapoa spp.
Discocactus spp.
Echinopsis famatimensis
Epithelantha spp.
Eriosyce spp. (most species), together with
Eriosyce imitans
Eriosyce napina
Eriosyce occulta
Escobaria leei
Escobaria minima
Ferocactus cylindraceus
Frailea castanea
Lophocereus schottii monstrose
Mammillaria guelzowiana
Mammillaria pectinifera
Mammillaria perezdelarosae

Mammillaria saboae var. haudeana
Mammillaria solisioides
Obregonia denegri
Ortegocactus macdougallii
Pediocactus simpsonii var. minor
Pelecyphora aselliformis
Pelecyphora strobiliformis
Rebutia rauschii
Turbinicarpus spp.
Uebelmannia spp.

SPECIES FOR SHADE

SUCCULENTS
These species will grow fairly well in low light.

Aloe (many species), including
Aloe barbadensis
Aloe distans
Aloe harlanii
Aloe humilis
Aloe x 'Doran Black'
Anacampseros rufescens 'Sunrise' and
    other large-leaved species
Bombax ellypticum
Dorstenia foetida
Echeveria spp.
Euphorbia (many species), together with
Euphorbia lactea variegata cristata
Euphorbia milii and its varieties
Euphorbia royleana
Euphorbia trapifolia cristata
Ficus spp.
Gasteria spp.
Graptopetalum spp.
x Graptoveria amethorum
x Graptoveria 'Silver Star'
Haworthia (particularly species with
    thinner leaves), together with

Haworthia bolusii var. bolusii
Haworthia cooperi
Haworthia cuspidata variegata
Haworthia limifolia
Haworthia reinwardtii var. chalumnensis
Haworthia viscosa var. caespitosa
Hoya spp.
Kalanchoe spp.
Monadenium coccineum
Monsonia vanderietiae
Operculicarya decaryi
Pachyphytum spp.
x Pachyveria (all cultivars)
Portulaca molokaiensis
Portulacaria afra
Portulacaria afra variegata
Sansevieria spp. (particularly thin-leaved
    species)
Sempervivum spp.
Senecio spp. (except for highly succulent
    species)
Trichodiadema spp.
Zamiacaulcas spp.

CACTI
These species will survive and, in some cases, flower in low light.

Aporocactus spp. and hybrids
Borzicactus samaipatanus
Cereus hildmannianus
Cereus hildmannianus monstrose
Epiphyllum spp. and hybrids
Gymnocalycium andrea var. grandiflorum
Gymnocalycium baldianum
Gymnocalycium bruchii
Hatiora salicornioides
Parodia graessneri
Parodia haselbergii
Rebutia (most species originally in
    Rebutia but not Sulcorebutia or
    Weingartia)
Rebutia graciliflora var. borealis
Rebutia marsoneri
Rebutia miniscula fma. senilis
Rebutia muscula
Rebutia narvaecensis
Rebutia wessneriana var. krainziana

COLD-TOLERANT SPECIES

SUCCULENTS
These species will tolerate at least brief periods of frost without damage.

Adromischus spp.
Agave americana and its forms
Agave angustifolia var. marginata
Agave colorata
Agave ferox
Agave macroacantha
Agave palmeri
Agave parryi var. hauchucensis
Agave parryi var. truncata
Agave victoria-reginae and varieties
Agave x 'Leopoldii'
Aloe humilis
Brachychiton rupestris
Calibanus hookeri
Cotyledon undulata
Dasylirion longissimum
Echeveria (most species), together with
Echeveria agavoides
Echeveria lilacina
Echeveria x 'Topsy Turvy'
Euphorbia horrida var. striata
Euphorbia royleana
Fouquieria fasciculata
Fouquieria splendens
Grahamia coahuilense
Graptopetalum bellum
x Graptoveria amethorum
x Graptoveria 'Silver Star'
Idria columnaris
Lampranthus spp.
Mestoklema spp.
Sedum spp. (all but tropical species)
Sempervivum spp.
Titanopsis spp.
Trichodiadema spp.
Yucca (all northern species),
    together with
Yucca carnerosana
Yucca rigida

CACTI
These species of cacti will tolerate at least some brief frost without damage.

Acanthocalycium violaceum
Ancistrocactus uncinatus var. wrightii
Ariocarpus fissuratus var. fissuratus
Ariocarpus retusus var. retusus

Astrophytum coahuilense
Astrophytum myriostigma
Astrophytum ornatum
Carnegiea gigantea (only as larger
   specimens)
Coryphantha clava
Coryphantha elephantidens
Coryphantha macromeris var. *runyonii*
Coryphantha ramillosa
Coryphantha sulcata
Echinocactus grusonii (only as larger
   specimens)
Echinocereus (northern species in
   particular), together with
Echinocereus neomexicanus
Echinocereus papillosus
Echinocereus pentalophus
Echinocereus pulchellus
Echinocereus reichenbachii
Echinocereus viridiflorus
Echinopsis (most species), together with
Echinopsis aurea
Echinopsis chamaecereus and its hybrids
Echinopsis huascha
Echinopsis peruvianus
Echinopsis smurzianus
Echinopsis x 'Glorious'
Echinopsis x 'Green Gold'
Echinopsis x 'Los Angeles'
Eriosyce (most species), together with
Eriosyce napina
Eriosyce occulta
Eriosyce senilis
Eriosyce subgibbosa var. *nigrihorrida*
Eriosyce subgibbosa var. *wagenknechtii*
Eriosyce villosa fma. *laniceps*
Escobaria (most northern species),
   together with
Escobaria hesteri

Escobaria leei
Escobaria minima
Escobaria roseana
Escobaria vivipara
Ferocactus (most species, particularly
   larger specimens)
Ferocactus cylindraceus
Ferocactus pilosus
Ferocactus rectispinus
Ferocactus wislizeni
Gymnocalycium (most southern
   species), together with
Gymnocalycium andrea var. *grandiflorum*
Gymnocalycium baldianum
Gymnocalycium bruchii
Gymnocalycium cardenasianum
Gymnocalycium erinaceum
Gymnocalycium manzanense
Gymnocalycium quehlianum
Gymnocalycium saglione
Gymnocalycium tillianum
Mammillaria (many species),
   together with
Mammillaria bocasana
Mammillaria bombycina
Mammillaria candida
Mammillaria carmenae
Mammillaria compressa
Mammillaria duwei
Mammillaria geminispina
Mammillaria hahniana
Mammillaria lauii fma. *subducta*
Mammillaria microthele
Mammillaria perbella fma.
   pseudoperbella
Mammillaria perezdelarosae
Mammillaria plumosa
Mammillaria pringlei
Mammillaria prolifera
Mammillaria supertexta
Mammillaria zeilmanniana
Opuntia (most northern species),
   together with
Opuntia fulgida var. *fulgida*
Opuntia invicta
Opuntia lindheimeri
Opuntia microdasys var. *alba* and
   Opuntia microdasys monstrosus
Opuntia tunicata
Opuntia vestita
Oreocereus (most species as larger
   specimens)
Oreocereus henricksenianus var.
   densilanatus
Oreocereus celsianus

Parodia (many species originally in
   Notocactus), together with
Parodia leninghausii
Parodia magnifica
Parodia tephracanthus
Parodia uebelmanniana
Pediocactus spp.
Rebutia (most species, except those
   originally in *Weingartia*)
Rebutia albissima
Rebutia arenacea
Rebutia graciliflora var. *borealis*
Rebutia heliosa var. *condorensis*
Rebutia marsoneri
Rebutia mentosa
Rebutia miniscula fma. *senilis*
Rebutia muscula
Rebutia narvaecensis
Rebutia rauschii
Rebutia steinbachii fma. *bicolor*
Rebutia wessneriana var. *krainziana*
Stenocactus spp.
Stetsonia coryne (only larger specimens)
Tephrocactus spp.
Thelocactus spp.

FREELY FLOWERING
SPECIES

SUCCULENTS
*These species all flower fairly easily and
often produce attractive displays.*

Adromischus spp.
Aloe (most species, dwarf species in
   particular), together with
Aloe barbadensis
Aloe harlanii
Aloe humilis
Aloe x 'Doran Black'
Anacampseros rufescens 'Sunrise'
Argyroderma spp.
Ceropegia (most vining species),
   together with
Ceropegia devechii
Ceropegia stapeliiformis
Conophytum (most species), together
   with
Conophytum ficiforme
Conophytum friedrichiae
Conophytum limpidum
Conophytum verrucosum
Cotyledon spp.
Crassula (most species), together with
Crassula x 'Morgan's Pink'

Echeveria spp.
Euphorbia milii and its varieties
Fenestraria rhopalophylla
Frithia pulchra
Fouquieria macdougallii
Lapidaria margaretae
Lithops spp.
Monsonia vanderietiae
Nananthus schooneesii
Othonna (most species), together with
Othonna clavifolia
Othonna herrei
Pachyphytum spp.
Pachypodium x 'Arid Lands' (*P. namaquanum* x *P. succulentum*)
x *Pachyveria* hybrids
Pelargonium (most species), together with
Pelargonium alternans
Pelargonium laxum
Pelargonium reniforme
Pleiospilos spp.
Portulaca molokaiensis
Titanopsis spp.
Trichodiadema bulbosum

CACTI

These species will often produce impressive displays of flowers, even under less-than-ideal conditions.

Acanthocalycium violaceum
Aporocactus (all species and hybrids)
Arrojadoa dinae
Arrojadoa penicillata
Astrophytum ornatum
Borzicactus samaipatanus
Cleistocactus (most species), together with
Cleistocactus baumannii
Copiapoa barquitensis
Copiapoa tenuissima
Echinocereus (many species), together with
Echinocereus luteus
Echinocereus pentalophus
Echinocereus reichenbachii
Echinocereus viridiflorus
Echinopsis (most smaller-growing species), together with
Echinopsis aurea
Echinopsis chameacereus and its hybrids
Echinopsis huascha
Echinopsis x 'Glorious'
Echinopsis x 'Green Gold'

Echinopsis x 'Los Angeles'
Eriosyce senilis
Eriosyce subgibbosa var. *nigrihorrida*
Eriosyce subgibbosa var. *wagenknechtii*
Escobaria hesteri
Escobaria vivipara
Ferocactus macrodiscus
Gymnocalycium spp.
Hatiora salicornioides
Mammillaria (many species), together with
Mammillaria bocasana
Mammillaria bombycina
Mammillaria candida
Mammillaria carmenae
Mammillaria duwei
Mammillaria geminispina
Mammillaria glasii
Mammillaria hahniana
Mammillaria huitzilopochtli
Mammillaria lauii fma. *subducta*
Mammillaria nivosa
Mammillaria perbella fma. *pseudoperbella*
Mammillaria perezdelarosae
Mammillaria pringlei
Mammillaria prolifera
Mammillaria saboae var. *haudeana*
Mammillaria schumannii
Mammillaria supertexta
Mammillaria zeilmanniana
Matucana aureiflora
Parodia (most species), together with
Parodia graessneri
Parodia haselbergii
Parodia herteri
Parodia horstii
Parodia mairanana
Parodia microsperma
Parodia punea
Parodia uebelmanniana
Rebutia (most species), together with
Rebutia albissima
Rebutia arenacea
Rebutia graciliflora var. *borealis*
Rebutia heliosa var. *condorensis*
Rebutia marsoneri
Rebutia mentosa
Rebutia miniscula fma. *senilis*
Rebutia muscula
Rebutia narvaecensis
Rebutia neocummingii
Rebutia steinbachii fma. *bicolor*
Rebutia wessneriana var. *krainziana*
Thelocactus bicolor var. *bolansis*

SPECIES WITH LARGE OR UNUSUAL FLOWERS

Although they don't flower so easily as many species, these are still worth a little extra effort.

SUCCULENTS

Adenium spp.
Bombax ellypticum
Caralluma spp.
Cephalopentandra ecirrhosa
Ceraria fruticosa
Dorstenia foetida
Duvalia spp.
Edithcolea grandis
Eulophia pettersii
Hoodia spp.
Huernia spp.
Jacaratia hasseleriana
Jatropha podagrica
x *Luckhoffia beukmannii*
Matelea (*Gonolobus*) *cyclophylla*
Momordica rostrata
Monsonia spp.
Orbeopsis spp.
Pachycormis discolor
Pachypodium spp.
Pedilanthus spp.
Piaranthus spp.
Pseudolithos spp.
Sansevieria spp.
Senecio spp.
Sesamothamnus spp.
Stapelia spp.
Stapelianthus spp.
Tavaresia spp.
Tomatriche spp.
Trichocaulon spp.
Uncarina spp.

249

CACTI

Ancistrocactus uncinatus var. *wrightii*
Ariocarpus spp.
Astrophytum spp.
Coryphantha elephantidens
Discocactus spp.
Echinocereus neomexicanus
Echinocereus pectinatus var. *rubispinus*
Echinocereus pentalophus
Echinocereus pulchellus
Epiphyllum spp. and their hybrids
Escobaria minima
Mammillaria guelzowiana
Mammillaria (Cochemiea) maritima
Mammillaria saboae var. *haudeana*
Matucana madisoniorum
Rebutia rauschii
Thelocactus macdowellii
Thelocactus rinconensis

SPECIES THAT WILL TOLERATE BRIGHT, HOT LIGHT

SUCCULENTS

Adenia spinosa
Agave (most species), together with
Agave americana and *A. americana* var. *mediopicta fma. alba*
Agave angustifolia var. *marginata*
Agave colorata
Agave ferox
Agave macroacantha
Agave palmeri
Agave parryi var. *hauchucensis*
Agave parryi var. *truncata*
Agave x 'Leopoldii'
Alluadia (all species), together with
Alluadia dumosa
Alluadia procera
Aloe (most larger species, including *Aloe barbadensis*, *Aloe dichotoma* and *Aloe ramosissima*)
Bombax ellypticum
Brachychiton spp.
Bursera spp.
Calibanus hookeri
Cissus tuberosus
Commiphora spp.
Cotyledon undulata
Cyphostemma juttae
Dasylirion spp.
Euphorbia (many species, particularly tree species)
Euphorbia horrida var. *striata*

Euphorbia royleana
Ficus palmeri
Fouquieria spp.
Hoodia macrantha
Idria columnaris
Jacaratia hasseleriana
Jatropha cordata
Jatropha cuneata
Matelea (Gonolobus) cyclophylla
Mestoklema tuberosa
Momordica rostrata
Moringa droughardtii
Operculicarya decaryi
Pachycormis discolor
Pachypodium geayi
Pachypodium namaquanum
Pachypodium saundersii
Pedilanthus macrocarpus
Portulacaria afra
Uncarina decaryi
Yucca spp.

CACTI

Acanthocalycium violaceum
Ancistrocactus uncinatus var. *wrightii*
Ariocarpus fissuratus var. *fissuratus*
Ariocarpus retusus var. *retusus*
Astrophytum coahuilense
Astrophytum myriostigma
Astrophytum ornatum
Carnegiea gigantea
Cephalocereus senilis
Cereus (most species)
Cleistocactus (most species)
Coryphantha (most larger species), together with
Coryphantha macromeris var. *runyonii*
Coryphantha ramillosa
Coryphantha sulcata

Echinocactus grusonii
Echinocereus (most larger-growing species), together with
Echinocereus neomexicanus
Echinocereus papillosus
Echinocereus pectinatus var. *rubispinus*
Echinocereus reichenbachii
Echinocereus viridiflorus
Echinopsis (most larger species originally in the genus *Trichocereus*), together with
Echinopsis huascha
Echinopsis x 'Los Angeles'
Echinopsis peruvianus
Echinopsis smurzianus
Epithelantha micromeris
Epithelantha micromeris var. *unguispina*
Escobaria hesteri
Escobaria vivipara
Ferocactus (most species), together with
Ferocactus cylindraceus
Ferocactus herrerae
Ferocactus pilosus
Ferocactus rectispinus
Ferocactus robustus
Ferocactus wislizenii
Gymnocalycium cardenasianum
Gymnocalycium saglione
Lophocereus schottii
Lophocereus schottii monstrose
Mammillaria bombycina
Mammillaria candida
Mammillaria compressa
Mammillaria geminispina
Mammillaria microthele
Mammillaria pringlei
Mammillaria schumannii
Myrtillocactus geometrizans cristata
Opuntia (most species)
Oreocereus (most species, when mature specimens)
Pachycereus pringlei
Pereskia weberiana
Pilosocereus alensis
Quiabentia chacoensis
Stenocactus coptonogonus
Stenocereus (most species)
Stetsonia coryne
Tephrocactus articulatus
Thelocactus (most species)

CAUDICIFORMS
Succulents that produce a caudex, above or below ground, which can be displayed for effect.

Adenia spp.
Adenium spp.
Bombax ellypticum
Brachychiton rupestris
Bursera spp.
Calibanus hookeri
Cephalopentandra ecirrhosa
Ceraria spp.
Cissus saundersii
Cissus tuberosus
Commiphora (many species), together with
Commiphora glandulosa
Cyphostemma spp.
Dioscorea elephantipes
Euphorbia (many species), together with
Euphorbia ambovombensis
Euphorbia balsamifera
Euphorbia cap-saintmariensis
Euphorbia cylindrifolia var. tuberifera
Euphorbia francoisii
Euphorbia persistens
Euphorbia piscidermis
Euphorbia tortirama
Ficus (most species), together with
Ficus palmeri
Ficus petiolaris
Fockea (most species)
Fouquieria fasciculata
Fouquieria macdougallii
Ibervillea spp.
Idria columnaris
Jacaratia hasseleriana
Jatropha cordata
Jatropha cuneata
Jatropha podagrica
Matelea (Gonolobus) cyclophylla
Mestoklema tuberosa
Momordica rostrata
Monadenium (many tuberous species), together with
Monadenium rubellum
Monsonia spp.
Moringa droughardtii
Nananthus schooneesii
Operculicarya decaryi
Othonna spp.
Pachycormis discolor
Pachypodium spp.
Pelargonium (most species)
Portulaca molokaiensis
Portulacaria afra
Raphionacme flanaganii
Senecio (many tuberous species), together with
Senecio ballyi
Sesamothamnus lugardae
Seyrigia humbertii
Talinum aurantiacum
Trichodiadema bulbosum
Tylecodon spp.
Uncarina decaryi

SPECIES SUITABLE FOR BONSAI TREATMENT

Bombax ellypticum
Brachychiton (several species, especially Brachychiton rupestris)
Bursera (all species), together with
Bursera fagaroides
Bursera hindsiana
Bursera microphylla
Bursera schlectendahlii
Ceraria fruticosa
Ceraria pygmeae
Commiphora glandulosa
Euphorbia ambovombensis
Euphorbia balsamifera
Euphorbia cap-saintmariensis
Euphorbia cylindrifolia var. tuberifera
Euphorbia francoisii
Ficus palmeri
Fouquieria diguetii
Fouquieria fasciculata
Fouquieria macdougallii
Jacaratia hasseleriana
Jatropha cordata
Jatropha cuneata

Mestoklema tuberosa
Monsonia vanderietiae
Operculicarya decaryi
Pachycormis discolor
Pelargonium (most shrubby species), together with
Pelargonium alternans
Pelargonium laxum
Pereskia weberiana
Portulaca molokaiensis
Portulacaria afra and Portulacaria afra variegata
Sesamothamnus lugardae
Trichodiadema bulbosum
Tylecodon paniculata
Uncarina decaryi

VINING SPECIES

SUCCULENTS
These species produce long, vining stems, often in great quantities, from a large caudex.

Adenia aculeata
Adenia glauca
Adenia venenata
Cephalopentandra ecirrhosa (annual)
Ceropegia (many species, some with annual growth)
Ceropegia devechii
Ceropegia stapeliiformis
Cissus saundersii (annual)
Cissus tuberosus (annual)
Dioscorea elephantipes (annual)
Fockea edulis
Hoya carnosa
Hoya imperialis
Ibervillea tennuisecta (annual)
Matelea (Gonolobus) cyclophylla (annual)
Momordica rostrata (annual)
Monadenium rubellum
Raphionacme flanaganii (annual)
Seyrigia spp.

CACTI
These species produce long stems and are suitable for hanging baskets.

Aporocactus spp. and their hybrids
Arrojadoa spp.
Echinoceurus papillosus
Echinopsis chamaecereus and its hybrids.

INDEX

Page numbers in *italics* refer to illustrations

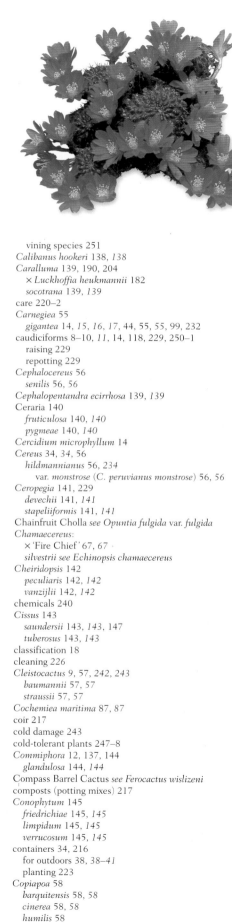

ACKNOWLEDGEMENTS
The publishers would like to thank the following picture libraries for supplying photographs for use in the book:
The Robert Harding Picture Library for pages 2, 15T, 116-117.
Harry Smith Horticultural Photographic Collection for pages 14 BL, 27T, 29, 37TL, 40-41B.
Peter Anderson for pages 26T, 27B, 28B, 30B, 33BR.
Tony Stone/ Getty Images for pages 16TL, 16TR, 16B, 17TL, 17TR.
Andrew Lawson photography for pages 16-17B, 26B, 31TR, 34TR, 38BR, 41.
The Garden Picture Library for page 28TR.